THE CITY & GUILDS TEXTBOOK

LEVEL 3 DIPLOMA IN
BRICKLAYING

JUSTIN BEATTIE
TONY TUCKER
MARTIN BURDFIELD
COLIN FEARN

**SERIES TECHNICAL EDITOR
MARTIN BURDFIELD**

About City & Guilds

City & Guilds is the UK's leading provider of vocational qualifications, offering over 500 awards across a wide range of industries, and progressing from entry level to the highest levels of professional achievement. With over 8500 centres in 100 countries, City & Guilds is recognised by employers worldwide for providing qualifications that offer proof of the skills they need to get the job done.

Equal opportunities

City & Guilds fully supports the principle of equal opportunities and we are committed to satisfying this principle in all our activities and published material. A copy of our equal opportunities policy statement is available on the City & Guilds website.

First edition 2015

ISBN 978-0-85193-303-0

Publisher: Charlie Evans
Content Project Managers: Jennie Pick and Frankie Jones
Production Editor: Lauren Cubbage

Cover design by Design Deluxe
Illustrations by Peter Bull Art Studio, Barking Dog Art and Palimpsest Book Production Ltd
Typeset by Saxon Graphics Ltd, Derby
Printed in the UK by Cambrian Printers Ltd

British Library Cataloguing in Publication Data

A catalogue record for this book is available from the British Library.

Publications

For information about or to order City & Guilds support materials, contact 0844 534 0000 or centresupport@cityandguilds.com. You can find more information about the materials we have available at www.cityandguilds.com/publications.

Every effort has been made to ensure that the information contained in this publication is true and correct at the time of going to press. However, City & Guilds' products and services are subject to continuous development and improvement and the right is reserved to change products and services from time to time. City & Guilds cannot accept liability for loss or damage arising from the use of information in this publication.

City & Guilds
1 Giltspur Street
London EC1A 9DD

0844 543 0033

www.cityandguilds.com

publishingfeedback@cityandguilds.com

CONTENTS

FOREWORD

Whether in good times or in a difficult job market, I think one of the most important things for young people is to learn a skill. There will always be a demand for talented and skilled individuals who have knowledge and experience. That's why I'm such an avid supporter of vocational training. Vocational courses provide a unique opportunity for young people to learn from people in the industry, who know their trade inside out.

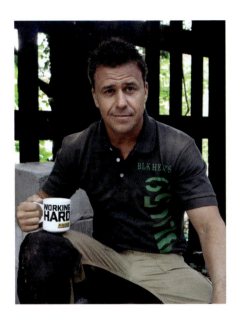

Careers rarely turn out as you plan them. You never know what opportunity is going to come your way. However, my personal experience has shown that if you haven't rigorously learned skills and gained knowledge, you are unlikely to be best placed to capitalise on opportunities that do come your way.

When I left school, I went straight to work in a butcher's shop, which was a fantastic experience. It may not be the industry I ended up making my career in, but being in the butcher's shop, working my way up to management level and learning from the people around me was something that taught me a lot about business and about the working environment.

Later, once I trained in the construction industry and was embarking on my career as a builder, these commercial principles were vital in my success and helped me to go on to set up my own business. The skills I had learned gave me an advantage and I was therefore able to make the most of my opportunities.

Later still, I could never have imagined that my career would take another turn into television. Of course, I recognise that I have had lucky breaks in my career, but when people say you make your own luck, I think there is definitely more than a grain of truth in that. People often ask me what my most life-changing moment has been, expecting me to say winning the first series of *Big Brother*. However, I always answer that my most life-changing moment was deciding to make the effort to learn the construction skills that I still use every day. That's why I was passionate about helping to set up a construction academy in the North West, helping other people to acquire skills and experience that will stay with them for their whole lives.

After all, an appearance on a reality TV show might have given me a degree of celebrity, but it is the skills that I learned as a builder that have kept me in demand as a presenter of DIY and building shows, and I have always continued to run my construction business. The truth is, you can never predict the way your life will turn out, but if you have learned a skill from experts in the field, you'll always be able to take advantage of the opportunities that come your way.

Craig Phillips

City & Guilds qualified bricklayer, owner of a successful construction business and television presenter of numerous construction and DIY shows

ABOUT THE AUTHORS

JUSTIN BEATTIE
CHAPTERS 4 AND 5

I grew up in London and eventually settled in Lincolnshire. My career in construction started as an apprentice bricklayer at the age of 16 working for a local building company and attending Grimsby College (now Grimsby Institute of Further & Higher Education), where I achieved my Advanced Craft City & Guilds qualification in Brickwork. During my time as an apprentice I twice won the South Humberside Local Joint Training Committee Cup.

Following my time at college I went on to work as a site foreman and project manager on several construction and regeneration projects. In 2007 I went full circle and returned to the college where I started as an apprentice, teaching all levels of bricklaying and specialising in advanced craft.

I find the role very rewarding and it gives me tremendous satisfaction to see learners developing confidence and skills to enable them to go on to have their own successful careers within construction.

In my spare time I enjoy reading and running a martial arts club.

TONY TUCKER
CHAPTERS 3 AND 6

I was born in the South West and I have spent most of my life there.

Construction has always played a big part in my life, my career began at the age of 15 as a bricklaying apprentice for a small local construction company. After completing my apprenticeship I moved on and worked for a range of larger companies on many interesting projects. In time I progressed to management and soon started to work for myself in building and development.

I started to teach bricklaying at the local college at a very early age and managed to continue my own education at the same time by completing my CIOB qualifications and a BA in Education. I gained a Fellowship of the Chartered Institute of Building in 2000. Working in construction has provided me with many opportunities and I have worked and travelled both nationally and internationally. I am a Past President of the Guild of Bricklayers and still work with them delivering conferences for bricklaying tutors.

I have worked on many interesting projects including building most of the homes that my family have lived in. I have truly loved all of the work that I have experienced in construction, in education, with the Guild of Bricklayers, the Chartered Institute of Building, and my work with City & Guilds.

There are many opportunities that working in construction can give to young people, enjoy your learning and use the knowledge that you gain well.

MARTIN BURDFIELD

CHAPTER 2 AND SERIES TECHNICAL EDITOR

I come from a long line of builders and strongly believe that you will find a career in the construction industry a very rewarding one. Be proud of the work you produce; it will be there for others to admire for many years.

As an apprentice I enjoyed acquiring new knowledge and learning new skills. I achieved the C&G Silver Medal for the highest marks in the Advanced Craft Certificate and won the UK's first Gold Medal in Joinery at the World Skills Competition. My career took me on from foreman, to estimator and then works manager with a number of large joinery companies, where I had the privilege of working on some prestigious projects.

Concurrent with this I began working in education. I have now worked in further education for over 35 years, enjoying watching learners' skills improve during their training. For 10 years I ran the SkillBuild Joinery competitions and was the UK Training Manager and Chief Expert Elect at the World Skills Competition, training the UK's second Gold Medallist in Joinery.

Working with City & Guilds in various roles over the past 25 years has been very rewarding.

I believe that if you work and study hard that anything is possible.

COLIN FEARN

CHAPTER 1

I was born, grew up and continue to live in Cornwall with my wife, three children, a Staffordshire bull terrier, a cat and three rabbits.

As a qualified carpenter and joiner, I have worked for many years on sites and in several joinery shops.

I won the National Wood Award for joinery work and am also a Fellow of the Institute of Carpenters, holder of the Master Craft certificate and have a BA in Education and Training.

I was until recently a full-time lecturer at Cornwall College, teaching both full-time students and apprentices.

I now work full-time as a writer for construction qualifications, practical assessments, questions and teaching materials for UK and Caribbean qualifications.

In my spare time I enjoy walks, small antiques and 'keeping my hand in' with various building projects.

HOW TO USE THIS TEXTBOOK

Welcome to your City & Guilds Level 3 Diploma in Bricklaying textbook. It is designed to guide you through your Level 3 qualification and be a useful reference for you throughout your career. Each chapter covers a unit from the 6705 Level 3 qualification, and covers everything you will need to understand in order to complete your written or online tests and prepare for your practical assessments.

Please note that not all of the chapters will cover the learning outcomes in order. They have been put into a logical sequence as used within the industry and to cover all skills and techniques required.

Throughout this textbook you will see the following features:

Superimposed hearth
A 'decorative feature' normally part of the 'fire surround' that is laid to protect the floor from sparks and embers

Useful words – Words in bold in the text are explained in the margin to help your understanding.

INDUSTRY TIP
On Flemish bond curved walling, lay all of the face headers and stretchers first before marking and cutting any bricks into the rear of the wall.

Industry tips – Useful hints and tips related to working in the construction industry.

ACTIVITY
In the workshop, practise cutting mitred bats on bricks and form an acute quoin in English and Flemish bond incorporating a birdsmouth feature.

Activities – These are suggested activities for you to complete.

FUNCTIONAL SKILLS
You have been asked to build a circular wall one brick thick using tapered joints. The wall is 1200mm high and the diameter is 2.1m. Calculate the number of bricks required to construct the wall.

Work on this activity can support FM2 (L2.2.2 and C2.7).

Functional Skills – These are activities that are tied to learning outcomes for the Functional Skills Maths, English and ICT qualifications.

STEP 1 Remove four bricks at DPC level using a jointing chisel.

STEP 2 After you've removed the bricks, clean the joints away.

Step by steps – These steps illustrate techniques and procedures that you will need to learn in order to carry out bricklaying tasks.

OUR HOUSE

Looking at 'Our House', can you describe the bonding arrangements that are displayed on the panels to the rear garden wall?

'Our House' – These are activities that tie in directly with 'Our House' on SmartScreen to help you put the techniques in the book in context. Ask your tutor for your log-in details.

Case Study: Dayne

Dayne's new brickwork company has really taken off and he is getting a lot of work. He has just started to work on his own after working for a local builder as a trainee for the last few years. His work keeps him busy as when he is not building he is either pricing up work or ordering materials.

Case Studies – Each chapter ends with a case study of an operative who has faced a common problem in the industry. Some of these will reveal the solution and others provide you with the opportunity to solve the problem.

Dog-tooth brickwork

A type of string course, where bricks are laid diagonally in relation to the face line of the wall to give the course a serrated effect.

Trade dictionary – This feature lists the key terms and tools that you will pick up from reading this book.

At the end of every chapter are some 'test your knowledge' questions. These questions are designed to test your understanding of what you have learnt in that chapter. This can help with identifying further training or revision needed. You will find the answers at the end of the book.

INTRODUCTION

This book has been written to support students studying bricklaying at Level 3. By studying this book, you should receive the more advanced skills and knowledge required to complete your course and either progress to further study, enter the workforce or, where you are already working, progress to a supervisory level. You will learn in more depth how work is acquired, the contract documents used, and how the requirements of planning for time, labour and materials allow the build to be constructed efficiently. Specifically, you will learn about radial and battered brickwork, decorative and reinforced brickwork and constructing fireplaces and chimneys.

As mentioned in the features listed on the previous pages, which are there to help you retain the information you will need to become a bricklayer, this textbook includes a large trade dictionary. Use this for reference in class and in the workshop. Become familiar with the terms and techniques, and pay attention to the skills you need to master. Bricklayers who study at this level are often promoted to site supervisors and, when further experienced, site managers. Over time you will become proud of the many buildings that you have helped to build and they will stand as a testament to your skill and knowledge.

ACKNOWLEDGEMENTS

To my lovely wife, best friend and soul mate, Linda, for your constant support and encouragement. I dedicate my work to my beautiful daughters, Lauren and Holly, and wish you the best in your future. And finally to all of my tutors and learners past, present and future who have taught me to never stop learning.

Justin Beattie

To my dear wife Jane, for her constant help and support, and to all of the friends and colleagues that I have had the great pleasure of working with in education over the last 25 years.

Tony Tucker

To my gorgeous wife Clare, without whose constant support, understanding and patience I would not have been able to continue. To Matthew and Eleanor: after not being there on too many occasions, normal service will be resumed. Finally, my parents, to whom I will always be grateful.

Martin Burdfield

I would like to thank my dear wife Helen for her support in writing for this book. I dedicate my work to Matt, Tasha and Daisy, and not forgetting Floyd and Mrs Dusty.

Colin Fearn

City & Guilds would like to sincerely thank the following:

For invaluable bricklaying expertise

David Griffin and Julian Walden.

For freelance editorial support

Cambridge Editorial Partnership Ltd (www.camedit.com) and Ben Gardiner.

For their help with photoshoots

Andrew Buckle (photographer), Garry Blunt, Ryan Kenneth, Nikesh McHugh, Luke Banneman, Joe Beckinsale, Adeel Qamer and the staff at Central Sussex College.

For supplying pictures for the book cover

Andrew Buckle.

TRADE DICTIONARY

Industry term	Definition and regional variations
Aggregates 	The coarse mineral material, such as sharp sand and graded, crushed stone (gravel), used in making mortar and concrete.
Angle finder 	Used in angled walling to set out and build acute and obtuse angles.
Approved Code of Practice (ACoP) 	ACoP gives practical advice for those involved in the construction industry in relation to using machinery safely. ACoP has a special legal status and employers and employees are expected to work within its guidelines.
Arch centre 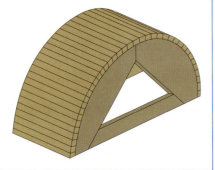	Timber frameworks that are used to support arches temporarily during construction. A temporary timber structure is used to support the arch bricks until the mortar has set and the arch becomes self-supporting. The folding wedges allow the centre to be eased (loosened) then struck (removed).

Industry term	Definition and regional variations
Architect 	A trained professional who designs a structure and represents the client who wants the structure built. They are responsible for the production of the working drawings. They supervise the construction of buildings or other large structures.
Architectural technician 	A draftsperson who works in an architectural practice. They usually prepare the drawings for a building.
Arris 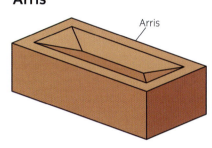	Any straight sharp edge of a brick formed by the junction of two faces.
Asbestos 	A naturally occurring mineral that was commonly used for a variety of purposes including: insulation, fire protection, roofing and guttering. It is extremely hazardous and can cause a serious lung disease known as asbestosis.
Attached pier 	Piers that are not free-standing and are used in a structure or wall to add strength or reinforcement. The term 'attached' means that the pier is bonded into the main section of masonry following the specified bonding arrangement.
Axed brick	A wedge-shaped or tapered brick. Also known as a 'voissoir'.

Industry term	Definition and regional variations
Back boiler	A unit built into the back of a solid fuel fireplace that heats water by heat transfer from the fire.
Banding	Whole sections of brickwork that differ in colour and stand out from the main body of work.
Bat	Part of a brick greater than one-quarter.
Bearing	The part of a lintel that is bedded on the actual wall at each end.
Bed	Mortar upon which the brick is laid or bedded.
Bed joint	Continuous, horizontal mortar joint supporting the bricks.
Bill of quantities	Produced by the quantity surveyor and describes everything that is required for the job based on the drawings, specification and schedules. It is sent out to contractors and ensures that all the contractors are pricing for the job using the same information.

Industry term	Definition and regional variations
Blind arch 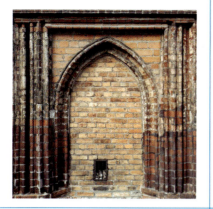	An arch whose centre has been filled in with brickwork.
Boat level 	A small level approximately 250mm long with three bubble chambers set at vertical, horizontal and 45° degrees. Boat levels are useful in checking the accuracy of individual bricks that have been laid.
Bolster 	A broad-bladed chisel used for cutting bricks and blocks.
Bond/bonding 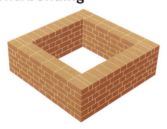	The arrangement or pattern of laying bricks and blocks to spread the load through the wall, also for strength and appearance.
Boundary	A line marking the end of an area.
Brick hammer 	A hammer used for rough cutting of bricks.
Brick-on-edge coping 	A masonry addition that protects the top of the wall from poor weather, where the bricks are laid on edge with the stretcher face uppermost. This type of coping can be used on walls greater than one-brick thickness by bonding the brick on edge (using Stretcher bond) across the top of the wall.

Industry term	Definition and regional variations
Brick trowel	Used to roll and spread the mortar for the bed joints for masonry work and to apply the perp joints. *Regional variation: walling trowel*
Bridged cavity	Something that touches both skins of a cavity wall, ie lintel, tie wire, cavity liner, mortar droppings.
British Standards Institute (BSI)	The authority that develops and publishes standards in the UK.
Broken bond	The use of part bricks to make good a bonding pattern where full bricks will not fit in.
Builder's square	A tool for checking corners. A builder's square that is set at an angle of 90° will form a right-angled quoin. *Regional variation: building square*
Building line	The front line of the building. Note that this can be on or behind the frontage line. (*See also* Line.)
Building Regulations	A series of documents that set out legal requirements for the standards of building work.
CAD drawings	Drawings which are created using computer-aided design.

Industry term	Definition and regional variations
Capping 	A brick, stone or concrete decorative feature on top of isolated piers which provides weather protection. They can incorporate a drip groove to shed water off the face of the pier.
Carbon neutral 	Carbon neutral, or having a net zero carbon footprint, refers to achieving net zero carbon emissions by balancing a measured amount of carbon released with an equivalent amount of carbon credits (planting of trees, etc) to make up the difference. It is used in the context of carbon dioxide dioxide-releasing processes associated with transportation and energy production.
Cast in situ	To form a shutter or box and cast in position.
Cavity tray 	Membrane placed over a bridged cavity. It directs any water present in the cavity to weep holes outside the skin. (*See also* Bridged cavity.)
Cavity wall 	Walls built in two separate skins/leaves (usually of different materials) with a void held together by wall ties.
Chimney stack 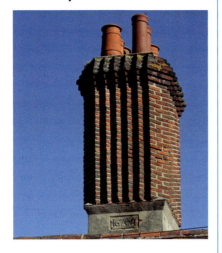	Part of a chimney enclosing one or more flues that rises above the roof of a building that includes the chimney terminal, but not the flue terminal.

Industry term	Definition and regional variations
Cladded	When a surface has been covered in another material, eg plastic or timber.
Clipper saw	This is a bench-type masonry saw used for wet cutting masonry. *Regional variation: masonry bench saw*
Closed lagged	Describing the unspaced timber laggings (laths) placed onto the upper surface of an arch centre or turning piece.
Club hammer	A weighted hammer is used with a bolster or chisel for cutting bricks, blocks and masonry. *Regional variation: lump hammer*
Common bricks	Bricks of medium quality used for ordinary walling work where no special face finish is required. Bricks are manufactured to dimensions and tolerances decided by official institutes. In the UK, this is the British Standards Institute.
Composite shapes	A shape that is made up from two or more different shapes. For instance, a gable end may have a triangular-shaped top section with a square or rectangular lower section.

Industry term	Definition and regional variations
Compression	A force squeezing a material.
Condensation	Water that collects as droplets on a cold surface when humid air is in contact with it; also the conversion of a gas to a liquid.
Contract documents	These comprise working drawings and schedules, specifications, bill of quantities and contracts.
Concrete	Material made up of cement, fine aggregate (sand) and course aggregate (stone) of varying sizes and in varying proportions. It is mixed with water.
Contractors	Workers or companies working to an agreement that is legally binding.
Control measures	Specific instructions to work to and control work practices.
Coping	A masonry addition that protects the top of a wall from poor weather. (*See also* Brick-on-edge coping.)

Industry term	Definition and regional variations
Corbelling 	A method of stepping brickwork across gradually in quarter-brick sections.
Corner blocks 	Corner blocks are plastic or wooden blocks used to hold the line on course at the quoins without the need to put the pin in the brick or block joint.
Corner profiles 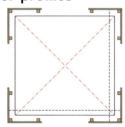	A type of profile used for marking the position of corners. Most bricklayers find corner profiles easier to use as they have level lines which can be used to form building lines in two directions. (*See also* Profiles.)
Course 	A horizontal row of blocks or bricks laid on a mortar bed.
Creepers 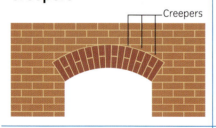	The cut bricks around the extrados of an arch.
Critical path analysis (CPA)	Programme to be followed. Not commonly used on 'everyday contracts'. It is very specialised, and it's easy to make mistakes unless experts are used to generate it. In construction, CPA tends to be used on long, logistically difficult projects such as high-rise commercial buildings (incorporating high-tech systems) in densely populated areas (eg an international bank headquarters in any major city of the world).

Industry term	Definition and regional variations
Cross-section 	A view that shows an imaginary slice through a structure to reveal interior details. (*See also* Section view.)
Cured 	A word that describes concrete that has set over time.
Damp proof course (DPC) 	A layer or strip of watertight material placed in a joint of a wall to prevent the passage of water. Fixed at a minimum of 150mm above finished ground level. Two types of DPC are rigid and flexible.
Dead load	The load of a structure itself and any other permanent fixtures.
Dead shore 	An upright timber used as a temporary support for the dead load of a building during structural alterations, commonly used to support a needle.
Deadmen 	Temporary brickwork built at the corner of a wall to place lines onto for ranging in a wall.

Industry term	Definition and regional variations
Debris 	Rubble or waste, eg which could be the product of cutting out a wall with a hammer and chisel.
Dense 	Material that is hard and heavy for its volume, ie dense blocks.
Dentil course 	Dentil courses are tooth-like projections in the brickwork produced by projecting alternate headers within a course of bricks from the face of the wall. Dentil courses should have at least one course of bricks laid over the top of them to protect the projecting brick from the elements.
Dimension paper	Paper with vertically ruled columns onto which building work is described, measured and costed.
Disc cutter 	A tool powered by electricity, petrol or air that is used to cut masonry or dense materials.
Dividers 	This tool can be used when producing templates to build arches. Once the arch has been drawn, dividers are used to space out evenly the bricks on the extrados of the arch.
Dogleg  © Rugby Brick Cutting	A special brick used on 135° obtuse corners, also known as an external angled brick.

Industry term	Definition and regional variations
Dog-tooth brickwork 	A type of string course, where bricks are laid diagonally in relation to the face line of the wall to give the course a serrated effect.
Double handling	Moving materials twice or even three times before use. This wastes time and energy when bricklaying.
Downdraught	The effect of wind on a flue that causes the flue gases to blow down the flue and into the room.
Dry bond	A method of spacing bricks or blocks without mortar to sort out potential problems with the bond.
Ear defenders	A means of personal protection from the harmful effects of noise.
Efflorescence	A white deposit which may form on the surface of new bricks if the latter contain a high proportion of mineral salts.
Elevation	A drawing showing any face of a building or wall or object.
Engineering bricks	Hard dense bricks of regular size used for carrying heavy loads, eg in bridge buildings, heavy foundations.

Industry term	Definition and regional variations
English bond	A type of one-brick bond. This bond is set out with alternating courses of headers and stretchers. It is the strongest bonding arrangement possible.
English garden wall bond	A type of one-brick bond. The arrangement consists of three, five or seven courses of stretchers to one course of headers.
Excavation	The process of removing subsoil to form a trench.
Expansion joint	An expansion joint separates masonry into segments to accommodate movement due to the increased volume of the wall structure. The joint allows the masonry to expand and contract.
Face	1 The surface presented to view; the front. 2 A brick has two faces, a long side called a stretcher face and a short side called a header face.
Face plane	The alignment of all the bricks or blocks in the face of a wall to give a uniform flat appearance.

Industry term	Definition and regional variations
Faceting 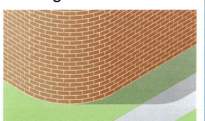	Maintaining an even surface with no protruding edges.
Fair face 	Indicating face work of neat appearance. Flemish bond is often referred to as fair-faced.
Flammable 	Describing material that will burn if it is in contact with fire.
Flashing 	Flashings are commonly made from lead and are used to provide waterproofing at joints where roofing materials meet walls and around chimneys. May also be made from zinc or copper.
Flat roofs 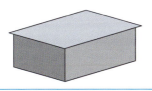	A flat roof is defined as a roof having a pitch of 10° or less. Flat roofs are similar in design to floors, in that they are made from joists decked with timber sheet material. A waterproof layer such as bituminous felt (made from tar), plastic or fibreglass is also used.
Flaunching 	The cement fillet at the junction around a chimney pot and chimney stack.

Industry term	Definition and regional variations
Flemish bond 	A type of one-brick bond that consists of alternating headers and stretchers within a course. The headers in a course are centred above the stretchers in the course below to give a strong quarter bond and also to produce an interesting pattern.
Flemish garden wall bond 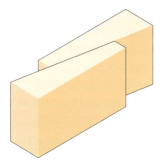	A type of one-brick bond. In this bond there is a pattern of three or five stretchers followed by one header repeated along the length of each course. The header face in a course should be centred above the middle stretcher of each group of three in the course below. One of a number of bonds used to provide a fair face on both sides of the wall, by reducing the number of headers passing through the width of the wall.
Folding wedges 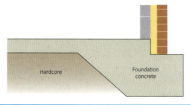	A pair of wedges used back to back to create a pair of parallel faces; by sliding one wedge against the other the total parallel thickness of the folding wedges can be adjusted to pack out the required gap.
Foundation 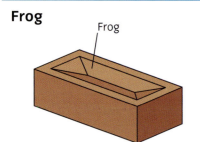	Used to spread the load of a building to the subsoil.
Frog 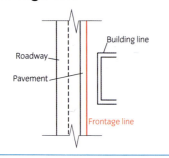	The indentation in a brick.
Frontage line	The front edge of the building plot, usually taken from the centre line of a road or kerb edge, from which the building line is established.

Industry term	Definition and regional variations
Full joint 	A joint that has no gaps or voids that will allow water penetration.
Gauge 	The dimensions of a bed joint (10mm) and a brick depth (65mm) added together (75mm). This needs to be kept uniform and accurate so that the final height of the wall is kept to specification. This is known as keeping to gauge and requires frequent checking with a tape measure or gauge rod.
Gauge rod 	This is used to check gauge of the work and to maintain even bed joints over the height of the wall.
Gothic arch 	Two segments of a circle joining at a pointed apex to form an arch shape. There are three main types of Gothic arch and they are named by the way they are set out. They are called equilateral, dropped and lancet and are different in their spans and heights. Gothic arches are always pointed at the crown of the arch.
Grinder 	This is a power tool used to grind and cut dense materials.
Half-bat 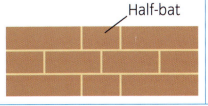	The smallest cut allowed in half-brick walling, it measures 102.5mm. This is the same width as the header face of a full brick.

Industry term	Definition and regional variations
Half-bond 	This is another term for Stretcher bond which is when bricks or blocks are arranged with an overlap the width of a brick or block. This means the perp joints are exactly halfway along the face of the stretchers in the course below. (*See also* Half-brick walling.)
Half-brick walling 	Stretcher bond is often called half-bond. Since the width of the wall is almost the same as half a brick, we refer to Stretcher bond as half-brick walling.
Half-round joint 	The concave shape of the finished bed and perp joints. This is the most common form of joint. *Regional variation: bucket handle*
Hammer drill 	A power tool used to drill holes in masonry or concrete.
Hand hawk 	Used to hold and pick up mortar when pointing or rendering.
Hardstanding	An area of ground where hardcore has been compacted for the placing of temporary buildings or materials.
Hatchings Brickwork	Patterns used on a drawing to identify different materials to meet the standard BS1192.

Industry term	Definition and regional variations
Header face	The end face of a brick, which is its shortest side. It is 102.5mm wide.
Hoarding	Barrier surrounding the site to protect against theft and unauthorised entry.
Hollow pier	A pier where the bricks are laid so that the inside of the pier is hollow.
Imposed load	Additional loads that may be placed on the structure, eg people, furniture, wind and snow.
Improvement notice	Issued by an HSE or local authority inspector to formally notify a company that improvements are needed to the way it is working.
Inclement weather	Weather that prevents building work from taking place, generally too cold, windy or wet, but could also be too hot.
Industrial standards	Minimum standards of quality of completed work universally adopted within the industry.

Industry term	Definition and regional variations
Insulation	Materials used to retain heat and improve the thermal value of the building. Can also be used in managing sound transfer.
Isolated piers	Piers that are built separate from other masonry structures and are often used in situations such as gated entrances on a drive or pathway. If the pier is built in 1½ or 2 brick thickness (or more), it has the advantage of allowing reinforcement to be introduced within the hollow centre. The pier can then support the weight of a heavy gate.
Isometric projection 30°	A drawing showing detail in three dimensions. The vertical lines in the structure will be drawn at 90° to the horizontal (or bottom edge of the page) and the horizontal lines of the structure will be drawn at 30° to the horizontal on the page.
Jointing chisel	A specially shaped chisel that is used to cut out joints in brickwork without damaging the brick's face.
Jointing iron	A tool used to provide a finish to the joints. It produces a concave finish to the mortar just before it begins to harden, to create a half-round joint. *Regional variation: jointer*
Jointing	To make a finish to the mortar faces as work proceeds, eg half-round jointing.

Industry term	Definition and regional variations
Kiln	A type of large oven, used to produce moulded clay facing bricks.
Kinetic lifting	A method of lifting that ensures the risk of injury is reduced.
Label course	This is either a stone or brick feature which sits on the extrados and forms a weathered feature over an arch. Often found in Gothic arches.
Lateral pressure Lateral force	Pressure that is exerted from a sideways, usually horizontal, direction.
Lead time	The delay between the initiation and execution of a process. For example, the lead time between the placement of an order for a staircase from a joinery manufacturer and its delivery may be anywhere from two to eight weeks.

Industry term	Definition and regional variations
Leaves	The two walls that make up a cavity wall to comply with current building regulations. They are tied together with wall ties. *Regional variation: skin*
Levelling	To make sure that two points are at the same height.
Lime	A fine powdered material traditionally used in mortars.
Line	The straightness of the block or brickwork.
Line and pins	String held with pins used to line and level the courses of bricks or blocks in position.
Lintel	A horizontal member for spanning an opening, such as a door, to support the structure above, usually made from steel or concrete. A lintel used in a cavity wall must always be protected with the use of a cavity tray. The tray is installed above the lintel and will help catch any moisture and direct it to the outside of the wall using weep holes.

Industry term	Definition and regional variations
Local exhaust ventilation (LEV) 	An engineering control system that reduces exposure to airborne contaminants by sucking the dust and fumes away from the workplace.
Manufacturer's instructions 	Guidelines given by the manufacturer on conditions of use.
Masonry saw 	A saw used to cut lightweight blocks.
Method statement (construction) 	This is a detailed breakdown of the labour and plant required for each bill item. This allows for accurate programming. *Regional variation: construction phase plan*

Industry term	Definition and regional variations
MEWPs 	An abbreviation for mobile elevated working platforms. A type of access equipment that will enable you to gain access to work at a higher level than you can reach from the floor.
Mixer 	Used to mix mortar and concrete on site. This can be powered by electricity, a diesel engine or a petrol engine.
Mortar 	A mixture of soft sand and cement mixed with water and other additives if required, eg plasticiser, colouring or lime. It is used for laying bricks.
Movement joint	A joint to allow thermal expansion in materials, enabling expansion and contraction. (*See also* Expansion joint.)
Offset props 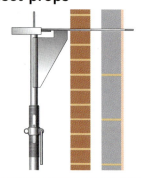	An adaptation that is added to an expanding prop to provide support for brick/block structures.

Industry term	Definition and regional variations
Open lagged 	Describing the spaced timber laggings (laths) placed onto the upper surface of an arch centre or turning piece. *Regional variation: hit and miss lagging*
Optical level 	A levelling operation using eyesight. The level is accurate up to 30m with a variation of +/–5mm. Bricklayers use optical levels when the length of construction exceeds the straight edge. The level is placed on a tripod and used with a staff or rod to transfer lines between two or more points.
Ordnance bench mark (OBM) 	They are a given height on an Ordnance Survey map. This fixed height is described as a value, eg so many metres above sea level (as calculated from the average sea height at Newlyn, Cornwall).
Orthographic projection 	A drawing where the front elevation of a structure has the plan view directly below it. The side or end elevations are shown directly each side of the front elevation. The most commonly used type of orthographic projection is called 'first angle projection'.
Overhand work	Facework executed from the back of the wall.
Oversailing courses 	Oversailing courses are brick courses that extend beyond the normal face of the wall. Unlike the other types of string course (dentil and dog-tooth) that have in-and-out patterns, oversailing courses are formed in a continuous line. Oversailing courses can also be used to increase the thickness of a wall.
Parged	A method of daubing lime mortar on the inside lining of the chimney flue to provide extra protection.

Industry term	Definition and regional variations
Perimeter	The distance around an object or room.
Permits to work	The permit to work is a documented procedure that gives authorisation for certain people to carry out specific work within a specified timeframe. It sets out the precautions required to complete the work safely, based on a risk assessment.
Perp joints	Vertical mortar joints which join two bricks or blocks together. They are at right angles (or perpendicular) to the bed.
Personal protective equipment (PPE)	This is defined in the Personal Protective Equipment at Work Regulations as 'all equipment (including clothing affording protection against the weather) which is intended to be worn or held by a person at work and which protects against one or more risks to a person's health or safety.' For example, safety helmets, gloves, eye protection, high-visibility clothing, safety footwear and safety harnesses.
Piers	Brickwork used for support in walls or as pillars, attached and detached.
Pinch rod	A piece of timber cut to the width of an opening and used to check that the opening size stays the same width over the full height of the opening.

Industry term	Definition and regional variations
Pitched roofs	Pitched roofs are constructed using rafters and come in a variety of designs, notably lean-to, gable and hipped.
Plasticiser	An additive that is used to make mortar pliable and easier to work with. This is safer and easier to use than the traditionally used hydrated lime in powder form.
Plinth	The projecting base of a wall or column.
Plinth bricks	Special bricks used to reduce the thickness of walls as they have a weathered finish. Plinth bricks are the preferred choice over tumbling in nowadays as the method of construction is much quicker and the finished appearance can look much better.
Plumb	The verticality of brickwork. Plumbing should be started from the second course, using a spirit level.
Pneumatic breaker	This is used for heavy breaking of concrete and roadways.

Industry term	Definition and regional variations
Pointing	The process of applying a finish to the joints in brickwork using mortar.
Pointing trowel	Used to apply a joint finish after completion of a wall.
Pre-cast	Formed in a mould until hard and then used as a solid item. Such items are often made in a factory, or can be made on site and fitted when cured.
Profiles	Boards fixed horizontally to ground pegs at the ends of a wall before construction commences in order that lines may be stretched across to mark the position of the foundations and wall. (*See also* Corner profiles.)
Programme of work	A series of events where the order of activities and the amount of time involved has been planned out. This is usually shown in the form of a bar or Gantt chart. *Regional variation: work schedule*
Prohibition notice	Issued by an HSE or local authority inspector when there is an immediate risk of personal injury. Receiving one means you are breaking health and safety regulations.
Quantity surveyor	A quantity surveyor will produce the bill of quantities and later works with a client to manage costs and contracts.
Quarter bond	Bonds in a wall that have a width equal to the length of the stretcher face of a brick (and are therefore referred to as 'one-brick' walling). The bonding arrangement shows bricks lapping each other by a quarter of a length (as in English and Flemish bond). Used where a thicker wall is needed for greater strength.

Industry term	Definition and regional variations
Queen closer 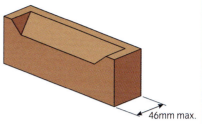	A brick split along its length to produce a cut of 46mm. It is cut to the size of half a header face, and is used next to quoin bricks to establish the start of a bonding arrangement. Also used in indents for junction walls.
Quoins 	The vertical external angles (corners) in walling. Builder's squares are used to check that the corner is square before you lay any blocks or bricks.
Racking back 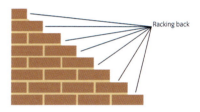	The process of building up the corners or the ends of a wall to produce a plumb reference point that guides accurate laying of the rest of the wall in between. *Regional variation: raking back*
Radial bricks 	Bricks manufactured in a curved shape.
Ranging line 	A line stretched between profiles to mark the position of a wall end or foundation. The line is made from nylon and is waterproof. *Regional variation: builder's line*
Rat trap bond 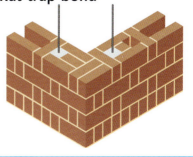	A brick bond incorporating reinforcement. Bricks are laid in rowlock and shiner positions.

Industry term	Definition and regional variations
Reclaim 	To re-use resources, eg to use crushed bricks for hardcore.
Reinforced 	Brickwork strengthened by adding steel and concrete.
Render 	This is a sand- and cement-based finish that is applied to a wall to give it a smooth finish.
Retaining wall 	A wall built to support or prevent the advance of a mass of earth or other material.
Return	The position where the inside leaf of a cavity wall returns to meet the outside leaf and seals the cavity.
Reveal	The masonry forming the side of a window or door opening.
Reverse bond 	In the same course, starting with a stretcher and ending with a header.
Risk assessment 	An assessment of the hazards and risks associated with an activity and the reduction and monitoring of them.

Industry term	Definition and regional variations
Rowlock face	A brick laid on its long narrow side on edge.
Sailor face	A brick laid vertically with the broad face exposed.
Scale Scale: 1:1250	The ratio of the size on a drawing to the size of the real thing that it represents. It is impossible to fit a full-sized drawing of a building onto a sheet of paper, so it is necessary to scale the size of the building to enable it to fit. Scale rules are used to draw scaled-down buildings on paper.
Scale rule	Used with drawings to measure the dimensional line to a scale.
Scutch hammer	A bricklayer's hammer with interchangeable finishing heads for trimming and tidying bricks and blocks. *Regional variation: comb hammer*

Industry term	Definition and regional variations
Section view 	Drawings that show a cut away view of a structure. (*See also* Cross-section.)
Segmental arch 	If a circle was drawn, this type of arch would be formed by a segment of the circle.
Semi-circular arch 	If a circle was drawn, this type of arch would be formed by half of the circle.
Services 	The utilities that serve a building such as water, gas, electricity and telephone.
Set square 	Used to draw lines at 90, 60, 45 and 30° on a drawing.

Industry term	Definition and regional variations
Setting out	A method of locating the position of building works ready for starting work. This involves marking and positioning where a structure will be built. Accuracy is very important when setting out as mistakes here can prove costly.
Settlement	The gradual distortions that are created in a building over time.
Shiner face	A brick laid on edge with the broad face of the brick exposed.
Sliding bevel	A sliding bevel is a square that can be set to different angles to aid marking out. It is constructed of a hardwood stock, a sliding blade and a locking screw. It is used to set out and mark the angle of the skewback on the brick when building arches.
Snap headers	Bricks cut in half and placed in one single skin of a wall. Mainly used in half-brick walling.
Soffit	The underside of a part of a building, such as an arch.
Soldier arch	Where bricks are laid on end with the stretcher face showing above an opening.
Soldier course	A decorative feature where bricks are laid on end with the stretcher face showing. A contrasting brick can be used to add to the decorative appearance and the bricks can be set to project a small distance from the face line of the main wall to add more detail.

Industry term	Definition and regional variations
Solid walls 	Walls of a thickness of one brick and greater. Unlike cavity walls, there are usually only two materials to consider; either bricks and mortar or blocks and mortar.
Spalling 	Where the faces of bricks are forced off by the effects of frost penetration; this is common in soft porous bricks. Spalling also occurs in concrete where steel expands due to corrosion and forces the face of the concrete to shell off under pressure.
Special bricks 	Also known as purpose-made bricks, these are bricks that are made for particular specific jobs, eg, bullnosed, single cants, squint bricks and doglegs.
Specification 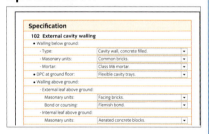	A contract document that gives information about the quality of materials and standards of workmanship required.
Spirit level 	A measuring tool to make sure the work is level and plumb. Spirit levels come in a range of sizes; the size most commonly used by bricklayers is 1.2m, but sometimes 2m spirit levels are used to help with the construction of blockwork.
Spot board 	A board made of durable material roughly 600mm x 600mm, on which mortar is placed. The boards are raised up from ground level by supporting it on blocks.

Industry term	Definition and regional variations
Springer brick 	The lowermost voussoir, located at the springing point of the arch.
Squint brick 	A special brick placed into the corner of a half-brick wall. Just like a normal quoin, the bonding arrangement is then worked out from there.
Stihl saw 	A tool used to cut very hard bricks.
Stitch drilling 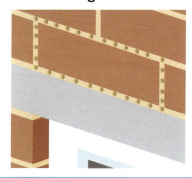	A method of drilling a number of holes along a joint to ease its removal.
Stitching 	A method of inserting reinforcement into the bed joints of a wall to provide added strength.

Industry term	Definition and regional variations
Storey rod	A rod that is used to check the vertical height of various aspects of the building during construction. The rod is normally marked with window heights, joist heights, door heights, etc.
Straight edge	An accurately proportioned implement with parallel edges made of timber or aluminium and up to 3m in length.
Stretcher bond	Bricks or blocks arranged with an overlap the width of a brick or block. This means the perp joints are exactly halfway along the face of the stretchers in the course below.
Stretcher face	The long face of a brick when laid. It measures 215mm wide.
String course	A long narrow course projecting from the general face of the brickwork.
Structural engineer	A person who calculates loads, stresses and strains that may be applied to a building and advises on designs to accommodate them.
Subfoundation	The ground that a foundation bears on. *Regional variation: natural foundation*

Industry term	Definition and regional variations
Subsidence 	This is the downward movement of the site on which a building stands, where the movement is not connected with the weight of the building.
Subsoil 	Earth covering the site, low compression strength.
Superimposed hearth 	A decorative feature, normally part of the fire surround, that is laid to protect the floor from sparks and embers.
Sustainability 	To continue to do something with minimal long-term effects on the environment. Building materials can be sustainable if they are chosen carefully.
Tape measure 	A measuring tool used to set out and check dimensions. A range of tape measures in various sizes is required when setting out a structure. Tape measures vary in range from 3m to 30m.
Temporary bench mark (TBM) 	Unlike an OBM, this is only temoprary and is set up on site. These can be timber pegs surrounded by concrete.

Industry term	Definition and regional variations
Tensile forces	A measure of the ability of material to resist a force that tends to pull it apart.
Tile creasing	Two courses of concrete or clay tiles, half-bonded and bedded in mortar. The creasing course oversails (projects) protecting the wall from water running down from the brick on edge course.
Tile cutter	A power tool used to cut ceramic wall and floor tiles.
Tingle plate	This is used on a long line when laying bricks or blocks to ensure that the line does not sag in the middle.
Tolerances	Allowable variations between the specified measurement and the actual measurement.
Toolbox talk	A health and safety talk carried out on site to highlight any potential hazards and precautions to be taken. This will usually be carried out by the site foreman and recorded in writing.

Industry term	Definition and regional variations
Trammel heads	Trammel heads are used to set out circular shapes. A pencil is placed into one end and the other end acts as a pivot point. The heads can be spaced along the timber rod to make a circle larger or smaller depending on the radius.
Trowel	Used to lay bricks. It has a 'blade', which allows you to manipulate the mortar when laying.
Turning pieces	A temporary timber support used when building segmental arches to support the arch bricks until the radius is complete from one side of the opening to the other.
Unit rate	The unit rate = the labour rate + the material rate
U-value	U-value, also known as thermal transmittance, is the rate of transfer of heat through a structure (in watts) or more correctly through one square metre of a structure divided by the difference in temperature across the structure. It is expressed in watts per metre squared kelvin, or W/m^2K.
Volatile organic compound (VOC)	The volatile organic compounds measure shows how much pollution a product will emit into the air when in use.
Walkthrough	An animated sequence as seen at the eye level of a person walking through a proposed structure.

Industry term	Definition and regional variations
Wall ties	Usually made of stainless steel, these are used to tie the two skins of a cavity wall together to strengthen it.
Weatherstruck joint	An angled joint, which means one side of the joint is pressed further into the joint than the other. This allows water to shed off the wall.
Weep holes	Small openings in a wall to permit the escape of water from the back of the wall.
Well graded sand	Sand that has large, medium and small grains, such as 'pit sand' or 'sea-dredged sand'. Used in mortar.
Withes	The thin division between adjoining flue liners, sometimes termed mid-feathers.

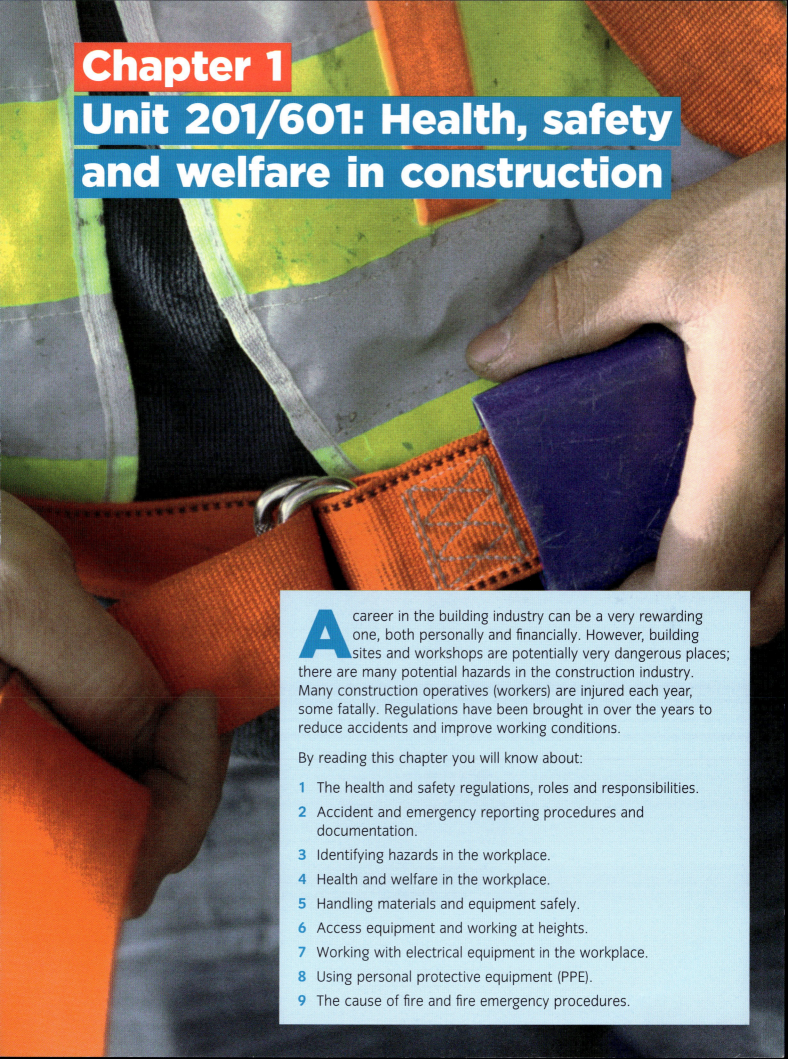

Chapter 1
Unit 201/601: Health, safety and welfare in construction

A career in the building industry can be a very rewarding one, both personally and financially. However, building sites and workshops are potentially very dangerous places; there are many potential hazards in the construction industry. Many construction operatives (workers) are injured each year, some fatally. Regulations have been brought in over the years to reduce accidents and improve working conditions.

By reading this chapter you will know about:

1 The health and safety regulations, roles and responsibilities.
2 Accident and emergency reporting procedures and documentation.
3 Identifying hazards in the workplace.
4 Health and welfare in the workplace.
5 Handling materials and equipment safely.
6 Access equipment and working at heights.
7 Working with electrical equipment in the workplace.
8 Using personal protective equipment (PPE).
9 The cause of fire and fire emergency procedures.

HEALTH AND SAFETY LEGISLATION

According to the Health and Safety Executive (HSE) figures, in 2012/13:

- Forty-six construction operatives were fatally injured. Twelve of these operatives were self-employed. This compares with an average of 50 fatalities over the previous five years, of which an average of 17 fatally injured construction operatives were self-employed.

- The rate of fatal injury per 100,000 construction operatives was 1.94, compared with a five-year average of 2.07.

- Construction industry operatives were involved in 27% of fatal injuries across all industry sectors and it accounts for the greatest number of fatal injuries in any industry sector.

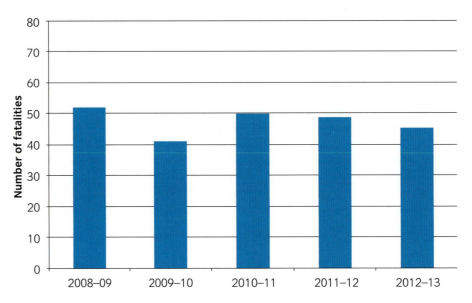

Number and rate of fatal injuries to workers in construction (RIDDOR)

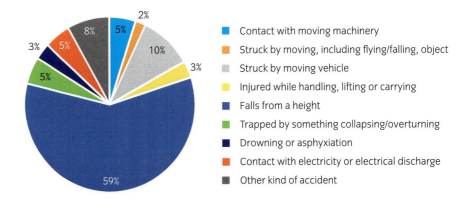

Proportion of fatalities in 2012/13 in construction

Health and safety legislation and great efforts made by the industry have made workplaces much safer in recent years. It is the responsibility of everyone involved in the building industry to continue to make it safer. Statistics are not just meaningless numbers – they represent injuries to real people. Many people believe that an accident will never happen to them, but it can. Accidents can:

- have a devastating effect on lives and families

- cost a lot financially in injury claims

- result in prosecution

- lead to job loss if an employee broke their company's safety policy.

Employers have an additional duty to ensure operatives have access to welfare facilities, eg drinking water, first aid and toilets, which will be discussed later in this chapter.

If everyone who works in the building industry pays close attention to health, safety and welfare, all operatives – including you – have every chance of enjoying a long, injury-free career.

UK HEALTH AND SAFETY REGULATIONS, ROLES AND RESPONSIBILITIES

In the UK there are many laws (legislation) that have been put into place to make sure that those working on construction sites, and members of the public, are kept healthy and safe. If these laws and regulations are not obeyed then prosecutions can take place. Worse still, there is a greater risk of injury and damage to your health and the health of those around you.

Standard construction safety equipment

The principal legislation which relates to health, safety and welfare in construction is:

- Health and Safety at Work Act (HASAWA) 1974

- Control of Substances Hazardous to Health (COSHH) Regulations 2002

- Reporting of Injuries, Diseases and Dangerous Occurrences Regulations (RIDDOR) 1995

- Construction, Design and Management (CDM) Regulations 2007

- Provision and Use of Work Equipment Regulations (PUWER) 1998

- Manual Handling Operations Regulations 1992

- Personal Protective Equipment (PPE) at Work Regulations 1992

- Work at Height Regulations 2005 (as amended)
- Lifting Operations and Lifting Equipment Regulations (LOLER) 1998
- Control of Noise at Work Regulations 2005
- Control of Vibration at Work Regulations 2005.

HEALTH AND SAFETY AT WORK ACT (HASAWA) 1974

The Health and Safety at Work Act (HASAWA) 1974 applies to all workplaces. Everyone who works on a building site or in a workshop is covered by this legislation. This includes employed and self-employed operatives, subcontractors, the employer and those delivering goods to the site. It not only protects those working, it also ensures the safety of anyone else who might be nearby.

KEY EMPLOYER RESPONSIBILITIES

The key employer health and safety responsibilities under HASAWA are to:

- provide a safe working environment
- provide safe access (entrance) and egress (exit) to the work area
- provide adequate staff training
- have a written health and safety policy in place
- provide health and safety information and display the appropriate signs
- carry out risk assessments
- provide safe machinery and equipment and to ensure it is well-maintained and in a safe condition
- provide adequate supervision to ensure safe practices are carried out
- involve trade union safety representatives, where appointed, in matters relating to health and safety
- provide personal protective equipment (**PPE**) free of charge, ensure the appropriate PPE is used whenever needed, and that operatives are properly supervised
- ensure materials and substances are transported, used and stored safely.

PPE

This is defined in the Personal Protective Equipment at Work Regulations 1992 as 'all equipment (including clothing affording protection against the weather) which is intended to be worn or held by a person at work and which protects against one or more risks to a person's health or safety.'

Risk assessments and method statements

The HASAWA requires that employers must carry out regular **risk assessments** to make sure that there are minimal dangers to their employees in a workplace.

Risk assessment

An assessment of the hazards and risks associated with an activity and the reduction and monitoring of them

Risk Assessment

Activity / Workplace assessed: Return to work after accident
Persons consulted / involved in risk assessment
Date:
Reviewed on:

Location:
Risk assessment reference number:
Review date:
Review by:

Significant hazard	People at risk and what is the risk Describe the harm that is likely to result from the hazard (eg cut, broken leg, chemical burn etc) and who could be harmed (eg employees, contractors, visitors etc)	Existing control measure What is currently in place to control the risk?	Risk rating Use matrix identified in guidance note Likelihood (L) Severity (S) Multiply (L) * (S) to produce risk rating (RR)				Further action required What is required to bring the risk down to an acceptable level? Use hierarchy of control described in guidance note when considering the controls needed	Actioned to: Who will complete the action?	Due date: When will the action be completed by?	Completion date: Initial and date once the action has been completed
			L	S	RR	L/M/H				
Uneven floors	Operatives	Verbal warning and supervision	2	1	2	M	None applicable	Site supervisor	Active now	Ongoing
Steps	Operatives	Verbal warning	2	1	2	M	None applicable	Site supervisor	Active now	Ongoing
Staircases	Operatives	Verbal warning	2	2	4	M	None applicable	Site supervisor	Active now	Ongoing

Severity		Likelihood		
		1 Unlikely	**2** Possible	**3** Very likely
1 Slight/minor injuries/minor damage		1	2	3
2 Medium injuries/significant damage		2	4	6
3 Major injury/extensive damage		3	6	9

Likelihood
3 – Very likely
2 – Possible
1 – Unlikely

Severity
3 – Major injury/extensive damage
2 – Medium injury/significant damage
1 – Slight/minor damage

1   – Low risk, action should be taken to reduce the risk if reasonably practicable
2, 3, 4 – Medium risk, is a significant risk and would require an appropriate level of resource
6 & 9 – High risk, may require considerable resource to mitigate. Control should focus on elimination of risk, if not possible control should be obtained by following the hierarchy of control

123 type risk assessment

A risk assessment is a legally required tool used by employers to:

- identify work hazards

- assess the risk of harm arising from these hazards

- adequately control the risk.

Risk assessments are carried out as follows:

1 Identify the hazards. Consider the environment in which the job will be done. Which tools and materials will be used?

2 Identify who might be at risk. Think about operatives, visitors and members of the public.

3 Evaluate the risk. How severe is the potential injury? How likely is it to happen? A severe injury may be possible but may also be very improbable. On the other hand a minor injury might be very likely.

4 If there is an unacceptable risk, can the job be changed? Could different tools or materials be used instead?

5 If the risk is acceptable, what measures can be taken to reduce the risk? This could be training, special equipment and using PPE.

6 Keep good records. Explain the findings of the risk assessment to the operatives involved. Update the risk assessment as required – there may be new machinery, materials or staff. Even adverse weather can bring additional risks.

A **method statement** is required by law and is a useful way of recording the hazards involved in a specific task. It is used to communicate the risk and precautions required to all those involved in the work. It should be clear, uncomplicated and easy to understand as it is for the benefit of those carrying out the work (and their immediate supervisors).

Inductions and toolbox talks

Any new visitors to and operatives on a site will be given an induction. This will explain:

- the layout of the site

- any hazards of which they need to be aware

- the location of welfare facilities

- the assembly areas in case of emergency

- site rules.

Toolbox talks are short talks given at regular intervals. They give timely safety reminders and outline any new hazards that may have arisen because construction sites change as they develop. Weather conditions such as extreme heat, wind or rain may create new hazards.

KEY EMPLOYEE RESPONSIBILITIES

The HASAWA covers the responsibilities of employees and subcontractors:

- You must work in a safe manner and take care at all times.

- You must make sure you do not put yourself or others at risk by your actions or inactions.

Method statement

A description of the intended method of carrying out a task, often linked to a risk assessment

INDUSTRY TIP

The Construction Skills Certification Scheme (CSCS) was set up in the mid-'90s with the aim of improving site operatives' competence to reduce accidents and drive up on-site efficiency. Card holders must take a health and safety test. The colour of card depends on level of qualification held and job role. For more information see www.cscs.uk.com

ACTIVITY

Think back to your induction. Write down what was discussed. Did you understand everything? Do you need any further information? If you have not had an induction, write a list of the things you think you need to know.

INDUSTRY TIP

Remember, if you are unsure about any health and safety issue always seek help and advice.

- You must co-operate with your employer in regard to health and safety. If you do not you risk injury (to yourself or others), prosecution, a fine and loss of employment. Do not take part in practical jokes and horseplay.

- You must use any equipment and safeguards provided by your employer. For example, you must wear, look after and report any damage to the PPE that your employer provides.

- You must not interfere or tamper with any safety equipment.

- You must not misuse or interfere with anything that is provided for employees' safety.

FIRST AID AND FIRST-AID KITS

First aid should only be applied by someone trained in first aid. Even a minor injury could become infected and therefore should be cleaned and a dressing applied. If any cut or injury shows signs of infection, becomes inflamed or painful seek medical attention. An employer's first-aid needs should be assessed to indicate whether a first-aider (someone trained in first aid) is necessary. The minimum requirement is to appoint a person to take charge of first-aid arrangements. The role of this appointed person includes looking after the first-aid equipment and facilities and calling the emergency services when required.

First-aid kits vary according to the size of the workforce. First-aid boxes should not contain tablets or medicines.

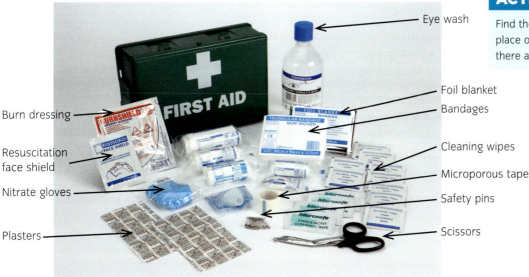

Burn dressing
Resuscitation face shield
Nitrate gloves
Plasters

Eye wash
Foil blanket
Bandages
Cleaning wipes
Microporous tape
Safety pins
Scissors

First-aid kit

SOURCES OF HEALTH AND SAFETY INFORMATION

Source	How they can help
Health and Safety Executive (HSE)	A government body that oversees health and safety in the workplace. It produces health and safety literature such as the **Approved Code of Practice** (ACoP).
Construction Skills	The construction industry training body produces literature and is directly involved with construction training.
The Royal Society for the Prevention of Accidents (ROSPA)	It produces literature and gives advice.
The Royal Society for Public Health	An independent, multi-disciplinary charity that is dedicated to the promotion and protection of collective human health and wellbeing.
Institution of Occupational Safety and Health (IOSH)	A chartered body for health and safety practitioners. The world's largest health and safety professional membership organisation.
The British Safety Council	It helps businesses with their health, safety and environmental management.

HEALTH AND SAFETY EXECUTIVE (HSE)

The HSE is a body set up by the government. The HSE ensures that the law is carried out correctly and has extensive powers to ensure that it can do its job. It can make spot checks in the workplace, bring the police, examine anything on the premises and take things away to be examined.

If the HSE finds a health and safety problem that breaks health and safety law it might issue an **improvement notice** giving the employer a set amount of time to correct the problem. For serious health and safety risks where there is a risk of immediate major injury, it can issue a **prohibition notice** which will stop all work on site until the health and safety issues are rectified. It may take an employer, employee, self-employed person (subcontractor) or anyone else

---

Approved Code of Practice

ACoP gives practical advice for those in the construction industry in relation to using machinery

INDUSTRY TIP

There are many other trade organisations, eg the Timber Research and Development Association (TRADA), which also offer advice on safe practices.

ACTIVITY

You have been asked to give a toolbox talk because of several minor injuries involving tripping on site. What topics would you include in this talk?

INDUSTRY TIP

To find out more information on the sources in the table, enter their names into a search engine on the internet.

Improvement notice

Issued by an HSE or local authority inspector to formally notify a company that improvements are needed to the way it is working

Prohibition notice

Issued by an HSE or local authority inspector when there is an immediate risk of personal injury. They are not issued lightly and if you are on the receiving end of one, you are clearly breaking a health and safety regulation

involved with the building process to court for breaking health and safety legislation.

The HSE provides a lot of advice on safety and publishes numerous booklets and information sheets. One example of this is the Approved Code of Practice (ACoP) which applies to wood working machinery. The ACoP has a special legal status and employers and employees are expected to work within its guidelines.

The duties of the HSE are to:

- give advice

- issue improvement and prohibition notices

- caution

- prosecute

- investigate.

The Approved Code of Practice booklet is available free online

CONTROL OF SUBSTANCES HAZARDOUS TO HEALTH (COSHH) REGULATIONS 2002

The Control of Substances Hazardous to Health (COSHH) Regulations 2002 control the use of dangerous substances, eg preservatives, fuels, solvents, adhesives, cement and oil-based paint. These have to be moved, stored and used safely without polluting the environment. It also covers hazardous substances produced while working, eg wood dust produced when sanding or drilling.

Hazardous substances may be discovered during the building process, eg lead-based paint or asbestos. These are covered by separate regulations.

When considering substances and materials that may be hazardous to health an employer should do the following to comply with COSHH:

- Read and check the COSHH safety data sheet that comes with the product. It will outline any hazards associated with the product and the safety measures to be taken.

- Check with the supplier if there are any known risks to health.

- Use the trade press to find out if there is any information about this substance or material.

- Use the HSE website, or other websites, to check any known issues with the substance or material.

When assessing the risk of a potentially dangerous substance or material it is important to consider how operatives could be exposed to it. For example:

Example of COSHH data sheet

- by breathing in gas or mist

- by swallowing it

- by getting it into their eyes

- through their skin, either by contact or through cuts.

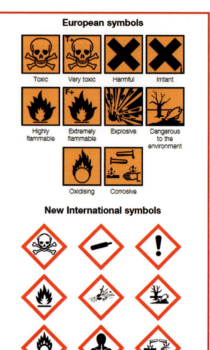

Safety data sheets

Products you use may be 'dangerous for supply'. If so, they will have a label that has one or more hazard symbols. Some examples are given here.

These products include common substances in everyday use such as paint, bleach, solvent or fillers. When a product is 'dangerous for supply', by law, the supplier must provide you with a safety data sheet. Note: medicines, pesticides and cosmetic products have different legislation and don't have a safety data sheet. Ask the supplier how the product can be used safely.

Safety data sheets can be hard to understand, with little information on measures for control. However, to find out about health risks and emergency situations, concentrate on:

- Sections 2 and 16 of the sheet, which tell you what the dangers are;
- Sections 4–8, which tell you about emergencies, storage and handling.

Since 2009, new international symbols have been gradually replacing the European symbols. Some of them are similar to the European symbols, but there is no single word describing the hazard. Read the hazard statement on the packaging and the safety data sheet from the supplier.

European symbols

Toxic Very toxic Harmful Irritant

Highly flammable Extremely flammable Explosive Dangerous to the environment

Oxidising Corrosive

New International symbols

Hazard checklist

☐ Does any product you use have a danger label?
☐ Does your process produce gas, fume, dust, mist or vapour?
☐ Is the substance harmful to breathe in?
☐ Can the substance harm your skin?
☐ Is it likely that harm could arise because of the way you use or produce it?
☐ What are you going to do about it?
  - Use something else?
  - Use it in another, safer way?
  - Control it to stop harm being caused?

CONTROL MEASURES

The control measures below are in order of importance.

1 Eliminate the use of the harmful substance and use a safer one. For instance, swap high **VOC** oil-based paint for a lower VOC water-based paint.

2 Use a safer form of the product. Is the product available ready-mixed? Is there a lower strength option that will still do the job?

VOC

The volatile organic compounds measure shows how much pollution a product will emit into the air when in use

INDUSTRY TIP

Product data sheets are free and have to be produced by the supplier of the product.

3 Change the work method to emit less of the substance. For instance, applying paint with a brush releases fewer VOCs into the air than spraying paint. Wet grinding produces less dust than dry grinding.

4 Enclose the work area so that the substance does not escape. This can mean setting up a tented area or closing doors.

5 Use extraction or filtration (eg a dust bag) in the work area.

6 Keep operatives in the area to a minimum.

7 Employers must provide appropriate PPE.

Paint with high VOC content

ACTIVITY

Think of three substances in your workplace or place of training that might be hazardous to health. Can you find a COSHH data sheet for each? (They can often be found on the internet if you search for the product.)

European symbols

New International symbols

COSHH symbols. The international symbols will replace the European symbols in 2015.

REPORTING OF INJURIES, DISEASES AND DANGEROUS OCCURRENCES REGULATIONS (RIDDOR) 1995

Despite all the efforts put into health and safety, incidents still happen. The Reporting of Injuries, Diseases and Dangerous Occurrences Regulations (RIDDOR) 1995 state that employers must report to the HSE all accidents that result in an employee needing more than seven days off work. Diseases and dangerous occurrences must also be reported. A serious occurrence that has not caused an injury (a near miss) should still be reported because next time it happens things might not work out as well.

Below are some examples of injuries, diseases and dangerous occurrences that would need to be reported:

- A joiner cuts off a finger while using a circular saw.

- A plumber takes a week off after a splinter in her hand becomes infected.

- A ground operative contracts **leptospirosis**.

- A labourer contracts dermatitis (a serious skin problem) after contact with an irritant substance.

- A scaffold suffers a collapse following severe weather, unauthorised alteration or overloading but no one is injured.

Leptospirosis

Also known as Weil's disease, this is a serious disease spread by rats and cattle

The purpose of RIDDOR is to enable the HSE to investigate serious incidents and collate statistical data. This information is used to help reduce the number of similar accidents happening in future and to make the workplace safer.

An F2508 injury report form

Although minor accidents and injuries are not reported to HSE, records must be kept. Accidents must be recorded in the accident book. This provides a record of what happened and is useful for future reference. Trends may become apparent and the employer may take action to try to prevent that particular type of accident occurring again.

ACTIVITY

You have identified a potential risk. What action should you take? Make notes.

CONSTRUCTION, DESIGN AND MANAGEMENT (CDM) REGULATIONS 2007

The Construction, Design and Management (CDM) Regulations 2007 focus attention on the effective planning and management of construction projects, from the design concept through to maintenance and repair. The aim is for health and safety considerations to be integrated into a project's development, rather than be an inconvenient afterthought. The CDM Regulations reduce the risk of harm to those that have to work on or use the structure throughout its life, from construction through to **demolition**.

The CDM Regulations play a role in safety during demolition

Demolition

When something, often a building, is completely torn down and destroyed

CDM Regulations protect workers from the construction to demolition of large and complex structures

The CDM Regulations apply to all projects except for those arranged by private clients, ie work that isn't in furtherance of a business interest. Property developers need to follow the CDM Regulations.

Under the CDM Regulations, the HSE must be notified where the construction work will take:

- more than 30 working days or

- 500 working days in total, ie if 100 people work for 5 days (500 working days) the HSE will have to be notified.

DUTY HOLDERS

Under the CDM Regulations there are several duty holders, each with a specific role.

Duty holder	Role
Client	This is the person or organisation who wishes to have the work done. The client will check that: - all the team members are competent - the management is suitable - sufficient time is allowed for all stages of the project - welfare facilities are in place before construction starts. HSE notifiable projects require that the client appoints a CDM co-ordinator and principal contractor, and provides access to a health and safety file.
CDM co-ordinator	Appointed by the client, the co-ordinator advises and assists the client with CDM duties. The co-ordinator notifies the HSE before work starts. This role involves the co-ordination of the health and safety aspects of the design of the building and ensures good communication between the client, designers and contractors.
Designer	At the design stages the designer removes hazards and reduces risks. The designer provides information about the risks that cannot be eliminated. Notifiable projects require that the designer checks that the client is aware of their CDM duties and that a CDM co-ordinator has been appointed. The designer will also supply information for the health and safety file.
Principal contractor	The principal contractor will plan, manage and monitor the construction in liaison with any other involved contractors. This involves developing a written plan and site rules before the construction begins. The principal contractor ensures that the site is made secure and suitable welfare facilities are provided from the start and maintained throughout construction. The principal contractor will also make sure that all operatives have site inductions and any further training that might be required to make sure the workforce is competent.
Contractor	Subcontractors and self-employed operatives will plan, manage and monitor their own work and employees, co-operating with any main contractor in relation to site rules. Contractors will make sure that all operatives have any further training that might be required to make sure they are competent. A contractor also reports any incidents under RIDDOR to the principal contractor.
Operatives	Operatives need to check their own competence: Can you carry out the task you have been asked to do safely? Have you been trained to do this type of activity? Do you have the correct equipment to carry out this activity? You must follow all the site health and safety rules and procedures and fully co-operate with the rest of the team to ensure the health and safety of other operatives and others who may be affected by the work. Any health and safety issues must be reported.

A client, a contractor and an operative looking over building plans ahead of construction

WELFARE FACILITIES REQUIRED ON SITE UNDER THE CDM REGULATIONS

The table below shows the welfare facilities that must be available on site.

Facility	Site requirement
Sanitary conveniences (toilets) 	■ Suitable and sufficient toilets should be provided or made available. ■ Toilets should be adequately ventilated and lit and should be clean. ■ Separate toilet facilities should be provided for men and women.
Washing facilities 	■ Sufficient facilities must be available, and include showers if required by the nature of the work. ■ They should be in the same place as the toilets and near any changing rooms. ■ There must be a supply of clean hot (or warm) and cold running water, soap and towels. ■ There must be separate washing facilities provided for men and women unless the area is for washing hands and the face only.

Facility	Site requirement
Clean drinking water 	■ This must be provided or made available. ■ It should be clearly marked by an appropriate sign. ■ Cups should be provided unless the supply of drinking water is from a water fountain.
Changing rooms and lockers 	■ Changing rooms must be provided or made available if operatives have to wear special clothing and if they cannot be expected to change elsewhere. ■ There must be separate rooms for, or separate use of rooms by, men and women where necessary. ■ The rooms must have seating and include, where necessary, facilities to enable operatives to dry their special clothing and their own clothing and personal effects. ■ Lockers should also be provided.
Rest rooms or rest areas 	■ They should have enough tables and seating with backs for the number of operatives likely to use them at any one time. ■ Where necessary, rest rooms should include suitable facilities for pregnant women or nursing mothers to rest lying down. ■ Arrangements must be made to ensure that meals can be prepared, heated and eaten. It must also be possible to boil water.

ACTIVITY

What facilities are provided at your workplace or place of training?

PROVISION AND USE OF WORK EQUIPMENT REGULATIONS (PUWER) 1998

The Provision and Use of Work Equipment Regulations (PUWER) 1998 place duties on:

■ people and companies who own, operate or have control over work equipment

■ employers whose employees use work equipment.

Work equipment can be defined as any machinery, appliance, apparatus, tool or installation for use at work (whether exclusively or not). This includes equipment employees provide for their own use at work. The scope of work equipment is therefore extremely wide. The use of work equipment is also very widely interpreted and, according to the HSE, means 'any activity involving work equipment and includes starting, stopping, programming, setting, transporting, repairing, modifying, maintaining, servicing and cleaning.' It includes equipment such as diggers, electric planers, stepladders, hammers or wheelbarrows.

Under PUWER, work equipment must be:

- suitable for the intended use

- safe to use

- well maintained

- inspected regularly.

Regular inspection is important as a tool that was safe when it was new may no longer be safe after considerable use.

Additionally, work equipment must only be used by people who have received adequate instruction and training. Information regarding the use of the equipment must be given to the operator and must only be used for what it was designed to do.

Protective devices, eg emergency stops, must be used. Brakes must be fitted where appropriate to slow down moving parts to bring the equipment to a safe condition when turned off or stopped. Equipment must have adequate means of isolation. Warnings, either by signs or other means such as sounds or lights, must be used as appropriate. Access to dangerous parts of the machinery must be controlled. Some work equipment is subject to additional health and safety legislation which must also be followed.

Employers who use work equipment must manage the risks. ACoPs (see page 9) have been developed in line with PUWER. The ACoPs have a special legal status, as outlined in the introduction to the PUWER ACoP:

> *Following the guidance is not compulsory and you are free to take other action. But if you do follow the guidance you will normally be doing enough to comply with the law. Health and safety inspectors seek to secure compliance with the law and may refer to this guidance as illustrating good practice.*

> **INDUSTRY TIP**
>
> Abrasive wheels are used for grinding. Under PUWER these wheels can only be changed by someone who has received training to do this. Wrongly fitted wheels can explode!

> **ACTIVITY**
>
> All the tools you use for your work are covered by PUWER. They must be well maintained and suitable for the task. A damaged head on a bolster chisel must be reshaped. A split shaft on a joiner's wood chisel must be repaired. Why would these tools be dangerous in a damaged condition? List the reasons.

MANUAL HANDLING OPERATIONS REGULATIONS 1992

Employers must try to avoid manual handling within reason if there is a possibility of injury. If manual handling cannot be avoided then they must reduce the risk of injury by means of a risk assessment.

An operative lifting heavy bricks

LIFTING AND HANDLING

Incorrect lifting and handling is a serious risk to your health. It is very easy to injure your back – just ask any experienced builder. An injured back can be very unpleasant, so it's best to look after it.

Here are a few things to consider when lifting:

- Assess the load. Is it too heavy? Do you need assistance or additional training? Is it an awkward shape?

- Can a lifting aid be used, such as any of the below?

Wheelbarrow

Scissor lift

Gin lift

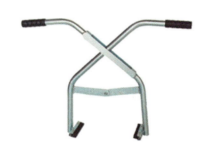

Kerb lifter

- Does the lift involve twisting or reaching?

- Where is the load going to end up? Is there a clear path? Is the place it's going to be taken to cleared and ready?

How to lift and place an item correctly

If you cannot use a machine, it is important that you keep the correct posture when lifting any load. The correct technique to do this is known as **kinetic lifting**. Always lift with your back straight, elbows in, knees bent and your feet slightly apart.

Kinetic lifting

A method of lifting that ensures that the risk of injury is reduced

THE CITY & GUILDS TEXTBOOK

Safe kinetic lifting technique

When placing the item, again be sure to use your knees and beware of trapping your fingers. If stacking materials, be sure that they are on a sound level base and on bearers if required.

Heavy objects that cannot easily be lifted by mechanical methods can be lifted by several people. It is important that one person in the team is in charge, and that lifting is done in a co-operative way. It has been known for one person to fall down and the others to then drop the item!

CONTROL OF NOISE AT WORK REGULATIONS 2005

Under the Control of Noise at Work Regulations 2005, duties are placed on employers and employees to reduce the risk of hearing damage to the lowest reasonable level practicable. Hearing loss caused by work is preventable. Hearing damage is permanent and cannot be restored once lost.

EMPLOYER'S DUTIES UNDER THE REGULATIONS

An employer's duties are:

- to carry out a risk assessment and identify who is at risk

- to eliminate or control its employees' exposure to noise at the workplace and to reduce the noise as far as practicable

- to provide suitable hearing protection

- to provide health surveillance to those identified as at risk by the risk assessment

- to provide information and training about the risks to their employees as identified by the risk assessment

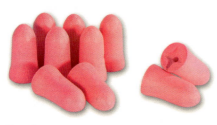

Ear defenders

Ear plugs

EMPLOYEES' DUTIES UNDER THE REGULATIONS

Employees must:

- make full and proper use of personal hearing protectors provided to them by their employer

- report to their employer any defect in any personal hearing protectors or other control measures as soon as is practicable

NOISE LEVELS

Under the Regulations, specific actions are triggered at specific noise levels. Noise is measured in decibels and shown as dB(A). The two main action levels are 80 dB(A) and 85 dB(A).

Requirements at 80 dB(A) to 85 dB(A):

- Assess the risk to operatives' health and provide them with information and training.

- Provide suitable ear protection free of charge to those who request ear protection.

Requirements above 85 dB(A):

- Reduce noise exposure as far as practicable by means other than ear protection.

- Set up an ear protection zone using suitable signage and segregation.

- Provide suitable ear protection free of charge to those affected and ensure they are worn.

PERSONAL PROTECTIVE EQUIPMENT (PPE) AT WORK REGULATIONS 1992

Employees and subcontractors must work in a safe manner. Not only must they wear the PPE that their employers provide but they must also look after it and report any damage to it. Importantly, employees must not be charged for anything given to them or done for them by the employer in relation to safety.

The hearing and respiratory PPE provided for most work situations is not covered by these Regulations because other regulations apply to it. However, these items need to be compatible with any other PPE provided.

The main requirement of the Regulations is that PPE must be supplied and used at work wherever there are risks to health and safety that cannot be adequately controlled in other ways.

The Regulations also require that PPE is:

- included in the method statement
- properly assessed before use to ensure it is suitable
- maintained and stored properly
- provided to employees with instructions on how they can use it safely
- used correctly by employees.

An employer cannot ask for money from an employee for PPE, whether it is returnable or not. This includes agency workers if they are legally regarded as employees. If employment has been terminated and the employee keeps the PPE without the employer's permission, then, as long as it has been made clear in the contract of employment, the employer may be able to deduct the cost of the replacement from any wages owed.

Using PPE is a very important part of staying safe. For it to do its job properly it must be kept in good condition and used correctly. If any damage does occur to an article of PPE it is important that this is reported and it is replaced. It must also be remembered that PPE is a last line of defence and should not be used in place of a good safety policy!

ACTIVITY

Check the date on your safety helmet. Always update your safety helmet if it is out of date.

INDUSTRY TIP

Remember, you also have a duty of care for your own health.

A site safety sign showing the PPE required to work there

The following table shows the type of PPE used in the workplace and explains why it is important to store, maintain and use PPE correctly. It also shows why it is important to check and report damage to PPE.

PPE	Correct use
Hard hat/safety helmet 	Hard hats must be worn when there is danger of hitting your head or danger of falling objects. They often prevent a wide variety of head injuries. Most sites insist on hard hats being worn. They must be adjusted to fit your head correctly and must not be worn back to front! Check the date of manufacture as plastic can become brittle over time. Solvents, pens and paints can damage the plastic too.
Toe-cap boots or shoes  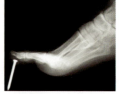 Safety boots	A nail in a construction worker's foot	Toe-cap boots or shoes are worn on most sites as a matter of course and protect the feet from heavy falling objects. Some safety footwear has additional insole protection to help prevent nails going up through the foot. Toe caps can be made of steel or lighter plastic.
Ear defenders and plugs   Ear defenders	Ear plugs	Your ears can be very easily damaged by loud noise. Ear protection will help prevent hearing loss while using loud tools or if there is a lot of noise going on around you. When using earplugs always ensure your hands are clean before handling the plugs as this reduces the risk of infection. If your ear defenders are damaged or fail to make a good seal around your ears have them replaced.
High-visibility (hi-viz) jacket 	This makes it much easier for other people to see you. This is especially important when there is plant or vehicles moving in the vicinity.
Goggles and safety glasses   Safety goggles	Safety glasses	These protect the eyes from dust and flying debris while you are working. It has been known for casualties to be taken to hospital after dust has blown up from a dry mud road. You only get one pair of eyes: look after them!

PPE	Correct use
Dust masks and respirators   Dust mask　　　　Respirator	Dust is produced during most construction work and it can be hazardous to your lungs. It can cause all sorts of ailments from asthma through to cancer. Wear a dust mask to filter this dust out. You must ensure it is well fitted. Another hazard is dangerous gases such as solvents. A respirator will filter out hazardous gases but a dust mask will not! Respirators are rated P1, P2 and P3, with P3 giving the highest protection.
Gloves   Latex glove　　　　Nitrile glove Gauntlet gloves　　Leather gloves	Gloves protect your hands. Hazards include cuts, abrasions, dermatitis, chemical burns or splinters. Latex and nitrile gloves are good for fine work, although some people are allergic to latex. Gauntlets provide protection from strong chemicals. Other types of gloves provide good grip and protect the fingers.  A chemical burn as a result of not wearing safety gloves
Sunscreen Suncream　　Melanoma	Another risk, especially in the summer months, is sunburn. Although a good tan is sometimes considered desirable, over-exposure to the sun can cause skin cancer such as melanoma. When out in the sun, cover up and use sunscreen (ie suncream) on exposed areas of your body to prevent burning.
Preventing HAVS 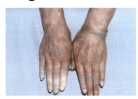	Hand–arm vibration syndrome (HAVS), also known as vibration white finger (VWF), is an industrial injury caused by using vibrating power tools (such as a hammer drill, vibrating poker and vibrating plate) for a long time. This injury is controlled by limiting the time such power tools are used. For more information see page 31.

For more information see page 31.

ACTIVITY

You are working on a site and a brick falls on your head. Luckily, you are doing as you have been instructed and you are wearing a helmet. You notice that the helmet has a small crack in it. What do you do?

1 Carry on using it as your employer will charge you for a new one: after all it is only a small crack.
2 Take it to your supervisor as it will no longer offer you full protection and it will need replacing.
3 Buy a new helmet because the old one no longer looks very nice.

INDUSTRY TIP

The most important pieces of PPE when using a disc cutter are dust masks, glasses and ear protection.

WORK AT HEIGHT REGULATIONS 2005 (AS AMENDED)

The Work at Height Regulations 2005 (as amended by the Work at Height (Amendment) Regulations 2007) put several duties upon employers:

- Working at height should be avoided if possible.

- If working at height cannot be avoided, the work must be properly organised with risk assessments carried out.

- Risk assessments should be regularly updated.

- Those working at height must be trained and competent.

- A method statement must be provided.

Workers wearing safety harnesses on an aerial access platform

Several points should be considered when working at height:

- How long is the job expected to take?

- What type of work will it be? It could be anything from fitting a single light bulb, through to removing a chimney or installing a roof.
  - ☐ How is the access platform going to be reached? By how many people?
  - ☐ Will people be able to get on and off the structure safely? Could there be overcrowding?

- What are the risks to passers-by? Could debris or dust blow off and injure anyone on the road below?

- What are the conditions like? Extreme weather, unstable buildings and poor ground conditions need to be taken into account.

A cherry picker can assist you when working at height

ACCESS EQUIPMENT AND SAFE METHODS OF USE

The means of access should only be chosen after a risk assessment has been carried out. There are various types of access.

Ladders

Ladders are normally used for access onto an access platform. They are not designed for working from except for light, short-duration work. A ladder should lean at an angle of 75°, ie one unit out for every four units up.

Strong upper resting point

Adequate lap on extension ladders

Ground back slope not exceeding 6°

Ground side slope not exceeding 16°, clean and free of slippery algae and moss

Using a ladder correctly

Roof ladder

Resting ladders on plastic guttering can cause it to bend and break

The following images show how to use a ladder or stepladder safely.

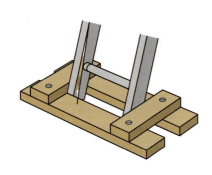

A ladder secured at the base.

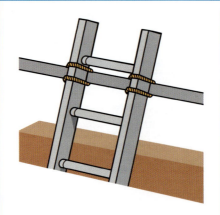

A ladder secured at the top of a platform for working from.

Access ladders should extend 1m above the landing point to provide a strong handhold.

Certain stepladders are unsafe to work from the top three rungs.

Don't overreach, and stay on the same rung.

Grip the ladder when climbing and remember to keep three points of contact.

INDUSTRY TIP

Always complete ladder pre-checks. Check the stiles (the two uprights) and rungs for damage such as splits or cracks. Do not use painted ladders because the paint could be hiding damage! Check all of the equipment including any stays and feet.

Stepladders

Stepladders are designed for light, short-term work.

Working from the side can make stepladders unstable. Do not overreach

Don't stand on the top three steps

Stepladder is fully open

Locked open firm and level on the ground

Using a stepladder correctly

Trestles

This is a working platform used for work of a slightly longer duration.

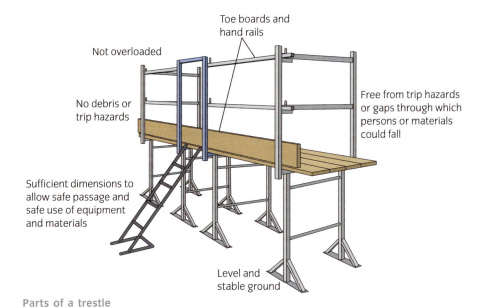

Not overloaded

Toe boards and hand rails

No debris or trip hazards

Free from trip hazards or gaps through which persons or materials could fall

Sufficient dimensions to allow safe passage and safe use of equipment and materials

Level and stable ground

Parts of a trestle

Tower scaffold

These are usually proprietary (manufactured) and are made from galvanised steel or lightweight aluminium alloy. They must be erected by someone competent in the erection and dismantling of mobile scaffolds.

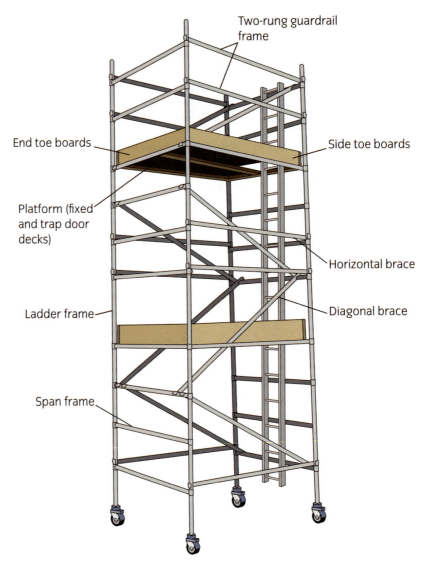

Two-rung guardrail frame

End toe boards

Side toe boards

Platform (fixed and trap door decks)

Horizontal brace

Ladder frame

Diagonal brace

Span frame

Parts of a tower scaffold

To use a tower scaffold safely:

- Always read and follow the manufacturer's instruction manual.

- Only use the equipment for what it is designed for.

- The wheels or feet of the tower must be in contact with a firm surface.

- Outriggers should be used to increase stability. The maximum height given in the manufacturer's instructions must not be exceeded.

- The platform must not be overloaded.

- The platform should be unloaded (and reduced in height if required) before it is moved.

- Never move a platform, even a small distance, if it is occupied.

INDUSTRY TIP

Remember, even a mobile access tower should have toe boards and guard rails fitted at all times when in use.

Tubular scaffold

This comes in two types:

- independent scaffold has two sets of standards or uprights

- putlog scaffold is built into the brickwork.

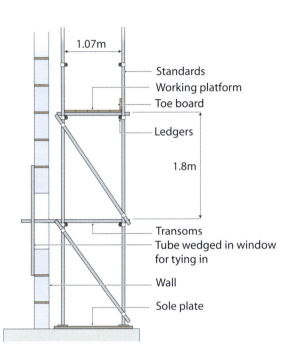

Independent tubular scaffold

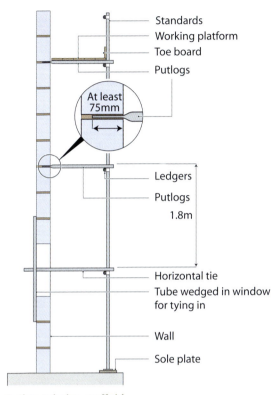

Putlog tubular scaffold

Tubular scaffold is erected by specialist scaffolding companies and often requires structural calculations. Only trained and competent scaffold erectors should alter scaffolding. Access to a scaffold is usually via a tied ladder with three rungs projecting above the step off at platform level.

OUR HOUSE

You have been asked to complete a job that requires gaining access to the roof level of a two-storey building. What equipment would you choose to get access to the work area? What things would you take into consideration when choosing the equipment? Take a look at 'Our House' as a guide for working on a two-storey building.

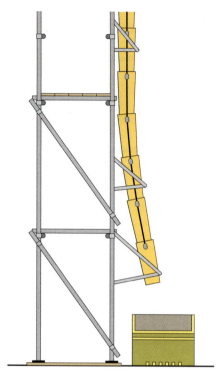

A debris chute for scaffolding

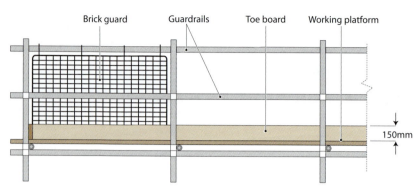

Brick guard   Guardrails   Toe board   Working platform

150mm

A safe working platform on a tubular scaffold

All scaffolding must:

- not have any gaps in the handrail or toe boards

- have a safe system for lifting any materials up to the working height

- have a safe system of debris removal.

Fall protection devices include:

- harnesses and lanyards

- safety netting

- air bags.

A harness and lanyard or safety netting will stop a person falling too far, leaving them suspended in the air. Air bags (commonly known as 'bouncy castles') are set up on the ground and inflated. If a person falls, they will have a soft landing. Air bags have fallen out of favour somewhat as some operatives use them as an easy way to get off the working platform – not the purpose they were intended for!

Using a scissor lift at height

LIFTING OPERATIONS AND LIFTING EQUIPMENT REGULATIONS (LOLER) 1998

The Lifting Operations and Lifting Equipment Regulations (LOLER) 1998 put responsibility upon employers to ensure that the lifting equipment provided for use at work is:

- strong and stable enough for the particular use and marked to indicate safe working loads

- positioned and installed to minimise any risks

- used safely, ie the work is planned, organised and performed by competent people

- subject to on-going thorough examination and, where appropriate, inspection by competent people.

THE CONTROL OF VIBRATION AT WORK REGULATIONS 2005

Vibration white finger or hand–arm vibration syndrome (HAVS) (see page 23) is caused by using vibrating tools such as hammer drills, vibrating pokers or hand held breakers over a long period of time. The most efficient and effective way of controlling exposure to hand-arm vibration is to look for new or alternative work methods that remove or reduce exposure to vibration.

An operative taking a rest from using a power tool

Follow these steps to reduce the effects of HAVS:

- Always use the right tool for each job.

- Check tools before using them to make sure they have been properly maintained and repaired to avoid increased vibration caused by faults or general wear.

- Make sure cutting tools are kept sharp so that they remain efficient.

- Reduce the amount of time you use a tool in one go, by doing other jobs in between.

- Avoid gripping or forcing a tool or work piece more than you have to.

- Encourage good blood circulation by:
  - □ keeping warm and dry (when necessary, wear gloves, a hat, waterproofs and use heating pads if available)
  - □ giving up or cutting down on smoking because smoking reduces blood flow
  - □ massaging and exercising your fingers during work breaks.

Damage from HAVS can include the inability to do fine work and cold can trigger painful finger blanching attacks (when the ends of your fingers go white).

Don't use power tools for longer than you need to

CONSTRUCTION SITE HAZARDS

DANGERS ON CONSTRUCTION SITES

Study the drawing of a building site. There is some demolition taking place, as well as construction. How many hazards can you find? Discuss your answers.

Dangers	Discussion points
Head protection	The operatives are not wearing safety helmets, which would prevent them from hitting their head or from falling objects.
Poor housekeeping	The site is very untidy. This can result in slips, trips and falls and can pollute the environment. An untidy site gives a poor company image. Offcuts and debris should be regularly removed and disposed of according to site policy and recycled if possible.
Fire	There is a fire near a building; this is hazardous. Fires can easily become uncontrollable and spread. There is a risk to the structure and, more importantly, a risk of operatives being burned. Fires can also pollute the environment.

Dangers	Discussion points
Trip hazards	Notice the tools and debris on the floor. The scaffold has been poorly constructed. There is a trip hazard where the scaffold boards overlap.
Chemical spills	There is a drum leaking onto the ground. This should be stored properly – upright and in a lockable metal shed or cupboard. The leak poses a risk of pollution and of chemical burns to operatives.
Falls from height	The scaffold has handrails missing. The trestle working platform has not been fitted with guard rails. None of the operatives are wearing hard hats for protection either.
Noise	An operative is using noisy machinery with other people nearby. The operative should be wearing ear PPE, as should those working nearby. Better still, they should be working elsewhere if at all possible, isolating themselves from the noise.
Electrical	Some of the wiring is 240V as there is no transformer, it's in poor repair and it's also dragging through liquid. This not only increases the risk of electrocution but is also a trip hazard.
Asbestos or other hazardous substances	Some old buildings contain **asbestos** roofing which can become a hazard when being demolished or removed. Other potential hazards include lead paint or mould spores. If a potentially hazardous material is discovered a supervisor must be notified immediately and work must stop until the hazard is dealt with appropriately.

Asbestos

A naturally occurring mineral that was commonly used for a variety of purposes including: **insulation**, fire protection, roofing and guttering. It is extremely hazardous and can cause a serious lung disease known as asbestosis

Insulation

A material that reduces or prevents the transmission of heat

FUNCTIONAL SKILLS

Using the data you collected in the Functional Skills task on page 3, produce a pie chart to show the proportion of occupational cancer that is caused by asbestosis.

Work on this activity can support FM L2.3.1 and C2.4.

Cables can be a trip hazard on site

Boiler suit

Hand cleaner

PERSONAL HYGIENE

Working in the construction industry can be very physical, and it's likely to be quite dirty at times. Therefore you should take good care with your personal hygiene. This involves washing well after work. If contaminants are present, then wearing a protective suit, such as a boiler suit, that you can take off before you go home will prevent contaminants being taken home with you.

You should also wash your hands after going to the toilet and before eating. This makes it safer to eat and more pleasant for others around you. The following steps show a safe and hygienic way to wash your hands.

STEP 1 Apply soap to hands from the dispenser.

STEP 2 Rub the soap into a lather and cover your hands with it, including between your fingers.

STEP 3 Rinse hands under a running tap removing all of the soap from your hands.

STEP 4 Dry your hands using disposable towels. Put the towels in the bin once your hands are dry.

WORKING WITH ELECTRICITY

Electricity is a very useful energy resource but it can be very dangerous. Electricity must be handled with care! Only trained, competent people can work with electrical equipment.

THE DANGERS OF USING ELECTRICAL EQUIPMENT

The main dangers of electricity are:

- shock and burns (a 230V shock can kill)

- electrical faults which could cause a fire

- an explosion where an electrical spark has ignited a flammable gas.

VOLTAGES

Generally speaking, the lower the voltage the safer it is. However, a low voltage is not necessarily suitable for some machines, so higher voltages can be found. On site, 110V (volts) is recommended and this is the voltage rating most commonly used in the building industry. This is converted from 230V by use of a transformer.

110V 1 phase – yellow

230V (commonly called 240V) domestic voltage is used on site as battery chargers usually require this voltage. Although 230V is often used in workshops, 110V is recommended.

230V 1 phase – blue

400V (otherwise known as 3 phase) is used for large machinery, such as joinery shop equipment.

Voltages are nominal, ie they can vary slightly.

BATTERY POWER

Battery power is much safer than mains power. Many power tools are now available in battery-powered versions. They are available in a wide variety of voltages from 3.6V for a small screwdriver all the way up to 36V for large masonry drills.

400V 3 phase – red

The following images are all examples of battery-powered tools you may come across in your workplace or place of training.

FIRE

Fire needs three things to start; if just one of them is missing there will be no fire. If all are present then a fire is unavoidable:

1 *Oxygen:* A naturally occurring gas in the air that combines with flammable substances under certain circumstances.

2 *Heat:* A source of fire, such as a hot spark from a grinder or naked flame.

3 *Fuel:* Things that will burn such as acetone, timber, cardboard or paper.

The fire triangle

If you have heat, fuel and oxygen you will have a fire. Remove any of these and the fire will go out.

PREVENTING THE SPREAD OF FIRE

Being tidy will help prevent fires starting and spreading. For instance:

- Wood offcuts should not be left in big piles or standing up against a wall. Instead, useable offcuts should be stored in racks.

- Put waste into the allocated disposal bins or skips.

- Always replace the cap on unused fuel containers when you put them away. Otherwise they are a potential source of danger.

- Flammable liquids (not limited to fuel-flammable liquids) such as oil-based paint, thinners and oil must be stored in a locked metal cupboard or shed.

- Smoking around flammable substances should be avoided.

- Dust can be explosive, so when doing work that produces wood dust it is important to use some form of extraction and have good ventilation.

FIRE EXTINGUISHERS AND THEIR USES

You need to know where the fire extinguishers and blankets are located and which fire extinguishers can be used on different fires. The table below shows the different classes of fire and which extinguisher to use in each case.

Fire blanket

Class of fire	Materials	Type of extinguisher
A	Wood, paper, hair, textiles	Water, foam, dry powder, wet chemical
B	Flammable liquids	Foam, dry powder, CO_2
C	Flammable gases	Dry powder, CO_2
D	Flammable metals	Specially formulated dry powder
E	Electrical fires	CO_2, dry powder
F	Cooking oils	Wet chemical, fire blanket

INDUSTRY TIP

Remember, although all fire extinguishers are red, they each have a different coloured label to identify their contents.

CO_2 extinguisher

Dry powder extinguisher

Water extinguisher

Foam extinguisher

It is important to use the correct extinguisher for the type of fire as using the wrong one could make the danger much worse, eg using water on an electrical fire could lead to the user being electrocuted!

EMERGENCY PROCEDURES

In an emergency, people tend to panic. If an emergency were to occur, such as fire, discovering a bomb or some other security problem, would you know what to do? It is vital to be prepared in case of an emergency.

It is your responsibility to know the emergency procedures on your work site:

- If you discover a fire or other emergency you will need to raise the alarm:
  - ☐ You will need to tell a nominated person. Who is this?
  - ☐ If you are first on the scene you will have to ring the emergency services on 999.
- Be aware of the alarm signal. Is it a bell, a voice or a siren?

- Where is the assembly point? You will have to proceed to this point in an orderly way. Leave all your belongings behind: they may slow you or others down.

- At the assembly point, there will be someone who will ensure everyone is out safely and will do so by taking a count. Do you know who this person is? If during a fire you are not accounted for, a firefighter may risk their life to go into the building to look for you.

- How do you know it's safe to re-enter the building? You will be told by the appointed person. It's very important that you do not re-enter the building until you are told to do so.

Emergency procedure sign

ACTIVITY

What is the fire evacuation procedure at your workplace or place of training?

SIGNS AND SAFETY NOTICES

The law sets out the types of safety signs needed on a construction site. Some signs warn us about danger and others tell us what to do to stay safe.

The following table describes five basic types of sign.

Type of sign	Description
Prohibition	These signs are red and white. They are round. They signify something that must *not* be done.
Mandatory	These signs are blue. They are round. They signify something that *must* be done.

Type of sign	Description
Caution 	These signs are yellow and black. They are triangular. These give warning of hazards.
Safe condition 	These signs are green. They are usually square or rectangular. They tell you the safe way to go, or what to do in an emergency.
Supplementary 	These white signs are square or rectangular and give additional important information. They usually accompany the signs above.

Case Study: Miranda

A site has a small hut where tools are stored securely, and inside the hut there is a short bench that has some sharpening equipment including a grinding wheel.

Miranda wished to grind her plane blade, but before using it found that the grinding wheel was defective as the side of the wheel had been used, causing a deep groove.

She found another old grinding wheel beneath the bench which looked fine. She fitted it to the grinder and used it.

Afterwards, she wondered if she should have asked someone else to change the wheel for her.

- What health and safety issues are there with this scenario?

- What training could Miranda undertake?

Work through the following questions to check your learning.

1   Which one of the following **must** be filled out prior to carrying out a site task?

   a   Invoice.

   b   Bill of quantities.

   c   Risk assessment.

   d   Schedule.

2   Which one of the following signs shows you something you **must** do?

   a   Green circle.

   b   Yellow triangle.

   c   White square.

   d   Blue circle.

3   Two parts of the fire triangle are heat and fuel. What is the third?

   a   Nitrogen.

   b   Oxygen.

   c   Carbon dioxide.

   d   Hydrogen sulphite.

4   Which of the following types of fire extinguisher would **best** put out an electrical fire?

   a CO_2.

   b   Powder.

   c   Water.

   d   Foam.

5   Which piece of health and safety legislation is designed to protect an operative from ill health and injury when using solvents and adhesives?

   a   Manual Handling Operations Regulations 1992.

   b   Control of Substances Hazardous to Health (COSHH) Regulations 2002.

   c   Health and Safety (First Aid) Regulations 1981.

   d   Lifting Operations and Lifting Equipment Regulations (LOLER) 1998.

6   What is the correct angle at which to lean a ladder against a wall?

   a   70°.

   b   80°.

   c   75°.

   d   85°.

7   Which are the **most** important pieces of PPE to use when using a disc cutter?

   a   Overalls, gloves and boots.

   b   Boots, head protection and overalls.

   c   Glasses, hearing protection and dust mask.

   d   Gloves, head protection and boots.

8   Which one of the following is **not** a lifting aid?

   a   Wheelbarrow.

   b   Kerb lifter.

   c   Gin lift.

   d   Respirator.

9   Which one of the following is a 3 phase voltage?

   a   400V.

   b   230V.

   c   240V.

   d   110V.

10   Above what noise level **must** you wear ear protection?

   a   75 dB(A).

   b   80 dB(A).

   c   85 dB(A).

   d   90 dB(A).

Chapter 2
Unit 301/701: Principles of organising, planning and pricing construction work

As you progress and gain responsibility within the industry you will be involved with interpreting a range of information. The understanding and communication of this information are crucial to the success of a building project. Mistakes made in interpreting information always prove costly in terms of labour, building materials and time. Whether reading a drawing, cross-checking information on a schedule, planning building work or working up a price, each process requires a methodical approach and should be able to be easily interpreted by those using the documentation. Much of this information is provided to you by the **contract documents**.

By reading this chapter you will know about:

1 Different types of drawn information in construction.

2 Energy efficiency and sustainable materials for construction.

3 Estimating quantities and price work for construction.

4 Planning work activities for construction.

5 Communicating effectively in the workplace.

DRAWN INFORMATION IN CONSTRUCTION

This section will discuss the different types of drawn information used and found in construction. In *The City & Guilds Textbook: Level 2 Diploma in Bricklaying* we have already looked at some of this information. Now we will recap this and look in a little more detail at how drawings are produced.

Drawings are required at every stage of building work. After the building has been designed and agreed with the client, drawings are required in order to apply for planning consent and Building Regulations approval. These drawings will show the size, position and general arrangement of the proposed construction and allow the Local Authority planning committee to decide whether approval should be given and whether the proposed building meets the current Building Regulations.

Flowchart of contracts documents

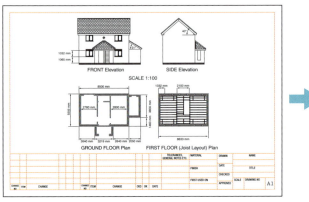

Project drawing:
1 Planning drawings: to a small scale.
2 Construction drawings: to a larger scale.

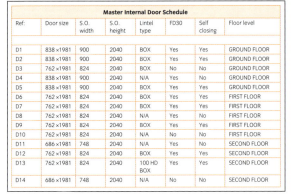

Schedules:
Information in a table form, taken from drawings and specifications, eg a door or decoration schedule.

Building Contract:
Gives details of start/end dates, conditions of work, methods of payment, etc.

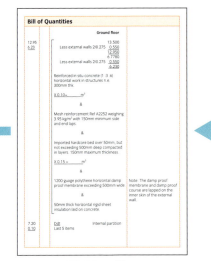

Bill of Quantities:
Written document prepared in accordance with the new Rules of Measurement Standard Information, used to provide pricing for a quote.

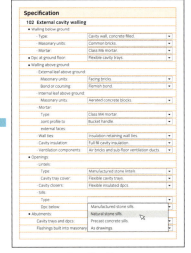

Specification:
Written document providing specific details of the materials and workmanship required.

TYPES OF DRAWING REQUIRED BY THE LOCAL AUTHORITY

LOCATION PLAN

This shows the proposed development in relation to its surrounding properties. It must be based on an up-to-date map and an identified standard metric **scale** (typically 1:1250 or 1:2500). The site of the proposed development needs to be outlined in red and any other land owned by the applicant that is close to or adjoining the site needs to be outlined in blue.

SITE PLAN

This shows the proposed development in relation to the property boundary (sometimes called a 'block plan'). Site plans are typically submitted at a scale of either 1:200 or 1:500 and should include the following:

- the size and position of the existing building (and any extensions proposed) in relation to the property boundary

- the position and use of any other buildings within the property boundary

- the position and width of any adjacent streets.

GENERAL ARRANGEMENT DRAWINGS

These include elevations and floor plans and sections of the proposed building. See page 49 for an example.

ELEVATIONS

These show the external appearance of each face of the building showing features such as slope of the land, doors, windows and the roof arrangement at a scale of 1:50 or 1:100 depending on the size of the project and the drawing sheet printed on.

FLOOR PLANS

These are used to identify the layout of the internal walls, doors, stairs and arrangement of bathrooms and kitchen. Again these will be drawn at a scale of 1:50 or 1:100.

SECTIONS

These are used to show vertical views through the building showing room heights and floor and roof constructions. These are generally drawn at a scale of 1:50.

Scale

A reduction in size by a given ratio, eg 1:5 means that the measurement on the scale is five times smaller than the real thing. So if the full-size object is 500mm long, the scaled-size object shown on the drawing would be 100mm long

ACTIVITY

Go to www.planningportal.gov.uk. Research what mandatory documents are required in a planning application.

Scale rule

ADDITIONAL DRAWINGS REQUIRED TO CONSTRUCT THE BUILDING

CONSTRUCTION DRAWINGS

These provide the detail required to construct a building. They provide the information required by individual trades to a larger scale and in more detail. They may include any or all of the following:

Assembly drawings

These types of drawings are used to show how various components fit together at various junctions. These are generally drawn at scales of 1:20, 1:10 and 1:5. Scale rules are used to draw scaled-down buildings on paper.

Component/range drawings

These supply information required by manufacturers producing various components for the finished building, eg purpose-made doors or kitchen units. A range drawing could also show a manufacturer's standard range of products available off the shelf, eg doors, windows and kitchen units. These are often shown at scales of 1:10 and 1:20. For instance, a range of doors or windows might be indicated on the floor plans with a simple code such as D1, D2, W1, W2, etc. These could also be shown on a door/window schedule including ironmongery and any glass requirements.

INDUSTRY TIP

Sketches can often be used to communicate information where a description is harder to understand. A picture paints a thousand words.

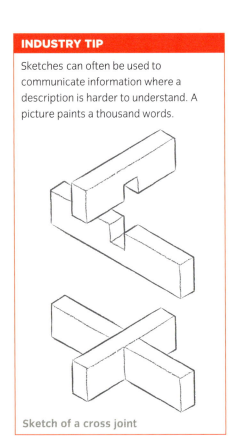

Sketch of a cross joint

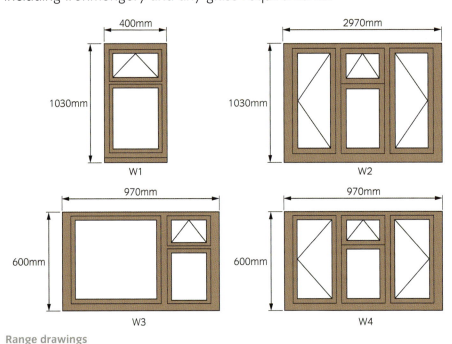

Range drawings

Detail drawings

Detail drawings show very accurate large-scale details of the construction of a particular item, eg a window or stair construction. Examples are joinery detailing and complex brickwork features. Typical scales are 1:2 and 1:5.

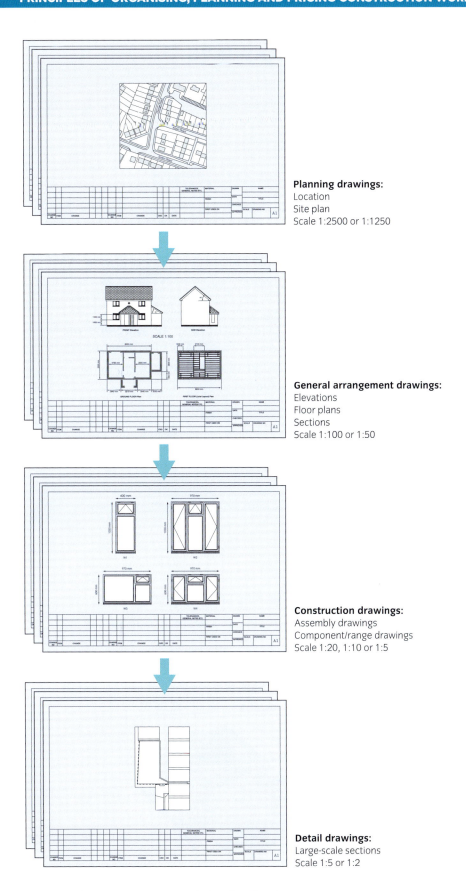

Planning drawings:
Location
Site plan
Scale 1:2500 or 1:1250

General arrangement drawings:
Elevations
Floor plans
Sections
Scale 1:100 or 1:50

Construction drawings:
Assembly drawings
Component/range drawings
Scale 1:20, 1:10 or 1:5

Detail drawings:
Large-scale sections
Scale 1:5 or 1:2

Flowchart showing progression of planning drawings

Parallel-motion drawing board

PRODUCTION OF DRAWINGS

Traditionally all drawings would have been produced by a draughtsperson by hand on large parallel-motion drawing boards. Some drawings are still produced this way but most are now produced using CAD (computer-aided design/drawing).

COMPUTER-AIDED DRAUGHTING

This is a method of producing drawings and designs using a design and drawing software package. These packages have been around for about 30 years now and have significantly improved during this period. They are now used by millions of people worldwide. Anything can be drawn using these software packages in either two or three dimensions.

Architectural technician

A technician who is employed by an architectural practice to produce construction drawings

All newly qualified architects or **architectural technicians** will produce drawings using CAD and this is the preferred method of production as they have a number of advantages over hand-produced drawings, which include:

- High quality drawings can be produced.
- Drawings can easily be magnified, manipulated and amended.
- Standard details can be saved and reproduced as any new contract requires.
- Drawing layers can be produced enabling particular details to be extracted.
- Objects can be viewed from any angle.
- Drawings can be archived without taking up valuable space.
- Drawings can be attached as files and sent via email.
- Three-dimensional virtual models and **walkthroughs** can be created.
- CAD can be used with other compatible software products to prepare schedules, specifications and CAM (computer-aided manufacturing) to produce products by machine.

Walkthrough

An animated sequence as seen at the eye level of a person walking through a proposed structure

Walkthrough illustration

While the advantages of CAD are significant there are a few disadvantages:

1 The initial outlay for the equipment required, eg:

- a central processing unit (computer)
- a visual display unit (VDU)
- a keyboard
- CAD software
- a plotter or printer.

2 The training of staff to use the software.

3 The cost of updating the software.

There are many CAD packages that can be purchased and downloaded free. Autodesk produces a range of programs which are used universally. AutoCAD is very popular. SketchUp, formerly owned by Google, is a free-to-download program. 'Our House' was drawn using this.

Typical CAD workstation with large screens

SketchUp software logo

OUR HOUSE

Log on to SmartScreen and open up 'Our House'. Explore the possibilities of this package – don't worry, you can't break it!

All drawings are produced on standard-sized sheets of paper.

Drawing paper		Other sized paper	
Name	**Size (mm)**	**Name**	**Size (mm)**
A0	1189 × 841	A5	210 × 148
A1	841 × 594	A6	148 × 105
A2	594 × 420	A7	105 × 74
A3	420 × 297	A8	74 × 52
A4	297 × 210		

FUNCTIONAL SKILLS

Use the internet to research the standard method for folding drawings allowing the information box to be shown when folded.

Work on this activity can support FICT L2 (4).

Examples of these paper sizes are shown on the next page.

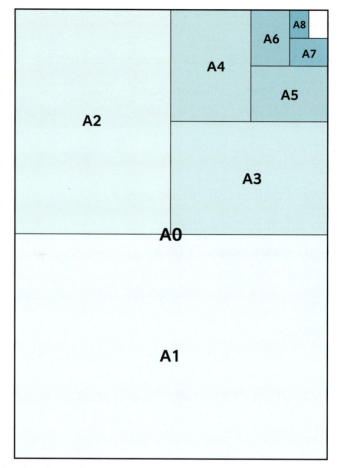

Standard drawing sheet sizes

DRAWING PROJECTION METHODS

ORTHOGRAPHIC PROJECTION

Most drawings are produced in two dimensions (length and width). These are called orthographic drawings. The only type of orthographic used in the UK is first angle orthographic. This shows how the views are projected on to a flat surface surrounding the object. The surface is then folded flat showing how the views are shown in first angle projection on a drawing.

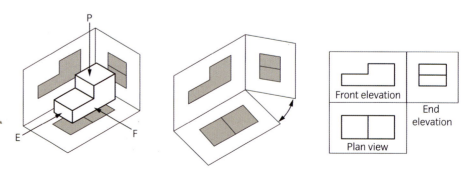

First angle orthographic

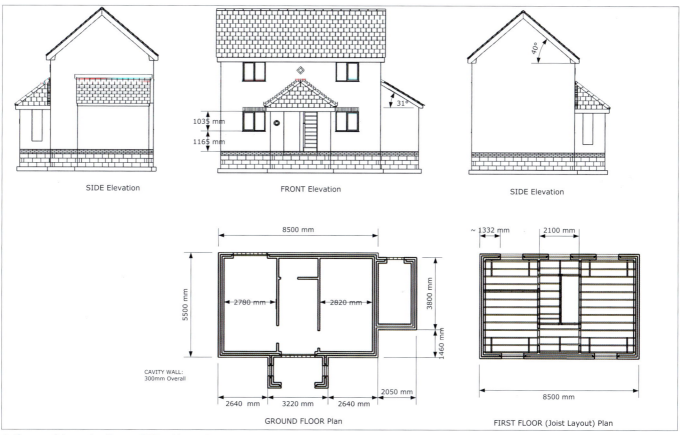

SIDE Elevation   FRONT Elevation   SIDE Elevation

GROUND FLOOR Plan   FIRST FLOOR (Joist Layout) Plan

Orthographic projections of 'Our House'

In construction most of the drawings we use are produced in orthographic projection. These show a front elevation, end elevation and plan views of our proposed building. Additional views can also be added to show detail as required. In order to produce these, the following information is required:

- overall sizes of the proposed building
- room dimensions
- position and sizes of doors and windows
- position of internal walls
- brickwork, carpentry and joinery specifications
- Building Regulations requirements.

THREE-DIMENSIONAL DRAWING

This type of drawing is often termed a pictorial drawing. These drawings can add considerable clarity to a two-dimensional drawing, allowing the viewer a more life-like representation of the building. They give the client, operatives, suppliers and non-technical personnel not involved with the construction process a better understanding of how the finished product will look or give more detail of what is required of a particular part of the construction. There are many types of three-dimensional drawing, but the most common types used in construction are isometric, oblique and perspective.

ACTIVITY

Practise drawing scaled orthographic views of the project you are currently working on in your training environment.

INDUSTRY TIP

Use a 4H grade pencil for construction lines and 2H for bold lines.

INDUSTRY TIP

Before starting a drawing, calculate the widths and heights of each elevation to ensure you start the drawing in the right place, otherwise you may run out of space on your drawing sheet.

ACTIVITY

Find out what type of drawing instrument can be set to draw any angle.

Isometric projection

This is the most commonly used and produces a life-like representation of the subject. To produce these, all lines are drawn vertical or to the left or right axis at 30° (using a standard 30°/60° set square). They are often used to show an overall view of the object and form the basis of most sketches.

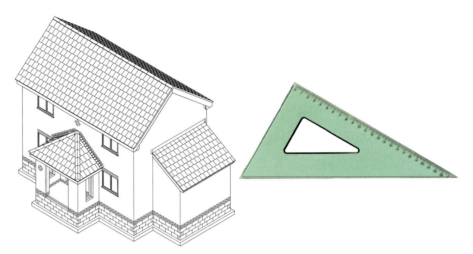

An isometric drawing of 'Our House'   30°/60° set square

Oblique projection

This is a less commonly used method of showing an object in three dimensions. The front elevation is drawn to its actual size and shape, with the third dimension (or depth) shown drawn back to either the left or right as required. The lines are drawn horizontally, vertically or at 45° axis to the left or right.

45° set square   An oblique projection of 'Our House'

Perspective drawings

These give the most realistic view of a building; lines are drawn vertically or drawn back to vanishing points (VP). The vanishing points can be positioned at any height but most commonly at the viewer's eye level.

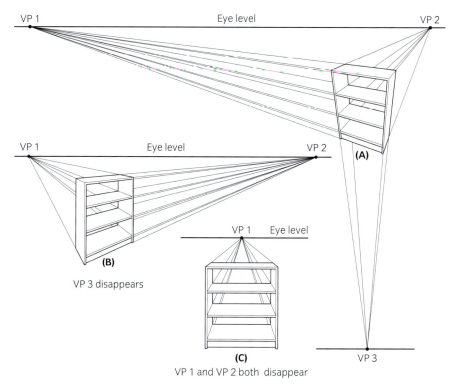

A perspective drawing

The same information is required to produce three-dimensional drawings as for two-dimensional drawings:

- dimensions
- scale required
- axis (30°, 45° or vanishing)
- position and required view of object.

An example of a perspective drawing

BASIC DRAWING SYMBOLS (HATCHINGS)

Standard symbols, also known as hatching symbols, are used on drawings as a means of passing on information simply. If all the parts of a building were labelled in writing, the drawing would soon become very crowded. Additionally, it is important to use standard symbols so that everyone can read them and they mean the same to everyone. The following images are just some of the standard symbols used.

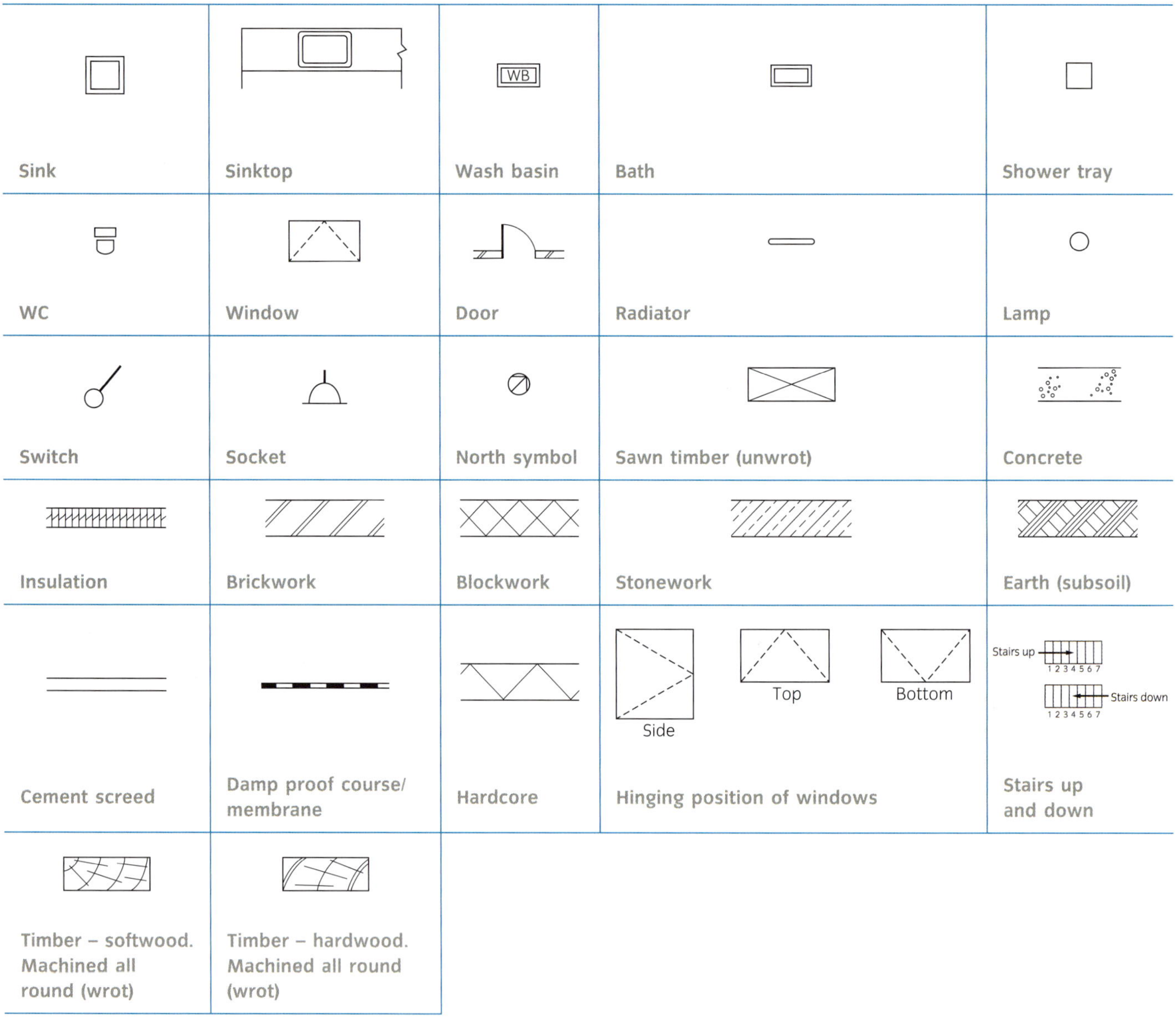
WB
Sink
Sinktop
Wash basin
Bath
Shower tray
WC
Window
Door
Radiator
Lamp
Switch
Socket
North symbol
Sawn timber (unwrot)
Concrete
Insulation
Brickwork
Blockwork
Stonework
Earth (subsoil)
Side
Top
Bottom
Stairs up
1 2 3 4 5 6 7
Stairs down
1 2 3 4 5 6 7
Cement screed
Damp proof course/ membrane
Hardcore
Hinging position of windows
Stairs up and down
Timber – softwood. Machined all round (wrot)
Timber – hardwood. Machined all round (wrot)

ESTIMATING QUANTITIES AND PRICING WORK FOR CONSTRUCTION

Before you can estimate quantities of construction materials, you need to know how to prepare a materials list using a schedule.

SCHEDULES

Drawings alone will not contain all the information required to carry out all operations efficiently. Drawings will show the positions of doors, windows, lintels and reinforcing, for example, but will not give specific detail. This information can be extracted and shown within a schedule. A schedule can be produced by a **quantity surveyor** as a part of their role. It is often read in conjunction with the range drawing. It provides an easy to handle and readable table. You can see an example on page 46.

A schedule records repeated design information that applies to a range of components or fittings, such as:

- windows
- doors
- reinforcement.

A schedule is mainly used on larger developments and contracts where there are multiples of several designs of houses, with each type having different components and fittings. It avoids a house being given the wrong component or fitting. On a typical plan, the doors and windows are labelled D1, D2, W1, W2, etc. These components would be included in the schedule, which would provide additional information about them.

To prepare a materials list to order from the schedules, you will need to use the information contained on them. This will include:

- quantity
- colour
- dimensions
- location
- installation details
- manufacturer.

Quantity surveyor

A quantity surveyor will produce the bill of quantities and later works with a client to manage costs and contracts

ACTIVITY

Produce a door schedule for at least five differently sized/types of doors within your college/training centre.

CALCULATING COSTS AND PRICING WORK

The calculation of costs for building work is carried out by an estimator. Every estimator builds their tender figures based on the information contained in the contract documents (drawings, bill of quantities and the specifications). We have already looked at drawings.

BILL OF QUANTITIES

Dimension paper

Paper with vertically ruled columns onto which building work is described, measured and costed

Taken off

Materials measured from the contract drawings

The quantity surveyor will have produced the bill of quantities. This describes on **dimension paper** each item, and the quantity of that item as '**taken off**' the drawing. The descriptions of the items that are listed for many years followed the SMM7 (Standard Method of Measurement 7) rule book. This is the standard method of measurement used in the construction of most architect-designed buildings. Through standardisation of their common features like the description of the brickwork and the quantities of that brickwork it leads to certainty of interpretation by all contractors when quoting for this work. This makes the process fair, as every contractor is pricing for the same items. The SMM7 was replaced by the NRM2 (New Rules of Measurement 2) from July 2013.

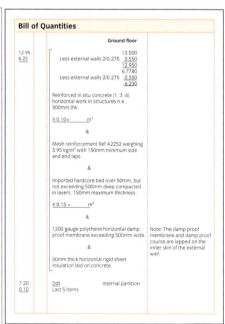

The NRM2 document is published by the Royal Institute of Charted Surveyors (RICS)

Extract from a bill of quantities

In addition to the standard items of work listed the bill of quantities will also contain information on:

Setting-up costs

These can include costs of hoarding, temporary services, temporary site accommodation, etc

- *Preliminaries:* these tend to be time-related costs that have to be built in such as management and supervision costs, **setting-up costs,** etc, rather than the costs of the actual building work.

- *Preambles:* these are statements that express the agendas and description of their accompanying documents. Therefore preambles in the bill of quantities refers to a tender letter that gives the description of the materials requirements for construction and it gives the quantity, type and characteristics of the materials required.

- *Provisional sum:* this refers to bills of work that is undefined. Such work does not have an accurate estimate and hence provisional sum best describes it. When giving a provisional sum, one has to include the type of work, how the work is to be done and the limitations likely to be encountered (such as the work hours being limited to night only).

- *Prime cost (PC):* PC sums cover work undertaken by nominated subcontractors, nominated suppliers and **statutory undertakings** and are based on quotations for items of work which can be populated into the quote.

Statutory undertakings

The various services that are brought to the site – water, electricity, etc

SPECIFICATION

This provides essential information to the contractor about the materials, finish and workmanship required for the building construction. The specification gives information that if noted on the drawing would clutter it and make it impossible to read as there would be more text than drawing. An example would be the type of brick or timber required.

On small projects the specification is written in the notes column above the information block on the drawing; on larger projects the specification is produced in a separate document.

Very often the description in the specification will be linked to the relevant British Standard.

Example of specification

THE TENDER PROCESS

The purpose of the tendering process is to provide the client with a number of estimates for the proposed work. The client will go out to known contractors, or for competitive tendering work it may be advertised and contractors come forward to quote for the work. Armed with the above contract documents the estimator will begin to build a tender cost. Each line of the bill will be costed. The figure used in the rate column will be an 'all-in rate' including:

- *Labour rates:* this will be calculated not at the operatives' hourly rate, but including costs such as annual holiday costs, employers' National Insurance contributions, pension contribution, sickness pay, bonuses, travelling time, etc.

- *Overheads:* manufacturing overheads include such things as electricity, gas, phone, insurance, plant and equipment, depreciation on equipment and buildings, factory supplies and factory personnel (other than direct labour).

- *Contingencies:* this is a small percentage added to cover unforeseen costs that may arise during the contract.

- *Profit:* the amount of money gained over and above direct costs. The rate applied will depend on a number of factors including current workload, the competition and the complexity of the project.

- *VAT* on materials.

Calculating a unit rate

Calculate a **unit rate** for brickwork using the following information.

- Facing brickwork (in half-brick walling) laid in 1:5 cement mortar

- Gang of two bricklayers, one labourer

- Hourly rate: bricklayer rate £15.00, labourer £8.00

- Production rate: 50 bricks/hr (per bricklayer)

- 60 bricks/m²

- Cost of bricks/1000 = £400 (includes 5% waste)

- Pre-mixed mortar on site £30/330 litre tub (60 litre of mortar m²/brickwork)

Unit rate

The unit rate = the labour rate + the material rate

Example

Labour rate

Labour (2 × 15) + 8 = £38 total hourly rate

$$\text{Production rate} = \frac{\text{bricks laid/hr}}{\text{bricks/m}^2} = \frac{100}{60} = 1.7\text{m}^2/\text{hr.}$$

$$\text{Labour rate} = \frac{\text{total hourly rate}}{\text{Production rate (m}^2/\text{hr)}} = \frac{38}{1.7} = £22.35/\text{m}^2$$

Materials rate

$$\text{Cost of bricks/m}^2: \frac{400}{1000} = 0.4 \text{ (each brick costs 40p)}$$

INDUSTRY TIP

Always double check all-in rates; if these are wrong the error in the costings will be considerable.

0.4 × 60 (bricks/m²) = Cost of bricks/m² = £24

Cost of mortar/m²: 1 litre/brick × 60 = 60 litres/m²

$\dfrac{30}{330} \times 60 = £5.45$

Cost of materials = 24 + 5.45 = £29.45

Unit rate

Total unit rate = labour rate + materials rate =
22.35 + 29.45 = **£51.80m²**

The total unit rate would now be used in the Rate column and would be multiplied by the Quantity column to produce the cost for this item. See the example below:

Extract from the bill of quantities

Number	Item description	Unit	Quantity	Rate	Amount	
					£	p
E.47	Half-brick walling	m²	75	51.80	3885	00

Each line of the bill should be completed and the last columns totalled to provide the final estimated cost. Once this has been completed, it should be reviewed by the management team prior to submitting to the client for consideration. It is common for a client to ask for three estimates; an estimator's job can involve a lot of work with very few contracts obtained. One in 10 jobs won would be a good success rate.

OTHER WAYS OF ESTIMATING COSTS

Traditionally many companies use a building price book, which is a complete guide for estimating, checking and forecasting building work. Again the figures in these books are established all-in rates which are updated on a yearly basis. To calculate the cost of proposed work you simply find the description of work requiring costing and use the figures in this row.

There are now also many software packages that can be purchased, which allow fixed unit rates to be used. Again enter the quantity in the correct row and the software will total up the work as you enter the work to be priced.

ACTIVITY

Produce a costing for the practical assignment you are currently working on.

INDUSTRY TIP

Set up a database of standard all-in rates as this can save a lot of time when estimating.

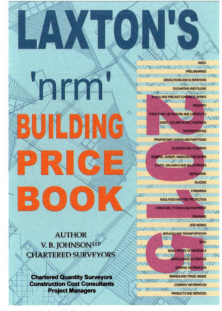

Typical building price book

Quotes

A & E BUILDERS LTD.

JOB ESTIMATE DATE:

An estimate

WHAT IS THE DIFFERENCE BETWEEN A *QUOTATION* AND AN *ESTIMATE*?

WHAT IS A QUOTATION?

A quotation (quote) is a document submitted in formal response to a request for the cost of specific work based on the contract documents supplied. In other words, it is a promise to do work at an agreed price. It should set out exactly what work will be done for that agreed price (based on the bill of quantities). Acceptance of this quotation by the client or their representative creates a binding agreement between the two parties. Any additional work requested by the client will not form part of this quote and should be costed separately.

WHAT IS AN ESTIMATE?

An estimate is exactly that: a best guess (sometimes referred to as a guesstimate) of how much specific work will cost or how long it will take to complete. Unlike a quote, it is not an offer to carry out this work for a fixed cost. This means that the job could cost either more or less than the estimated cost. Any charges expected to be above the estimate are best flagged up as early as possible to avoid possible later disputes.

SOURCING SUPPLIERS

This is often done during the pre-contract planning phase of the contract. Local suppliers are contacted and asked for quotes and their ability to supply materials to a given schedule. It pays to set up an early working relationship with your suppliers to ensure a good service.

PREFERRED SUPPLIERS

Suppliers can become 'preferred' in a number of ways; for example, your organisation may have used them before, they may have approached you or your technical colleagues with details of their proposition, they may have made a previously unsuccessful tender, or they may have been recommended by a similar organisation. The term *preferred supplier* does not in itself guarantee a level of business, but instead should be thought of as a guide to your thinking when considering a sourcing strategy. If there are several suppliers from which you can source the same materials, the preferred supplier may be one that consistently gives the best price or the one that is most reliable and always delivers on time.

ESTIMATING QUANTITIES OF CONSTRUCTION MATERIALS

At Level 2 you will have carried out a number of calculations for quantifying materials (see Chapter 2, page 57, *The City & Guilds Textbook: Level 2 Diploma in Bricklaying*). These workings are generally based on either linear, squared or volume calculations.

UNITS OF MEASUREMENT

The construction industry uses metric units as standard; however, you will occasionally come across imperial units as these are still used in common parlance in our industry. Material sizes in particular are often still referred to in imperial units even though they are now sold in metric units. An example of this is 8ft × 4ft sheets of ply where the correct size is 2,440mm × 1,220mm.

ACTIVITY

Use an internet search engine to research:
- What imperial unit was paint purchased in?
- How many millimetres are there in a foot?
- How many inches are there in a metre?

Units for measuring	Metric units	Imperial units
Length	millimetre (mm) metre (m) kilometre (km)	inch (in) or " eg 6" (6 inches) foot (ft) or ' eg 8' (8 ft)
Liquid	millilitre (ml) litre (l)	pint (pt)
Weight	gramme (g) kilogramme (kg) tonne (t)	pound (lb)

Units for measuring	Quantities	Example
Length	There are 1,000mm in 1m There are 1,000m in 1km	1mm × 1,000 = 1m 1m × 1,000 = 1km 6,250mm can be shown as 6.250m 6,250m can be shown as 6.250km
Liquid	There are 1,000ml in 1l	1ml × 1,000 = 1l
Weight	There are 1,000g in 1kg There are 1,000kg in 1t	1g × 1,000 = 1kg 1kg × 1,000 = 1t

INDUSTRY TIP

When ordering remember that products can be bought cheaper in large quantities.

CALCULATING VOLUMES

Volume is measured in cubes (or cubic units). How many cubes are in this rectangular prism (cuboid)?

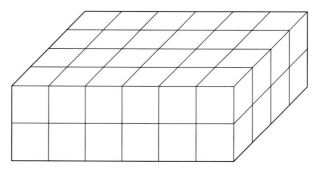

We can count the cubes although it is quicker to take the length, width and height and use multiplication. The rectangular prism above has a volume of 48 cubic units.

The volume of a rectangular prism is = length × width × height.

To calculate the volume of a rectangular prism we need to do two multiplications. We calculate the area of one face (or side) and multiply that by its height. The example below shows how the method for doing this.

FUNCTIONAL SKILLS

Calculate the cost of concrete required for a foundation 600mm wide and 300mm thick with a centre line measurement of 29.2m. Concrete costs £90m³.

Work on this activity can support FM2 (C2.7 and C2.8).

Answer: Volume: 29.2 × 0.6 × 0.3 = 5.256m³. Cost: 5.256 × 90 = £473.04

FUNCTIONAL SKILLS

Calculate the cost of timber required for 240m of 225mm × 50mm softwood floor joisting. Softwood costs £450m³.

Work on this activity can support FM2 (C2.7).

Answer: Volume: 240 × 0.225 × 0.05 = 2.7m³. Cost: 2.7 × 450 = £1,215.

Example

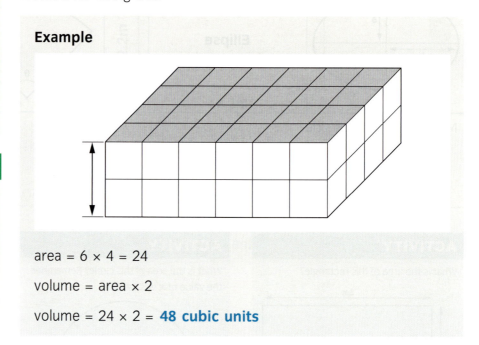

area = 6 × 4 = 24

volume = area × 2

volume = 24 × 2 = **48 cubic units**

WASTAGE

No matter how carefully we work there will be some waste involved in the construction process. There will always be offcuts of wood left over, we may not require all the mortar that has already been mixed or we may have part-full tins of paint left. Much of this unavoidable waste can be accounted for in the estimate by adding an extra allowance for this waste. Avoidable wastage can have a considerable effect on the overall profit a company makes (or loses).

How much we allow for natural waste will depend on the product. Typically we would allow an additional 5% for bricks, blocks and timber for construction purposes. This does not work for all materials; eg, if six rolls of wallpaper are required for a room, 5% would be 0.3 of a roll. As we can't order part of a roll, we would have to order a complete roll.

Calculating waste percentages

Percentage means per hundred, or *part of a hundred*.

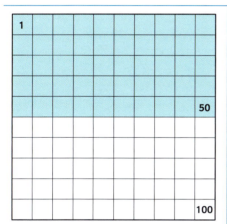

So **50%** means 50 per 100 (50% of this box is blue)

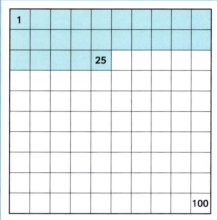

And **25%** means 25 per 100 (25% of this box is blue)

FUNCTIONAL SKILLS

Calculate the following:

a   40% of 240
b   30% of 300
c   57% of 1,140

Work on this activity can support FM2 (C2.4).

Answers: a) 96, b) 90, c) 649.8

Examples

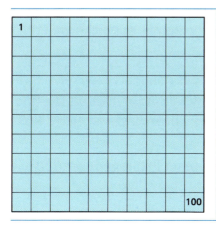

100% means all.

Example:

100% of 80 is $\dfrac{100}{100} \times 80 = $ **80**

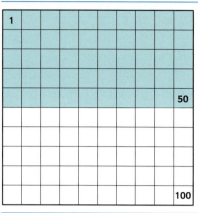

50% means half.

Example:

50% of 80 is $\dfrac{50}{100} \times 80 = \mathbf{40}$

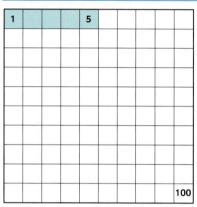

5% means 5 per 100.

Example:

5% of 80 is $\dfrac{5}{100} \times 80 = \mathbf{4}$

Waste does not just include materials but idle labour also.

Waste can be largely minimised by using common sense and having good management of **resources**.

This includes:

■ ordering materials just in time for their use; this will avoid materials being damaged or stolen in storage

■ having secure storage for high-value items

■ using a robust method of checking in materials on delivery, recording discrepancies and reporting errors; this will ensure that goods not received are not paid for and that the balance of the goods required is timely delivered

■ using an internal requisition system for materials required (large sites or joiner's shops commonly use this system); a supervisor will be required to sign the requisition prior to goods being given out by a store keeper

■ ensuring a first-in first-out (FIFO) system of storage is used to avoid materials being stored beyond their use-by date.

Resources

This can include materials, personnel and equipment

INDUSTRY TIP

'To fail to plan is to plan to fail.' Plan the amount of materials you need and arrange delivery times carefully. Having no or not enough materials to work with will hold up the labour force or leave them without productive work to do.

PLANNING WORK ACTIVITIES

To ensure that work can be completed on schedule within the given budget considerable planning of the building process is required. Good management is a prerequisite for a successful build; good or bad management will determine whether a profit is made and whether the company can remain in business.

Planning should take place at various stages during the contract:

- Pre-tender planning includes deciding whether this is the type of work that can be undertaken and whether there is the capability to achieve it within the time scale, then preparation of an estimate into the tender bid.

METHOD STATEMENT

Revision Date:	Revision Description:		Approved By:
Work Method Description	Risk Assessment	Risk Levels	Recommended Actions* (Clause No.)
1.			
2.			
3.			
4.			

RISK LEVELS: Class 1 (high)   Class 2 (medium)   Class 3 (low)   Class 4 (very low risk)

Engineering Details/Certificates/Work Cover Approvals:		Codes of Practice, Legislation:	
Plant/Equipment:		Maintenance Checks:	

Sign-off

Print Name:	Print Name:	Print Name:	Print Name:
Signature:	Signature:	Signature:	Signature:
Print Name:	Print Name:	Print Name:	Print Name:
Signature:	Signature:	Signature:	Signature:

Method statement

- Pre-contract planning occurs after the contract has been won and takes place prior to the build starting. The contractor may have up to six weeks to plan the commencement of work on site. During this time the following occur:
  - ☐ placing of orders for subcontractors
  - ☐ planning of the site layout in terms of temporary site buildings, storage of resources, traffic routes, position of crane, etc
  - ☐ laying on of temporary services
  - ☐ preparation of the work programme
  - ☐ production of **method statements**
  - ☐ sourcing of suppliers and labour.

- Contract planning is required to order the work in a logical sequence, determine labour, resource and plant requirements, maintain control and ensure work progresses as planned to meet the handover date.

Generally it is only the contract planning that concerns us, not in terms of producing a contract plan at this stage but in terms of knowing what one looks like and interpreting the information contained on it.

Method statement

This is a detailed breakdown of the labour and plant required for each bill item. This allows for accurate programming

INDUSTRY TIP

Every job and every site is different so method statements should always be site specific and should be compiled by a competent person who is familiar with health and safety guidelines, the process of works and the site characteristics.

SITE LAYOUT AND ORGANISATION

As a construction worker you may be involved in the planning or setting up of the site layout. As mentioned earlier, on large sites this may form part of the pre-contract planning, while on smaller sites this would be planned by the site manager.

The purpose of site planning is to ensure that the layout, positions of the temporary site buildings, stationary plant, storage areas, any cranes, welfare facilities and site routes are placed in their most strategic and convenient positions with the overall aim of providing the best conditions for maximum economy, continuity, safety and tidiness. Site routes should be kept clear and not impede the building being constructed. Planning should include the minimal movement of materials to save double handling. Considerable additional costs can be incurred if portable buildings or materials have to be relocated. A site plan should be produced showing where all these should be positioned. Fencing or hoarding may be required. If this has to be positioned on or over a public highway a hoarding licence must be applied for from the Local Authority and displayed on the hoarding. Each authority has its own rules about how the hoarding is to be lit, decorated and formed. The hoarding must have warning signs on display at the entrance providing information to visitors and workers alike.

Safety notices

ITEMS included on SITE LAYOUT PLAN

Site security fencing.

Entrance gates.

A   Welfare facilities.

B   Site offices.

C   Stores - lock up.

D   Storage racking for finishing materials.

E   Brick storage area on hardstanding.

F   Formwork/reinforcement fabrication areas.

G   General hardstanding area - formed up on commencement of contract.

H   Area for subcontractor's accommodation and storage.

I   Bagged aggregates and cement storage

●   Mortar mixing area.

⊠   Position of tower crane

  Car parking spaces.

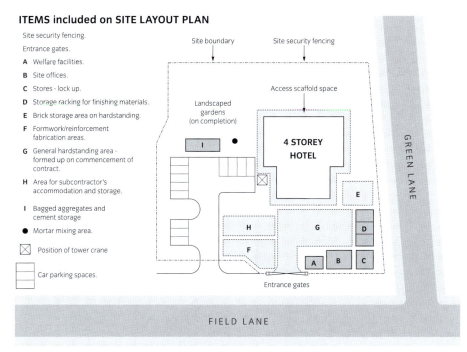

SITE LAYOUT PLAN: 4 STOREY HOTEL

Typical site layout

ACCESS AND TRAFFIC ROUTES

Consideration should also be given to how the site is accessed from the road. In some cases temporary roads have to be constructed to allow access to the site by plant and delivery lorries. Wherever possible, permanent roads should be used as the temporary roads or **hardstandings**. Permission must be obtained from the Local Authority for access over or encroachment of a public footpath. Traffic routes on site can be two way, but often there is only room for one-way traffic. Traffic routes should be clearly identified and where possible pedestrian routes provided separating them from the dangers of moving plant.

TEMPORARY SITE BUILDINGS

These are required for the management team, welfare facilities (including canteen and toilets) and storage. Where space on site is limited it can be stacked with suitable stair access. Larger sites have gatekeepers who monitor and record all comings and goings of staff, materials and visitors to the site. The buildings should be kitted out to allow each to fulfil its function effectively. Offices should be well lit with all services required laid on. The canteen should be suitably furnished, adequately heated and with facilities for drying clothes. Larger sites may have a separate facility for storing and drying clothes. The toilets should be cleaned and disinfected daily.

Temporary road access

Hardstanding

An area of ground where hardcore has been compacted for the placing of temporary buildings or materials

Site manager's office

Typical site accommodation set up as rest facilities

Typical clothes storage and drying facilities

Typical site accommodation set up as a meeting room facility

MATERIALS STORAGE AND HANDLING

Planning will help minimise wastage and losses arising from careless handling, poor storage, theft and double handling. Storage containers are required for high-value and fragile items, and for those that deteriorate when exposed to the weather. Open storage areas are required for bulk items such as timber, bricks, drainage pipes and roof trusses. Some items can be stored in the building as it is completed. It is essential that all materials are stored as required by the manufacturers' requirements to ensure they remain fit for purpose, do not become damaged or deteriorate.

Construction crane

STATIONARY PLANT

Careful planning and positioning of the site crane will allow materials to be offloaded, stored and taken to the final position efficiently and avoid double handling. The crane is often centrally positioned on the site to allow for the whole site to be encompassed by its radius. Mortar/concrete mixing or plant should of course be placed where the aggregate is stored.

PLANNING WORK ACTIVITIES

PROGRAMMES OF WORK

There are a number of different methods of programming building work. The most common is using some form of bar chart. Each company is likely to have its own variation of this. Traditionally this bar chart is referred to as a Gantt bar chart (as developed by Henry Gantt in the early twentieth century). Critical path analysis is another method employed to programme work but is not used much as it is more difficult to interpret the information.

Offloading construction materials from a lorry

Gantt bar chart programming

The programme of work is the key to a successful and efficiently run contract and will help the site manager and supervisors follow a set plan of action. The programme will show:

- the start date
- the sequence in which the building operations will be carried out
- an estimated time for each operation
- the labour required
- the plant required
- when materials require delivering
- the contract end date
- any public holidays.

Preparing the programme

The programme is prepared based on past experience, method statements and the measured rates from the estimate. In order to arrive at a basic programme for all trades, times are often based on a previous similar project.

Example: a small building contractor constructing a four-bedroom, brick-built house in 15 weeks.

Total time to build	100%	15 weeks (75 days)
Start to DPC	15%	11 days
DPC to watertight	45%	34 days
Internal work and finishing	40%	30 days

The programme shown above is based on the following breakdown of tasks.

Operation number	Description	Trade	Comment
1	Site preparation and setting out	Labourer, carpenter	Start to DPC
2	Excavation and concrete to foundations and drains	Labourer	
3	Brickwork to DPC	Bricklayer, labourer	
4	Back fill and ram	Labourer	
5	Hardcore and ground floor slab	Labourer, bricklayer	
6	Brickwork to first lift	Bricklayer, labourer	DPC to watertight
7	Scaffolding	Subcontractor, labourer	
8	Brickwork to first floor	Bricklayer, labourer	
9	First floor joisting	Carpenter, labourer	
10	Brickwork to eaves	Bricklayer, labourer	
11	Roof structure	Carpenter, labourer	
12	Roof tile	Subcontractor, labourer	
13	Windows fitted	Carpenter, labourer	
14	Carpentry first fix	Carpenter, labourer	Internal work and finishing
15	Plumbing first fix	Subcontractor, labourer	
16	Electrical first fix	Subcontractor, labourer	
17	Services	Subcontractor, labourer	
18	Plastering	Subcontractor, labourer	
19	Second fix carpentry	Carpenter, labourer	
20	Decoration	Subcontractor, labourer	
21	External finishing	Subcontractor, labourer	

These items of work can now be used on the bar chart.

Planned activities, labour and plant shown on a programme/progress chart

	Task	Week no	1	2	3	4	5	6	7	8	9	10	11	12	13	14	15
	Activity																
1	Site preparation and setting out		■														
2	Excavation/concrete to foundations and drains		■														
3	Brickwork to DPC			■													
4	Back fill and ram			■													
5	Hardcore and ground floor slab			■													
6	Brickwork to first lift				■												
7	Scaffolding					■							■				
8	Brickwork to first floor						■										
9	First floor joisting						■										
10	Brickwork to eaves						■	■									
11	Roof structure								■								
12	Roof tile									■							
13	Windows fitted									■							
14	Carpentry first fix									■	■						
15	Plumbing first fix/second fix									■			■				
16	Electrical first fix/second fix										■			■			
17	Services											■		■			
18	Plastering												■				
19	Second fix carpentry												■	■			
20	Decoration														■		
21	External finishing/snagging															■	
	Labour requirements																
	Labourer		2 2	2 2	2 2	1 2	2 2	2 2	1 1	1 1	1 1	1	1	1	1	1	
	Carpenter		1 1					2		2 2	3 3	3 3	2 2	2 2		1 1	
	Bricklayer			2 2	2 2		4 4	4 4 4									
	Subcontractors																
	Scaffolding, roof tiler, services, plumber, electrician, plasterer, painter and decorater, landscaper.					▌				▌	▌	▌	▌	▌	▌	▌	
	Plant requirements																
	Ground works plant		▌													▌	
	Cement mixer			▌	▌ ▌	▌ ▌	▌ ▌	▌									
	Scaffolding				▬	▬ ▬	▬ ▬	▬ ▬	▬ ▬								

Inclement weather

Weather that prevents building work from taking place, generally too cold, windy or wet, but could also be too hot

As you can see, the bar chart shows the sequence of operations and the labour and plant requirements very clearly. The second row of each activity line is used to measure progress against the planned activities. This will be shaded in another colour, usually green, as the build progresses. Careful monitoring of this progress line and early intervention of any slippage will ensure the contract remains on time. Generally, unless insufficient time has been allowed, **inclement weather**, staff sickness or lack of materials to work with will be the cause of delays. In order to 'catch up' it is likely that either extra labour is brought in, a more reliable supplier is found, or both.

Critical path analysis (CPA)

CPA is not commonly used on 'everyday contracts'. It is very specialised, and it's easy to make mistakes unless experts are used for generating it. In construction, CPA tends to be used on long, logistically difficult projects such as high-rise commercial buildings (incorporating high-tech systems) in densely populated areas (eg an international bank headquarters in any major city of the world).

CPA is used in a similar way to a bar chart to show what has to be done and by when, and what activities are critical. CPA is generally shown as a series of circles called 'event nodes'.

The key rules of a CPA

- Nodes (circles on the path) are numbered to identify each one and show the earliest start time (EST) of the activities that immediately follow the node, and the latest finish time (LFT) of the immediately preceding activities. Each node is split into three: the top shows the event/node number, the bottom left the EST, and the bottom right shows the LFT.

- The CPA must begin and end on one node.

- The nodes are joined by connecting lines which represent the task being planned. Each activity is labelled with its name, eg 'Brickwork to DPC', or it may be given a label, such as 'D', below.

- The length of the task is shown in the bottom of the node.

For example:

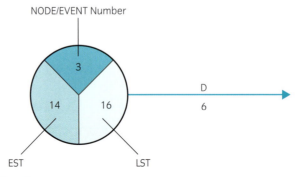

Example of CPA node

- The node is number 3.

- The EST for the following activities is 14 days.

- The LFT for the preceding activities is 16 days.

- There is 2 days' **float** in this case.

- The activity that follows the node is labelled 'D' and will take 6 days.

Every contract will have overlapping activities being carried out by various tasks, particularly large contracts. On a CPA this is shown by splitting the line.

The following CPA example shows the everyday task of making a cup of tea.

Float

In critical path analysis, the difference between the earliest start time (EST) and the latest finishing time (LFT)

	Method statement	**Secs**
1	Fill kettle	10
2	Boil water	90
3	Place tea bag in cup	10
4	Add milk	10
5	Add sugar	10
6	Pour water	10
7	Let tea brew	30
8	Remove tea bag from cup	10
9	Stir tea	10
10	**Hand over to client**	160

Making a cup of tea

Following this example you will see:

- Node 1 is the starting point where the kettle is filled.

- Node 2 is where the kettle is switched on for the water to boil (this node is 'critical' for the programme to work effectively and not to fall beyond time).

- Activities in nodes 3–5 can be carried out while the kettle is boiling.

- The split line shown dotted (often called a 'dummy line') links nodes 2 and 6, node 6 being pouring the boiling water onto the tea bag in the cup.

ACTIVITY

Following this example, produce a CPA for the start-to-DPC section of the bar chart on page 75.

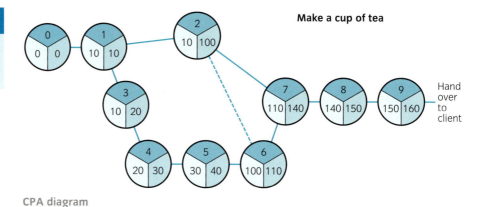

Make a cup of tea

CPA diagram

Hired plant

PAT (portable appliance testing)

There is a legal requirement for all portable electrical appliances to be tested on a regular basis (dependent on use). Most companies test annually

PLANT

During the pre-contract planning a decision will be made as to what items of plant will be purchased or hired. Some plant may already be owned by the company (cement mixers, power tools, etc) while others may not have been purchased due to their storage requirements and/or whether their initial cost can be recovered over a period of time.

HIRE OR PURCHASE?

- A crane, for example, would usually be hired as it would be cheaper to hire than purchase and does not have any storage requirements when not in use.

- Hired plant will always be supplied tested (**PAT**) and ready to use (see page 37).

- The hiring can be terminated when not in use, saving costs.

- There are no ongoing maintenance costs for hired equipment.

- Repeated use of hired equipment may be more expensive than the initial cost of outright purchase.

BUYING MATERIALS AND STOCK SYSTEMS

The programme will also allow the site manager or company buyer to plan for the advance ordering of materials (depending on the size of the company). It is good practice during the pre-contract planning to source suppliers that can provide all the materials required for the contract. In some cases these may be nominated suppliers. Most sites have limited space for storage so materials will be delivered on a regular basis. Some materials may have a long **lead time**. It is essential to know what lead times are required for all the materials needed for the project. Often discounts can be obtained if one builder's merchant is used to supply all materials required for a contract; knowledge of the reliability of this supplier is an important factor to avoid delays. As we mentioned earlier 'just-in-time' delivery methods work well to avoid wastage, damage and the need for storage space.

Lead time

The delay between the initiation and execution of a process. For example, the lead time between the placement of an order for a staircase from a joinery manufacturer and its delivery may be anywhere from two to eight weeks

SITE COMMUNICATION AND ADMINISTRATION

In *The City & Guilds Textbook: Level 2 Diploma in Bricklaying*, Chapter 2, we looked at common methods of communicating information on site and the use of standard documentation to help to make communication clear, simple and accurate. Earlier in this chapter we also looked at drawings, which are one of the most informative methods of communicating information. As you will see, there is a lot of paperwork floating around every workplace and this needs careful managing. The following table shows most of the standard forms of documentation found on site or in a joiner's shop:

SITE DOCUMENTATION

Type of documentation	Description
Timesheet **Timesheet** Employer: CPF Building Co. Employee Name: Louise Miranda Week starting: 1/6/15 Date: 21/6/13 	Day	Job/Job Number	Start Time	Finish Time	Total Hours	Overtime
Monday	Penburthy, Falmouth 0897	9am	6pm	8	
Tuesday	Penburthy, Falmouth 0897	9am	6pm	8	
Wednesday	Penburthy, Falmouth 0897	8.30am	5.30pm	8	
Thursday	Trelawney, Truro 0901	11am	8pm	8	2
Friday	Trelawney, Truro 0901	11am	7pm	7	1
Saturday	Trelawney, Truro 0901	9am	1pm	4	
Totals				43	3 | Employee's signature:_____ Supervisor's signature: _____	Used to record the hours completed each day, and is usually the basis on which pay is calculated. Timesheets also help to work out how much the job has cost in working hours, and can give information for future estimating work when working up a tender.

Type of documentation	Description
Delivery record	Every month a supplier will issue a delivery record that lists all the materials or hire used for that month.

Davids & Co
Monthly delivery record

Customer name and address:	Customer order date:
CPF Building Co Penburthy House Falmouth Cornwall	28th May 2015

Item number	Quantity	Description	Unit Price	Date Delivered
BS3647	2	1 tonne bag of building sand	£60	3/6/15
CM4324	12	25kg bags of cement	£224	17/6/15

Customer Signature: ....

Print name: ....

Date: ....

Invoice	Sent by a supplier. It lists the services or materials supplied along with the price the contractor is requested to pay. There will be a time limit within which to pay. Sometimes there will be a discount for quick payment or penalties for late payment.

Davids & Co
Invoice

Invoice number: 75856   Date: 2nd April 2015
PO number: 4700095685

Company name and address:	Customer name and address:
Davids & Co 228 West Retail Park Ivybridge Plymouth	CPF Building Co Penburthy House Falmouth Cornwall

VAT registration number: 663694542

For:

Item number	Quantity	Description	Unit Price
BS3647	2	1 tonne bag of building sand	£30
CM4324	12	25kg bags of cement	£224

Subtotal	£2748.00
VAT	20%
Total	£3297.60

Please make cheques payable to Davids & Co

Payment due in 30 days

Type of documentation	Description
Site diary 	This will be filled out daily. It records anything of note that happens on site such as deliveries, absences or occurrences, eg delay due to the weather.
Method statement 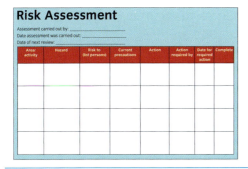	There are two types of method statement in common use. The first includes a risk assessment. This would be written during the pre-contract stage of the work programming. The second is more traditionally used to accurately estimate the time that each operation in the building process will take and is related to the bill of quantities. It is used as a guide to completing the work programme.
Risk assessment	An assessment of the hazards and risks associated with an activity and the reduction and monitoring of them. Applying risk assessments and maintaining high standards of health and safety is the responsibility of everybody working in construction.

Type of documentation	Description
Permit to work **PERMIT TO WORK** 1. Area / 2. Date 3. Work to be Done / 4. Valid From / 5. Valid To 6. Company 7. Man in Charge / 8. No of Men 9. Safety Precautions 10. Safety Planning Certificate (cancelled if alarm sounds) I have inspected the above job which has been safely prepared according to requirements of a safety planning certificate Signed .... 11. Approval of Permit to Work I am satisfied that this permit is properly authorised, that safe access is provided, and that all persons affected by this job have been informed Signed .... 12. Electrical Equipment All power has been isolated/locked/tagged/tried* Circuits are live for troubleshooting only Signed .... 13. Acceptance of Permit to Work I/we* have read and understood the above precautions and will observe them. All equipment complies with relevant standards. I understand the site emergency plan. Signed .... 14. Completion of Permit to Work I/we* certify that this job is complete/incomplete*, all guards have been replaced and secured and all equipment has been removed. The job site has been left clean and tidy. Signed .... 15. Renewal of Permit to Work (same day only) Approved until .... Signed .... Approved until .... Signed .... If the alarm sounds / If you discover a fire 1. Stop Work / 1. Break fire point 2. Make equipment safe / 2. Leave the building 3. Leave the building by the nearest exit / 3. Ring 222 and give name, position, description etc 4. Make your way to the main car park / 4. Report to incident controller in Main car park Do not re-enter any building until you are told it is safe	A permit to work is a documented procedure that gives authorisation for certain people to carry out specific work within a specified period of time. It sets out the precautions required to complete the work safely, based on the risk assessment.

Manufacturer's instructions

MANUFACTURERS' INSTRUCTIONS

It is important to follow manufacturers' instructions for your own safety and to protect your product or purchase. Some instructions are in warning form while others are explanations of how to use that product. Warning instructions such as 'do not place in contact with fire' mean that the product is flammable, and not following this instruction could cause an explosion resulting in injuries. Other examples of manufacturers' instructions are:

- information on the back of a paint tin showing drying times, types of solvents required for cleaning brushes, etc

- information supplied as a user manual for powered equipment such as a mixer or chop saw

- information on how to use a brick cleaner safely or how to use a two-part epoxy adhesive.

Not following these instructions can lead to the invalidation of a **warranty**, lead to misuse of the product or the product not performing as expected.

Warranty

An assurance of performance and reliability given to the purchaser of a product or material. If the item should fail within the warranty period, it entitles the purchaser to a replacement

OTHER DOCUMENTS FOUND ON SITE

Minutes

Minutes of meetings normally include the following information:

- the time, date and place of the meeting

- a list of the people attending

- a list of absent members of the group

- approval of the previous meeting's minutes, and any matters arising from those minutes

- for each item in the agenda, a record of the principal points discussed and decisions taken and who is responsible for actioning any discussed items

- any other business (AOB)

- the time, date and place of the next meeting

- the name of the person taking the minutes.

Before each meeting an agenda should be drawn up, detailing the matters to be discussed. A set of minutes provides a record of what happened at the meeting, what actions are required, who is responsible for carrying them out and by what date.

Set of minutes

INDUSTRY TIP

Distribute (by email) the agenda before the meeting, so that members of the group have a chance to prepare for the meeting. After the meeting, follow up any action points set.

Memo

A memo, short for **memorandum,** is a brief document or note informing or reminding the receiver of something that has to be done. Memos have virtually been replaced by emails now.

Memorandum

Latin for 'to be remembered'

Memo

Hi Clare, Just to let you know that the client will be joining us at the review meeting on site next Monday.

Kind regards, Martin.

Organisational chart

An organisational chart is a diagram that shows the structure of an organisation and the relationships and relative ranks of its parts and positions/jobs.

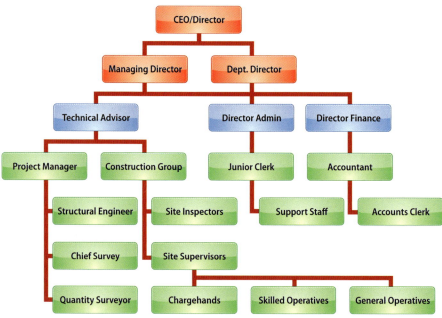

Organisational chart

SITE INDUCTION

Before starting work on site (or even when visiting) everyone should receive a site induction. This should give information on the following:

- a general introduction to the project and staff
- details of welfare facilities, site access and parking arrangements
- what to do in the case of an accident, designated first aiders, etc
- procedures for reporting accidents and near misses
- fire procedure and muster points
- notification of daily hazards such as working at height or moving vehicles
- notification about method statements and risk assessments
- site rules including those concerning drug or alcohol abuse, bullying, etc
- any other site-specific requirements.

There should be a record kept of who was inducted and when. It is in everyone's interest to ensure working on site is as safe as possible.

TOOLBOX TALKS

As mentioned in Chapter 1, a 'toolbox talk' is a short presentation given to a workforce on a single aspect of health and safety. A toolbox talk is prepared by either a company's safety officer, by a manufacturer's representative about a product being used or by a site supervisor. It should give timely safety reminders and outline any new hazards that the workforce may come into contact with. This may be new materials to be used, changes to or new risk assessments arising from an accident or near miss or working in inclement weather.

The HSE has prepared a number of standard **PowerPoint** presentations and **PDFs**; these will save companies the time and effort required in writing them from scratch.

Health and Safety
Executive

HSE

Welfare facilities on small construction sites

Presented by

Martin Burdfield

HSE standard PowerPoint slide

PowerPoint

The name of a proprietary commercial presentation program developed by Windows. It presents a series of slides on an electronic whiteboard or screen

PDF (portable document format)

A file format used to represent documents in a manner independent of application software, hardware and operating system. It presents information in a fixed-layout flat document, including the text, fonts and graphics

ACTIVITY

Research what toolbox talks are available at www.hse.gov.uk.

DEFECTS SURVEY

Prior to a final certificate being written to sign off a contract, a defects survey should be carried out. Larger contracts should have a defects liability period (sometimes called a rectification period). This is a set period of time after a construction project has been completed during which a contractor is responsible for remedying defects. A typical defects liability period lasts for 12 months. A sum of money (typically 5%) is normally retained until after this period has come to an end. This will ensure that any necessary work is carried out.

To determine the work required a defects survey will need to be carried out. This could be done by a building surveyor, clerk of the works or maintenance manager. This will identify:

- poor standards of work

- poor quality of materials used

- damaged materials (damaged in construction not afterwards)

- human error.

A comprehensive list/table is collated on a schedule of outstanding works (this is commonly called a snagging list). The work identified is systematically worked through; this is often carried out by a snagging supervisor.

Schedule of outstanding works		Harold Court, Clacton-on-Sea
Location	**Defect**	**Remedial action**
Front entrance	Entry phone not working properly	Contact Door Services Ltd to send out an engineer to solve problem and recommission
First flight	Loose vinyl tiles on treads 4 and 6	Remove and bond new tiles to both steps
Front door to flat 3	Door twisted and not closing correctly	Contact Speedy Joinery to request replacement

TYPES OF COMMUNICATION

The importance of good communication cannot be overemphasised. Using effective communication skills is crucial to relationships and to success at work. There are, of course, many types of communication. We use verbal communication, non-verbal communication (eg using body language and facial expressions), written communication and many forms of each of those.

As we have said before, drawings are probably the most common means of giving information in our industry. The information shown on a drawing will communicate its contents to a speaker of any language. It is important for any communication to convey information without ambiguity.

WRITING LETTERS

Sometimes it is necessary to put in writing a permanent record of a complaint or concern. This is often the case where it is thought that a court case could ensue. Such a letter should then be sent using a method that requires the recipient to sign to say they have received it. Letters are almost exclusively word processed now and rarely hand written. A letter should be set out with the following layout and information.

Operative typing a letter

Your address

Your address, also known as the 'return address', comes first (leave this off if you're using letter-headed paper). Your return address should be on the right.

The date

Directly below your address, the date on which the letter was written should be given.

Recipient's name and address

The recipient's name and address should be positioned on the left-hand side.

The greeting

After the recipient's address, you should leave a line's space, then put 'Dear Mr Jones', 'Dear Bob' or 'Dear Sir/Madam' as appropriate.

The subject

You may want to include a subject for your letter — this is often helpful to the recipient to identify the order number or job concerned. This should be centred on the page.

The text of your letter

This should be:

- *Concise:* letters that are clear and brief can be understood quickly.

- *Authoritative:* letters that are well written and professionally presented have more credibility and are taken more seriously.

- *Factual:* accurate and informative letters enable the reader to see immediately the relevant details, dates and requirements, and to justify action to resolve the complaint.

- *Constructive:* letters with positive statements, suggesting concrete actions, encourage action and quicker decisions.

- *Friendly:* letters with a considerate, cooperative and complimentary tone are prioritised because the reader responds positively to the writer and wants to help.

The closing phrase and your name and signature

After the body of text, your letter should end with an appropriate closing phrase such as 'Yours sincerely'.

Leave several blank lines after the closing phrase (so that you can sign the letter after printing it), then type your name. You can optionally put your job title and company name on the line beneath this.

> **INDUSTRY TIP**
>
> If your letter is addressed to someone whose name you know (eg 'Dear Mrs Smith'), end it with 'Yours sincerely'.
>
> If your letter is addressed to someone whose name you don't know (eg 'Dear Sir/Madam'), end it with 'Yours faithfully'.

MB Construction
1 High Street
London
EC12 D34

01.12.2014

Mr Dawson
Scales Joinery Ltd
14 Riverside Way
Dalston Lane
Hackney E1

RE: 3 Harold Court (order 1629)

Dear Mr Dawson

Following our recent phone conversation I am writing to confirm that on further inspection the front door to 3 Harold Court is still not closing correctly. Our snagging supervisor has checked to see that the frame has been fixed plumb and informs me that it is. He has tried to ease the rebates to allow it to close more easily but the owner is still having difficulty.

Can I request that when you are delivering the paladin bin store doors you take the opportunity to have a look? If you can reliably confirm that your company will be able to rectify this problem without it re-occurring, please go ahead. Otherwise I would request that it is replaced by the 14.01.2015.

Yours sincerely,

E G Martin

E G Martin
Managing Director

ACTIVITY

Using the information on writing letters, reply to this letter, outlining what you will do as the joinery contractor to solve this issue.

FUNCTIONAL SKILLS

Draft a letter to a supplier informing them that two pallets of bricks out of 14 were badly damaged on the bottom two layers and that replacements are required.

Work on this activity can support FE2 (2.3.3a/2.3.4a).

A similar format to this letter can be used for defective or damaged materials or delivery problems.

It is important to state clearly what action you expect and in what time frame.

VERBAL COMMUNICATION

We looked at this at *Level 2* in Chapter 2. Talking face to face or on the phone is still the most common form of communication. Unfortunately there is rarely a record of these conversations; with this in mind you need to remember the following:

- Think before you speak, so that you get across exactly what you want to say.
- Be clear and concise in what you say.
- Ask for confirmation that what you have said has been understood.

BODY LANGUAGE

Body language refers to different forms of non-verbal communication. This often reveals an unspoken intention. Examples include:

- Rolling your eyes (to an onlooker meaning 'here we go again')
- Yawning   (indicating boredom)
- Hands in pocket   (indicating lack of interest)
- Crossed arms   (indicating disagreement with what is being said)
- Smiling   (indicating happiness)
- Frowning   (indicating unhappiness).

Types of body language

Everyone has the right to be treated with respect and this will always create a productive environment. Aggression breeds aggression and leads to poor working relations and levels of production and a poor image to customers.

INDUSTRY TIP

You will always get the best from people if you treat them as you would like to be treated yourself.

ENERGY-EFFICIENT BUILDING

There is an infinite supply of materials available to us and it is our responsibility to make the most of what we have. By using sustainable products we can control the rate of consumption of resources and conserve our natural assets. Constructing buildings using these methods will pay dividends. There are a number of organisations that can help us achieve this. The Energy Saving Trust is a social enterprise with a charitable foundation. It offers impartial advice to communities and households on how to reduce carbon emissions, use water more sustainably and save money on energy bills.

They offer three main services:

- *EST endorsed products:* Setting standards for best in class for products such as boilers and glazing.
- *EST listed:* Products are listed in a directory approach and checked against quality and safety standards. Aimed at housing associations and other house builders.
- *Verified by EST:* Test reports are verified by EST to provide assurance on products' energy saving claims.

ACTIVITY

Go to www.energysavingtrust.org.uk to see how an existing cavity wall can be insulated.

INDUSTRY TIP

You can view the different EST logos at this webpage: www.energysavingtrust.org.uk/businesses/certification

HEAT LOSS FROM BUILDINGS

Heat can be lost through buildings as shown. The improved insulation of these areas will improve the energy efficiency of buildings.

Sources of heat loss from a house

In addition heat flows from a building as shown below so it makes sense to insulate the structure to minimise this.

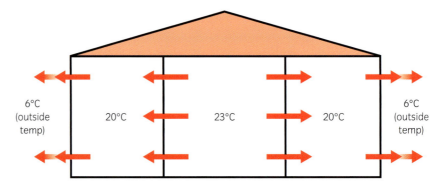

Heat flowing from a building

BUILDING REGULATIONS

Approved Document Part L, 'The Conservation of Fuel and Power in Buildings', is the standard that applies to construction projects that are new, extended, renovated, refurbished or involve a change of use.

To achieve compliance with Part L, the standard approach is to follow the guidance set out in the Government's Approved Documents, of which there are four:

- ADL1A New Dwellings

- ADL1B Existing Dwellings (extensions, renovations, change of use or energy status)

- ADL2A New Non Domestic Buildings

- ADL2B Existing Non Domestic Buildings (extensions, renovations, change of use or energy status).

Government Approved Documents

The route to compliance for new buildings and extensions is through the use of the national calculation methodology (NCM) software which calculates a dwelling or building's carbon dioxide emission rate and compares it against the target emission rate also calculated in the software for the same building. The relevant calculations are:

- SAP (Standard Assessment Procedure) for ADL1 and

- SBEM (Simplified Building Energy Model) for ADL2.

There are specialist companies that will carry out these calculations for you or you can use guidance documents that will show you how the requirements of the Approved Documents can be met.

Architects will produce their construction drawings and specifications to meet these requirements and this will be checked by the Local Authorities Building Control when a planning application and Building Regulations approval is sought.

Energy released by poorly insulated buildings can have a number of **detrimental** effects.

Highly insulated structures will help to:

- prevent heat loss

- reduce the size of heat-providing appliances

- reduce costs to the user

- help the environment

- reduce the country's energy demands.

INDUSTRY TIP

Invest in the best insulation affordable. It will save you money on energy in the long term.

Detrimental

Causing damage or harm

Watt

A unit of power

ACTIVITY

Go to www.planningportal.gov.uk and look up the minimum U-value required for a roof.

THERMAL TRANSMITTANCE

Thermal transmittance, also known as U-value, is the rate of transfer of heat through a structure (in **watts**) or more correctly through one square metre of a structure divided by the difference in temperature across the structure. It is expressed in watts per metre squared kelvin, or W/m²K. Well insulated parts of a building have a low thermal transmittance whereas poorly insulated parts of a building have a high thermal transmittance. The lower the U-value, the greater the insulation properties of the structure.

This chart shows the thermal conductivity of commonly used building structures.

Structure	U-value in W/m²K
Single-glazed windows, allowing for frames	4.5
Double-glazed windows, allowing for frames	3.3
Double-glazed windows with advanced coatings and frames	1.2
Triple-glazed windows, allowing for frames	1.8
Triple-glazed windows, with advanced coatings and frames	0.8
Well insulated roofs	0.15
Poorly insulated roofs	1.0
Well insulated walls	0.25
Poorly insulated walls	1.5
Well insulated floors	0.2
Poorly insulated floors	1.0

So as you will see, the Approved Documents will inform what U-value a structure must meet in order to comply with the Building Regulations.

Infra red image of heat escaping from a house

EXAMPLES OF U-VALUES REQUIRED IN A MODERN BUILDING

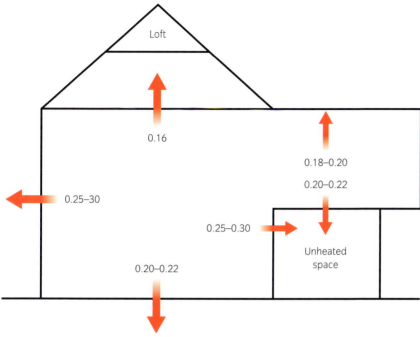

Heat lost in a typical house

The following table shows typical values of specifically constructed structures.

Element	Construction type	U-value (W/m²K)
Solid wall	Brickwork 215mm, plaster 15mm	2.3
Cavity wall	Brickwork 103mm, clear cavity 50mm, lightweight concrete block 100mm	1.6

Element	Construction type	U-value (W/m²K)
Cavity wall 	Brickwork 103mm, insulation 50mm, lightweight concrete block 100mm, lightweight plaster	0.48
Cavity wall 	Brickwork 103mm, insulation 100mm full cavity fill, lightweight concrete block 100mm, lightweight plaster	0.28
Cavity wall – timber frame 	Brickwork 103mm, clear cavity 14 studwork filled with PIR insulation	0.28
Timber frame and clad 	Tiles, render or cladding on battens	0.28

Element	Construction type	U-value (W/m²K)
Pitched roof	Tiles on battens, felt, ventilated loft airspace, 100mm mineral wool between joists, 170mm mineral wool over joists, plasterboard 13mm	0.16
Warm deck flat roof	150 PIR over joists 13mm plasterboard	0.18

ACTIVITY

Research two additional types of wall construction that will meet the current Building Regulations for a residential property.

INSULATION MATERIALS

The following types of materials are available to designers to reduce heat loss to achieve the Approved Document requirements.

Type of insulation	Description
Blue jean and lambswool 	Lambswool is a natural insulator. Blue jean insulation comes from recycled denim.
Fibreglass/mineral wool 	This is made from glass, often from old recycled bottles or mineral wool. It holds a lot of air within it and therefore is an excellent insulator. It is also cheap to produce. It does however use up a fair bit of room as it takes a good thickness to comply with Building Regulations. Similar products include plastic fibre insulation made from plastic bottles and lambswool.
PIR (polyisocyanurate) 	This is a solid insulation with foil layers on the faces. It is lightweight, rigid and easy to cut and fit. It has excellent insulation properties. Polystyrene is similar to PIR. Although polystyrene is cheaper, its thermal properties are not as good.

Type of insulation	Description
Multifoil 	A modern type of insulation made up of many layers of foil and thin insulation layers. These work by reflecting heat back into the building. Usually used in conjunction with other types of insulation.
Double glazing and draught proofing measures 	The elimination of draughts and air flows reduces heat loss and improves efficiency.
Loose-fill materials (polystyrene granules) 	Expanded polystyrene beads (EPS beads) are also used as cavity wall insulation. These are pumped into the wall cavity, mixed with an adhesive which bonds the beads together to prevent them spilling out of the wall. This type of insulation can be used in narrower cavities than mineral wool insulation and can also be used in some stone-built properties.

Type of insulation	Description
Expanded polystyrene boards 	A graphite-impregnated expanded polystyrene bead board, designed to provide enhanced thermal performance. Lightweight, easy to handle, store and cut on site.
Autoclaved aerated concrete blocks 	Autoclaved aerated concrete blocks are excellent thermal insulators and are typically used to form the inner leaf of a cavity wall. They are also used in the outer leaf, where they are usually rendered.
Materials formed on site (expanded foam) 	Spray foam insulation is an alternative to traditional building insulation such as fibreglass. A two-component mixture composed of isocyanurate and polyol resin comes together at the tip of a gun and forms an expanding foam that is sprayed onto the underside of roof tiles, concrete slabs, into wall cavities, or through holes drilled into a cavity of a finished wall.
Double and triple glazing 	Single glazing has a U-value of 5, older double-glazing about 3 and new modern double glazing a U-value of 1.6, which is mainly due the fact that the cavity is gas filled improving the efficiency of the units. An added advantage of triple glazing over double is the improved reduction of external noise.

ENERGY PERFORMANCE CERTIFICATES (EPCS)

Energy performance certificates (EPCs) are needed whenever a property is:

- newly built
- placed on the market for sale
- placed on the market as a rental property.

They were introduced as a result of a European Union Directive relating to the energy performance of buildings and have been a legal requirement since 2008 for any property, whether commercial or domestic, that is to be sold or rented. Since April 2012, legislation has been set in place that makes it illegal to market a property without a valid EPC.

EPCs give potential buyers an upfront look at how energy efficient a property is, how it can be improved and how much money this could save.

The document is valid for 10 years and shows how good – or bad – the energy efficiency of your property is. It grades the property's energy efficiency from A to G, with A being the highest rating.

If you have a brand new home it's likely to have a high rating. If you have an older home it's likely to be around D or E. EPCs for a property can be obtained through specialist companies. A surveyor will be sent out and details of the structure, the heating system and even the light bulbs will be taken. A software program or tables can be used to obtain a **holistic** value to grade the property.

Holistic

Meaning overall, taking everything into account

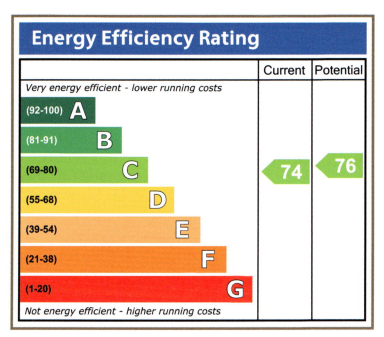

Rating chart

The chart on the previous page shows an example of a current rating and the potential improvement once changes have been made. The energy performance certificate also lists the ways to improve the rating – such as installing double glazing or loft, floor or wall insulation.

SUSTAINABLE MATERIALS

We all have to embrace reduction in energy consumption, whether this is by being limited to buying energy-efficient light bulbs or buying an 'A'-rated electrical appliance to cut down the fuel bills.

An energy-efficient light bulb

There are things we can opt into and things that are decided for us. The construction methods we use today are all decided for us, whether by codes of practice or Building Regulations. So these decide the minimum performance levels a building has to perform to for our comfort, safety and, of course, to conserve fuel and power.

Building materials can be sustainable if they are chosen carefully. For example, the process of manufacturing concrete uses considerable fuel and produces a lot of carbon dioxide (a gas that contributes to damaging the climate and our environment). On the other hand trees absorb carbon dioxide through the process of **photosynthesis** as they grow and can be grown sustainably. Trees look nice, make you feel good and they can be used to make a range of products (eg furniture, building products, paper products, medicines, cosmetics and rubbers). Some timber, however, is harvested from rainforests without thought for the surrounding environment, the life it supports or the fact that some species are close to extinction.

Photosynthesis

The process of converting light energy to chemical energy

Brick manufacturers are doing a lot to ensure the manufacture of bricks is sustainable. They achieve this by continuous improvement of their extraction and manufacturing processes and by providing products that contribute to sustainable construction. The clay is sourced from areas local to manufacturing plants so minimising the transport required.

MANAGED TIMBER SOURCES

Managed forests where trees are replanted after harvesting provide a sustainable source of timber. The Forest Stewardship Council (FSC) is an international non-profit organisation dedicated to promoting responsible forestry. The FSC® certifies forests all over the world to ensure they meet the highest environmental and social standards.

The system has two key components:

1 Forest Management and Chain of Custody certification. This system allows consumers to identify, purchase and use timber and forest products produced from well managed forests.

ACTIVITY

In pairs research three sustainable construction materials. Discuss the findings with your group.

Converted timber stamped showing certification

2 The FSC®'s 'tick tree' logo is used on product labels to indicate that the products are certified under the FSC® system. When you see the FSC® logo on a label you can buy timber and other wood products, such as paper, with the confidence that you are not contributing to the destruction of the world's forests.

FSC® logo

THE CODE FOR SUSTAINABLE HOMES™

The Code for Sustainable Homes™ is the national standard for the sustainable design and construction of new homes. It aims to reduce carbon emissions and promote higher standards of sustainable design above the current minimum standards set out by the Building Regulations. This is currently in the process of being wound down and will be replaced as a result of a Housing Standards review.

Code for Sustainable Homes™ logo

The code currently provides nine measures of sustainable design:

- energy/CO_2
- water
- materials
- surface water run-off (flooding and flood prevention)
- waste
- pollution
- health and well-being
- management
- ecology.

It uses a 1 to 6 star system to rate the overall sustainability performance of a new home against these nine categories.

The aim of this and other organisations is to prove the construction of **carbon-neutral** homes.

RECYCLED MATERIALS

A building that is sustainable must, by nature, be constructed using locally sustainable materials, ie materials that can be used without any adverse effect on the environment, and which reduce the distance travelled of those materials. When using locally sustainable materials it is essential that those materials are renewable, non-toxic and therefore safe for the environment. Ideally, they will be **recycled**, as well as recyclable.

Consideration should also be given to the extent a building material will contribute to the maintenance of the environment in years to come. Alloys and metals will be more damaging to the environment over a period of years as they are not biodegradable, and are not easily recyclable, unlike wood, for example. Also to what extent can the material be replenished? If the material is locally sourced and is likely to be found locally for the foreseeable future, travelling will be kept to a minimum, reducing harmful fuel emissions.

Examples of recycled building materials
- Crushed concrete or bricks for hardcore

- Reuse of tiles or slates

- Bricks cleaned up and reused

- Steel sections shot-blasted and refabricated

- Crushed glass recycled as sand or cement replacement or for the manufacture of kitchen worktops

Carbon neutral

Carbon neutral, or having a net zero carbon footprint, refers to achieving net zero carbon emissions by balancing a measured amount of carbon released with an equivalent amount of carbon credits (planting of trees, etc) to make up the difference. It is used in the context of carbon dioxide-releasing processes associated with transportation and energy production

Recycled

Manufactured from used or waste materials that have been reprocessed, eg bench seating made from recycled carrier bags

- Reuse of doors

- Panel products with chipped recycled timber

- Reused timber sections or floorboards

- Reuse of period architectural features

- Reuse of period fixtures and fittings (ironmongery, etc).

INDUSTRY TIP

Any number of items available can be sourced from local architectural salvage yards.

Recycled bricks

Case Study: Clare

Clare has been appointed as the site manager for the building of four two-bedroom bungalows. The company she works for has a history of constructing a range of standard dwellings. This is Clare's first role as a project manager and she is keen to show that she is capable of the task. To ensure everything runs smoothly and to time she gathers information from previous projects and plans the programme armed with this information.

There are differences, however, as this site is a little off the beaten track and the long-range weather forecast for the winter of the build is poor. Clare researches all the local suppliers and asks them to quote for the staged delivery of the materials required for the contract. She has the option of using company staff or local labour. Company staff will work out more expensive as accommodation costs will have to be paid. Local labour will be cheaper but will not have the experience of this specific work and the quality of their work will be unknown. On balance Clare chooses to use known company labour. An added advantage of using them is that if they are staying away from home they are more likely to put in extra hours if required. Finally Clare has to decide whether some of the smaller plant required should be purchased or hired. She gets quotes and decides on this occasion to use one of the material suppliers she has already contacted as she gets a preferential deal because they are also supplying the building materials.

All Clare's planning will pay dividends and should provide enough information to put together an accurate programme for the building work.

Work through the following questions to check your learning.

1   Which one of the following is an advantage of using CAD?

    a   Software is not required.

    b   Objects can be reproduced quickly.

    c   Drawing technicians are not required.

    d   Lines can be drawn quickly with set squares.

2   Which one of the following scales is used to produce a location plan?

    a   1:5.

    b   1:100.

    c   1:1250.

    d   1:4500.

3   Which one of the following is the **largest** drawing size?

    a   A0.

    b   A1.

    c   A2.

    d   A3.

4   Which one of the following three-dimensional drawings has the lines drawn back at 30°?

    a   Oblique.

    b   Isometric.

    c   Perspective.

    d   Orthographic.

5   Which one of the following is a document which promises to carry out work for a specific sum?

    a   Estimate.

    b   Quotation.

    c   Specification.

    d   Bill of quantities.

6   Which one of the following sections would setting-up costs be included in, within the bill of quantities?

    a   Preambles.

    b   Preliminaries.

    c   Provisional sum.

    d   Prime cost.

7   Who produces the bill of quantities?

    a   Builder.

    b   Architect.

    c   Clerk of works.

    d   Quantity surveyor.

8   Which one of the following **best** describes a fixed price for building work?

    a   Quote.

    b   Estimate.

    c   Guesstimate.

    d   Prime cost.

9   At what stage would the orders for subcontractors be placed?

    a   Preliminary.

    b   Pre-contract.

    c   Programming.

    d   Pre-tendering.

10 A detailed description of how a task will be carried out is called a

    a   programme

    b   specification

    c   risk assessment

    d   method statement.

11 The time it takes for a product to be manufactured is called the

    a   quote

    b   estimate

    c   lead time

    d   time delay.

12 Which one of the following is a disadvantage of hiring plant and equipment?

    a   Costs are reduced in the long term.

    b   Costs are increased in the long term.

    c   It is returned at the end of the contract.

    d   Replacement parts have to be purchased.

13 Which one of the following items will be required to document a client's request for a change to the work required?

    a   Memorandum.

    b   Specification.

    c   Variation order.

    d   Method statement.

14 The order of new-build work will be listed on a

    a   snagging list

    b   risk assessment

    c   method statement

    d   materials schedule.

15 Information on how to use a new product on site safely will be given

    a   by letter

    b   by email

    c   during an induction

    d   during a toolbox talk.

16 What is put on the top right-hand side of the page when writing a letter?

    a   Greeting.

    b   Signature.

    c   Sender's address.

    d   Recipient's address.

17 Triple-glazed windows help reduce

    a   dry rot

    b   heat loss

    c   wet rot

    d   efflorescence.

18 Which of the following construction methods has the **best** thermal value?

    a   Timber frame.

    b   Concrete wall.

    c   Brick wall.

    d   Stone wall.

19 Energy performance certificates are rated from grades

    a   A–D

    b   A–F

    c   A–G

    d   A–J.

20 Which Approved Document covers 'Conservation of fuel and power'?

    a   K.

    b   L.

    c   M.

    d   N.

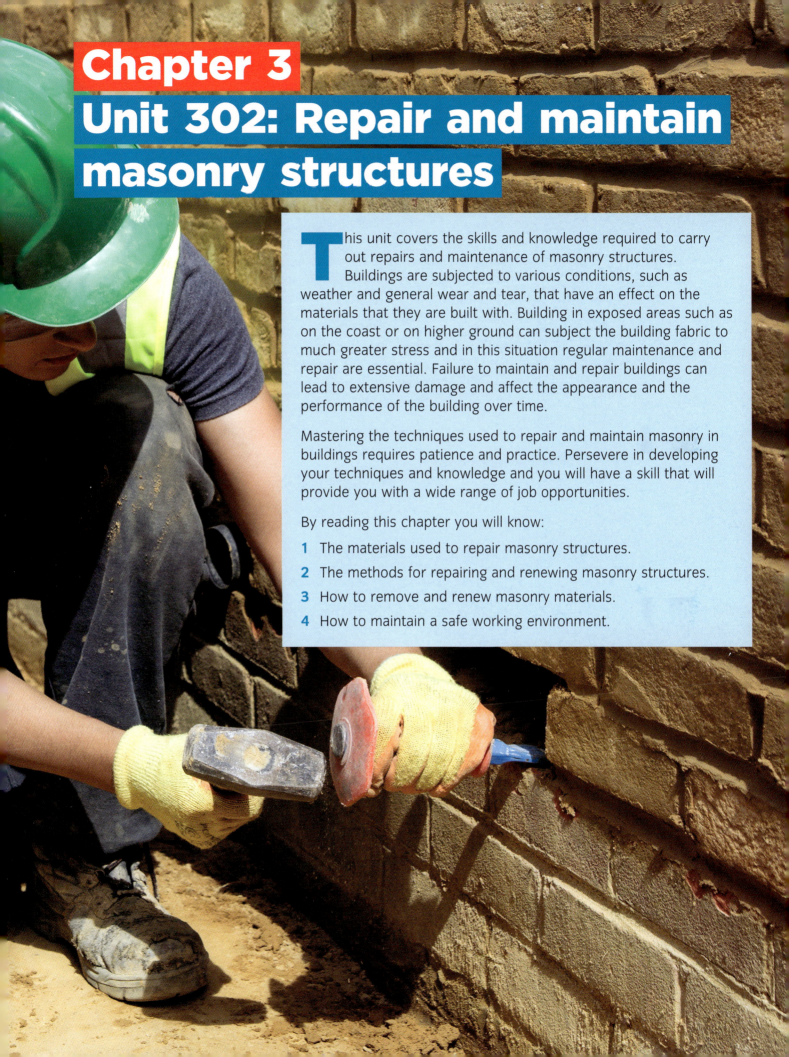

Chapter 3
Unit 302: Repair and maintain masonry structures

This unit covers the skills and knowledge required to carry out repairs and maintenance of masonry structures. Buildings are subjected to various conditions, such as weather and general wear and tear, that have an effect on the materials that they are built with. Building in exposed areas such as on the coast or on higher ground can subject the building fabric to much greater stress and in this situation regular maintenance and repair are essential. Failure to maintain and repair buildings can lead to extensive damage and affect the appearance and the performance of the building over time.

Mastering the techniques used to repair and maintain masonry in buildings requires patience and practice. Persevere in developing your techniques and knowledge and you will have a skill that will provide you with a wide range of job opportunities.

By reading this chapter you will know:

1 The materials used to repair masonry structures.

2 The methods for repairing and renewing masonry structures.

3 How to remove and renew masonry materials.

4 How to maintain a safe working environment.

MATERIALS USED TO REPAIR AND MAINTAIN MASONRY STRUCTURES

With most activities in life, the key to success is preparation. Carrying out maintenance and repairs is no exception; preparation is crucial. Before we consider repairs, it is essential that we identify the cause of the damage. Sometimes buildings are damaged because they were poorly designed or the wrong materials were used to construct them. The weather also has an influence on the condition of buildings and the effects of severe weather may create many problems. Proper maintenance will extend the useful life of a structure and its appearance.

Maintenance of buildings can be *preventative* or *responsive*. Preventative maintenance is carried out to avoid the building falling into disrepair. Responsive maintenance is carried out after a fault has occurred.

Masonry maintenance falls into three main categories:

- repair
- replace
- rebuild.

Examples of these are as follows:

- *Repair:* repairing damage to masonry that has cracked.
- *Replace:* replacing bricks that have **spalled** or suffered frost or water damage.
- *Rebuild:* rebuilding a chimney that had suffered severe weather damage or mortar failure.

Spalled

Damaged by frost, which forces the face of the brick to shell off

SELECTION OF MATERIALS

There are many materials that are used in the maintenance of buildings. The ones you need to know are covered in the following table.

Material	Description
Bricks  Perforated bricks (top left), frogged bricks (top right), engineering bricks (bottom left) and older imperial-size bricks (bottom right)	Bricks come in a variety of finishes and strengths. Older bricks are larger than newer bricks so it is important to identify the correct bricks for repair work.
Concrete blocks   100 × 225 × 450mm block (top) and 150 × 225 × 450mm block (bottom)	Blocks come in various strengths and sizes. They are used in structural walls.
Insulation blocks  Thermalite (top) and Celcon (bottom)	These are used in cavity walling to form an insulating leaf.

Material	Description
Mortar 	This is used as a bedding material for bricks and blocks.
Concrete 	This is used as a structural material for foundations, floor slabs and many other applications in construction.
Timber 	Timber is used for structural timberwork such as partitions, floors and roof structures.
Lintels 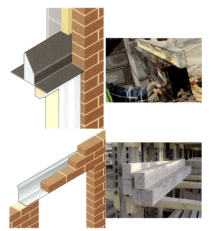 Steel lintel (top left), catnic lintel (top right), IG lintel (bottom left) and reinforced concrete lintel (bottom right)	Lintels are made of reinforced concrete and steel and are used to bridge openings.

Material	Description
Damp proof course (DPC) 	This is made from plastic or bitumen material and is used to provide a damp proof barrier in walls.
Trays 	These are used as a horizontal DPC in cavity walls to prevent moisture from travelling through the outer skin and direct it outwards.
Fixings 	These are used to fit window and door frames and secure them in openings.
Cavity ties 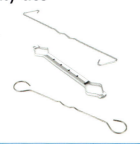	These are used in cavity walls to tie the two leaves together and provide extra stability to a cavity wall while preventing the passage of moisture from the outer to the inner leaf.
Pier caps 	Concrete cappings are used to protect the top of a pier and incorporate a drip groove to shed water off the face of the pier.
Copings 	These are used to protect the top of a wall and shed water off the wall. They are fitted with a drip groove to ensure that water is directed away from the face of the wall.

Material	Description
Special bricks  Special squint brick (top left), single cant brick (top right), bullnosed brick (bottom left) and dogleg brick (bottom right), © Rugby Brick Cutting	Specials are purpose-made bricks that add a feature to a wall. These include squint bricks, bullnosed bricks and doglegs.
Insulation 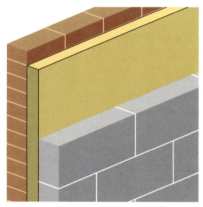	Insulation is used in cavity walls to increase their thermal properties. It can be made of compressed glass fibre, polystyrene or mineral wool.
Render 	This is a sand and cement-based finish that is applied to a wall to give it a smooth finish.
Flashings 	These are normally made from lead and fitted in to brickwork to prevent water penetration.

When selecting materials to carry out maintenance and repairs to structures, there are several important considerations that need to be made. Buildings requiring maintenance are often old and the materials used to construct them may no longer be manufactured. Some older bricks and blocks were made in **imperial** sizes and identical replacements may not be available. Some examples of older type bricks are shown in the pictures below.

Imperial

System of measurement that was used before the metric system was introduced in 1970

A modern, metric-size brick

Older, hand-made bricks were often much larger than modern bricks

Often it is necessary to use **reclaimed** materials as these are more likely to match the existing materials in colour and size. In the case of **special bricks**, it is sometimes necessary to have new ones made but this can be an expensive process for a small number of units.

Remember that the majority of materials used for construction are heavy and care should be taken when preparing them for use. Remember to use proper manual handling methods and to use lifting aids where you can. Further information can be found in Chapter 1. Placement of materials as near as possible to the work will help you to carry out the work more efficiently and safely.

Concrete copings and cappings that are damaged can generally be replaced but can also be cast **in situ.**

Mortar used for maintenance and repairs should wherever possible match the existing. Using aggregate of the correct grade and colour will produce a close match. It is good practice to trial several small mixes to try to create a close match to the mix originally used. Alternatively, where larger quantities are required, they can be sourced from local quarries.

Reclaimed

Referring to materials that have been used in a building previously

Special bricks

Also known as purpose-made bricks, these are bricks that are made for particular specific jobs, eg, bullnosed, single cants, squint bricks and doglegs

In situ

In position

INDUSTRY TIP

Cappings go on a pier whereas copings are laid along a wall.

COMMON MASONRY DEFECTS

It is necessary to maintain the masonry in buildings for a number of reasons. Buildings suffer wear over time because of the effects of weather and through general use. Some common defects in masonry are discussed below.

CRACKING

Cracking in a wall is generally caused by movement or expansion. The joints of a masonry wall should always be weaker than the structural units, ie the bricks, as this will allow a certain amount of movement in a structure without the walling material cracking. If individual bricks crack under movement, then the wall will no longer effectively spread the load of the structure.

It is important to study cracks and to establish whether they are structural or non-structural. A structural crack is a crack that has affected the body of the material, ie cracked the brick, block or stone. A non-structural crack is one that follows the joint line and therefore allows the wall to continue to spread the load across the length of the wall through the walling units.

If you are uncertain whether the structure is still moving, you can apply a 'tell-tale' to the wall over the crack. This will measure the movement over a period of time and the amount of movement can be recorded. A tell-tale is made of two pieces of overlapping plastic with a cross on one and a marked grid on the other. Once fixed, a reading is taken. Further readings can be recorded over a period of time. This will establish whether the crack is increasing.

Tell-tale applied over a crack in a wall

Types of cracks in brickwork

SETTLEMENT

Settlement is the gradual distortion of a building due to either unequal compression of its foundations or shrinkage within its structure. This is a normal process to some degree but when it is excessive it can be disruptive.

SUBSIDENCE

Subfoundation

The ground that a foundation bears on

Subsidence

This is the downward movement of the site on which a building stands, where the movement is not connected with the weight of the building

This occurs when the **subfoundation** of a building fails to support the foundation and causes the structure to subside or drop. This often causes severe cracking of the structure. There are several reasons why **subsidence** can occur and some are beyond our control. In areas of high clay concentration in the subsoil, long dry spells can cause the clay to shrink and this can cause foundations to drop. Large trees can also draw water from subsoil and undermine foundations. Underground springs and leaking pipes can also cause the subfoundation to deteriorate and cause it to fail. In some areas where there has been previous mining activity, movement may occur over time and cause subsidence.

Effects of subsidence in brickwork

Effects of settlement in brickwork

THERMAL EXPANSION

Very often the walls of a building will absorb heat due to exposure to direct sunlight. Large areas of masonry may experience expansion when they are subjected to rises in temperature. The movement caused by this expansion of materials can result in cracking.

In very large areas of masonry and walls that have a large number of openings for windows and doors, **expansion joints** are built in to allow for this change to be accommodated (for more information, see *The City & Guilds Textbook: Level 2 Diploma in Bricklaying*, page 222).

MORTAR FAILURE

Mortar failure is the breaking down of mortar joints causing water penetration and loosening of the walling units (bricks, blocks, stones). Mortar failure is also common in chimney stacks where the carbon from the soot generated by fires breaks down the mortar.

SULPHATE ATTACK

Sulphate attack is commonly seen in chimneys where the exposed position of the masonry causes soluble salts within the masonry to react with tricalcium aluminate, which is a constituent in the cement within the mortar. The result is the formation of ettringite, a calcium sulphoaluminate, a crystal that expands during its formation causing cracking in the joints. Prevention can be achieved by using denser materials that are less absorbent, as this will prevent the reaction. Sulphate-resistant cement can also be used.

Expansion joint

An expansion joint separates masonry into segments to accommodate movement due to the increased volume of the wall structure. The joint allows the masonry to expand and contract

Loose and crumbling brickwork

SPALLING

Spalling is where the faces of bricks are forced off by the effects of frost penetration; this is common in soft porous bricks. Spalling also occurs in concrete where steel expands due to corrosion and forces the face of the concrete to shell off under pressure.

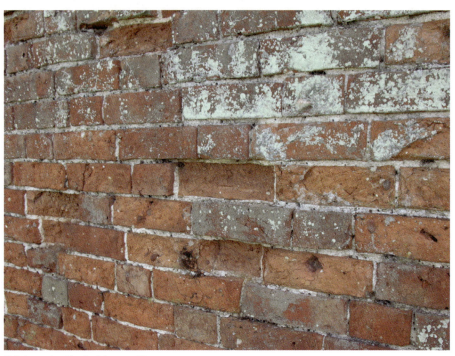

Brickwork affected by spalling

STAINING

Unsightly staining on the face of a wall is caused by constant water penetration.

Brickwork stained by water from leaking gutter

Brickwork stained by water from ineffective capping

EFFLORESCENCE

Efflorescence is white staining on the face of a wall caused by water passing through the material carrying soluble salts to the surface. This leaves a white powder on the wall surface as it dries out.

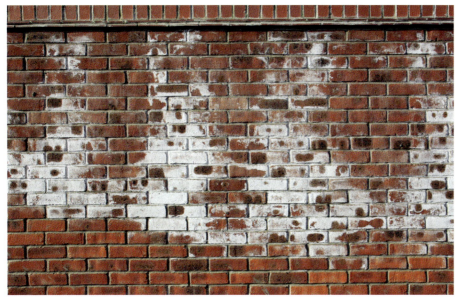

Efflorescence

METAL CORROSION

Corrosion of steel reinforcement in lintels results in the steel expanding in size inside the concrete forcing the concrete to crack and shell off, often resulting in the need for replacement.

Metal fixtures such as wall ties can break down through **oxidisation** resulting in the need to replace them.

Concrete erosion in a lintel

Oxidisation

The chemical term for the combination of a substance with oxygen; on metals this is a corrosive effect

BULGING

Bulging is when the face of a wall is forced out by pressure from above or behind. This can sometimes be caused by excessive load being applied to the back of a retaining wall, or excessive load being **imposed** on the top of the wall. The extent of the bulging will determine whether the brickwork will need to be replaced or whether it can be restrained or reinforced. This may need advice from a **structural engineer** who will calculate the loads and provide guidance on how the repair should be carried out.

Buildings are subject to a variety of forces; we normally refer to these as loads. Loads are divided into the following types:

- *Dead load:* this is the load of a structure itself and any other permanent fixtures.

- *Live load* or *imposed load:* this is the load that is applied to the building in use. It could be the weight of people using the building or the load imposed by weather, eg wind or snow.

Imposed

Applied to a point on a building from above

Structural engineer

A person who calculates loads stresses and strains that may be applied to a building and advises on designs to accommodate them

Bulging in a wall

STONE EROSION

Stone erosion is natural erosion in stone caused by weather, wear or breakdown in the material. For instance, lamination of slate is where the natural layers of the stone separate, crumble and become **porous**. Softer stone features such as cills or copings can deteriorate through the action of frost or acid rain.

Porous

Describing a material that admits the entry of gas or liquid through tiny holes

Stone coping that has suffered from erosion

DAMPNESS

Dampness can be found inside buildings through a variety of reasons. It is generally noticeable as wet patches or mould growth on the inside of the building. This can be both unsightly and cause **condensation** inside the building. Damp proof courses (DPC) that have failed allow water to track upwards causing rising damp. Internal walls of buildings may show signs of dampness because the property is constructed of solid walling or where a cavity wall has been poorly constructed and mortar has built up and bridged the cavity. In this latter situation it is common to see the inside leaf of a cavity showing damp patches where moisture has tracked across. Cavity walls can also allow water to pass through them where wall ties have been left dirty during construction. All of these are common faults in buildings and can be cured through carefully planned maintenance and repair.

Some repairs and maintenance are monitored by Local Authority Building Control, which regulates the design and construction of buildings, making sure they meet the minimum standards set out in the Building Regulations. Building Regulations are designed to ensure:

- the health and safety of people in and around buildings

- energy conservation

- access for all.

Building inspectors will inspect construction work and check that regulations have been adhered to.

Condensation

Water that collects as droplets on a cold surface when humid air is in contact with it; also the conversion of a gas to a liquid

Mould growth due to condensation

CALCULATE MATERIALS REQUIRED FOR MASONRY REPAIRS

We covered calculations involving linear measurement, volume and area, and quantities of material, in the previous chapter. Let's look at some examples for calculating quantities of material in the context of repairing and renewing masonry structures.

Example 1

A gable end of a residential property is south facing and has suffered severe spalling of the bricks.

It is estimated that 20% of the bricks in the wall will need to be replaced. From the measurements on the drawing below, we can calculate the number of bricks that will be required to carry out the work. In this situation we would normally add 5% for cutting and waste.

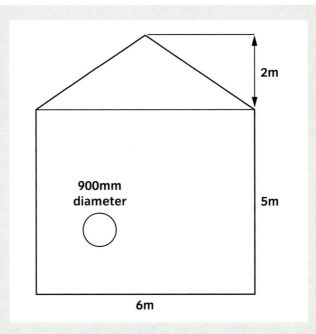

Step 1

Work out the area of the main wall and the gable.
Main wall: 6m × 5m = 30m²
Gable: (2m × 6m) ÷ 2 = 6m²

Add these areas together.

30m² + 6m² = 36m²

Total area = 36m²

Step 2

Take out the area of the circular window. To do this you must first work out the area of the window, using the formula πr^2.

Work out the radius: 900mm ÷ 2 = 450mm

Use the formula for the area of a circle; remember to convert the measurements for millimetres into metres, as this is what the main wall and gable are calculated in.

$$3.142 \times (0.450 \times 0.450m) = 0.636m^2$$

Subtract the area of the circle from the total area of the wall.

$$36m^2 - 0.636m^2 = 35.36m^2$$

Step 3

Now we know the total area of the wall using bricks, we need to find out 20% of this area, as 20% of the bricks need to be replaced.

$$35.36m^2 \times 0.2 = 7.07m^2$$

Then add on the 5% for wastage.

$$7.07 \times 1.05 = \mathbf{7.42m^2}$$

Example 2

A wall 6.5m long has suffered frost damage to the concrete and will need to be replaced.

Calculate the number of coping stones 450mm long that will need to be ordered to carry out the work. Remember to use the same unit of measurement for this calculation.

$$6.5m \div 0.45m = 14.4$$

Required coping stones = **15**

Example 3

A concrete driveway 6.5m long and 3m wide has cracked badly as it was not laid on a **compacted** base. The concrete is to be removed, the base compacted and new concrete laid to a depth of 100mm. Calculate the volume of concrete that will be needed for the job. Remember to use the same unit of measurement in your calculation.

$$\text{volume} = \text{length} \times \text{breadth} \times \text{height}$$

$$6.5 \times 3 \times 0.1 = \textbf{1.95m}^3$$

Compacted

Treated by exerting force so that the material increases in density

MIXING MORTAR FOR REPAIRS TO MASONRY

The method of mixing mortars for repairs and maintenance will vary according to the quantity required. For small-scale repairs, the mortar can be mixed on a mixing board with a shovel; larger quantities can be mixed in a small electric or petrol mixer. The selection of type will depend on whether there is a power source available. Remember that petrol mixers are not designed to be used in enclosed areas, so for inside work an electric mixer is a better option.

Mortar will need to be **gauged** to ensure that a consistent mix is achieved – gauging is normally carried out by volume. Quantities may be measured by use of a suitably sized container such as a bucket. Remember that it is essential to use clean (**potable**) water when mixing mortar, as use of polluted or dirty water can affect the strength and the colour of the mix. (See *The City & Guilds Textbook: Level 2 Diploma in Bricklaying*, pages 213–215 for more information on mixing mortar.)

When preparing to carry out maintenance or repairs, it is essential to establish exactly how the work will be carried out. To ensure that

Gauging materials

Gauged

Mixed in specific proportions

Potable

Describing water that is safe to drink

you are fully aware of what has to be done you will need to make reference to the job documentation. This may be a drawing or specification on a larger contract, or a job card for smaller works. The documentation will clarify the work that has to be carried out and specify the materials that will be used to complete the work.

PROTECTION OF COMPLETED WORK

Always remember that it is important to plan the job from start to finish and that it is vital to protect new work when completed from the effects of weather conditions. This may be the heat of the sun in summer, or rain or frost in the winter. Covering work with hessian cloth, plastic sheeting, timber boards or insulation can provide protection from these conditions. It is also important to protect the work from damage from passers-by. To ensure the security of the site, signs, notices and barriers should be put up. These will help by warning people of work that is being, or has been, carried out.

Brickwork covered to protect it from frost

METHODS FOR REPAIRING AND RENEWING MASONRY STRUCTURES

TOOLS USED FOR REPAIRS AND MAINTENANCE OF MASONRY STRUCTURES

There are a wide range of tools that can be used for maintenance and repair and correct selection will ensure that the work is carried out efficiently and safely. Tools can be divided into two categories.

HAND TOOLS

Hand tools are *not powered by any other source* and are used by hand. The hand tools you will use are covered in the following table.

Tool	Description
Brick trowel	This is used to roll and spread the mortar for the bed joints for masonry work and to apply the perp joints.
Pointing trowel	This is used to apply a joint finish after completion of a wall.
Lump/club hammer	A hammer is used with a bolster or chisel for cutting bricks, blocks and masonry.
Bolster	A bolster is a broad-bladed chisel used for cutting bricks and blocks.
Chisel	These come in a variety of sizes and are used for cutting holes in masonry.
Scutch/comb hammer	This is a hammer with interchangeable finishing heads used for trimming and tidying bricks and blocks.

Tool	Description
Brick hammer 	This is a hammer used for rough cutting of bricks.
Line and pins 	These are used while building a wall to line and to level bricks and blocks.
Corner blocks 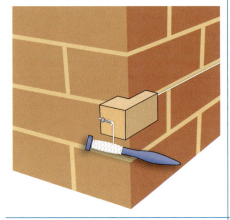	Corner blocks are plastic or wooden blocks used to hold the line on course at the quoins without the need to put the pin in the brick or block joint.
Spirit level 	This is a level used to establish level and plumb while constructing walls.

Tool	Description
Jointing chisel	A specially shaped chisel that is used to cut out joints in brickwork without damaging the brick's face.
Boat/pocket level	This is used to level bricks and blocks and for limited spaces. It is a small level approximately 250mm long with three bubble chambers set at vertical, horizontal and 45°.
Hand hawk	A hand hawk is used to hold and pick up mortar when pointing or rendering.
Tape measure	An expanding tape measure is used to measure work.
Building square	This is used to set out and build right-angled corners.
Tingle plate	This is used on a long line when laying bricks or blocks to ensure that the line does not sag in the middle.

Tool	Description
Jointing iron	A jointing iron is used to apply a half-round joint finish as the work proceeds.
Gauge rod 	This is used to check gauge of the work and to maintain even bed joints over the height of the wall.
Storey rod 	A rod that is used to check the vertical height of various aspects of the building during construction. The rod is normally marked with window heights, joists heights, door heights, etc.
Sealant gun 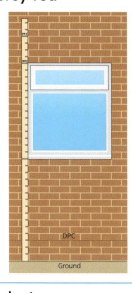	A tool used to hold and apply sealant.

POWER TOOLS

A power tool is any tool that is operated by an additional power source and mechanism other than solely by manual labour.

Tool	Description
Disc cutter	This is a tool powered by electricity, petrol or air that is used to cut masonry or dense materials.
Masonry bench saw/clipper saw	This is a bench-type masonry saw used for wet cutting masonry.
Hammer drill	A hammer drill is used for drilling holes in masonry.

Tool	Description
Tile cutter 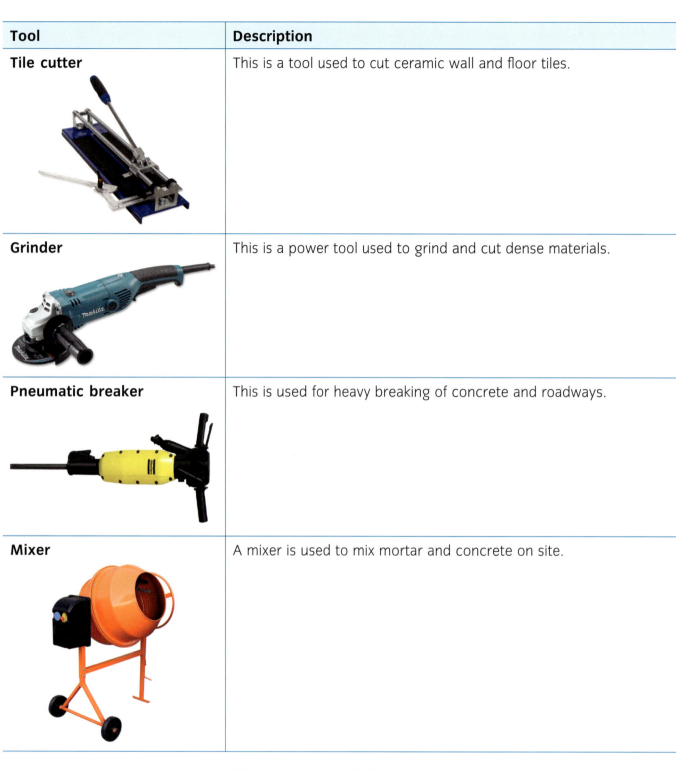	This is a tool used to cut ceramic wall and floor tiles.
Grinder	This is a power tool used to grind and cut dense materials.
Pneumatic breaker	This is used for heavy breaking of concrete and roadways.
Mixer	A mixer is used to mix mortar and concrete on site.

When selecting tools for work activities, always ensure that you follow the manufacturer's safety instructions and wear suitable PPE. Remember that cutting masonry generates dust and you must ensure that you protect yourself from inhaling particles. This should be covered in the risk assessment for the job.

Looking after your tools and equipment and keeping them clean and safely stored when not in use will ensure that they last longer and do not get stolen.

SAFETY AND PREPARATION

When planning any work you must ensure that you consider the wide range of hazards that may exist in the working environment. Every site has different hazards that you need to be aware of; many of these hazards are explained to you during a site induction. Ensure that you listen to the information given in the induction and act on the information provided. This will ensure that you keep yourself safe and also your colleagues and others who may be affected by what you are doing. This could be people who are working nearby or the general public. Chapter 1 provides a lot of important detail about the many laws and regulations dealing with safety at work.

Hazards include:

- falling objects – such as particles of masonry that could fall from above when working in the vicinity of a scaffold

- flying **debris** – generated by cutting masonry

- dust generated by cutting equipment such as a masonry saw or disc cutter

- skin damage, from harmful materials and also from exposure to sunlight that can have dangerous long-term effects; always wear gloves and ensure that your skin is properly protected from direct sunlight

- fire and risk of fire from storage of petrol that may be used to run a masonry saw or mixer

- contact with services such as water, electricity and gas whilst excavating

- slips, trips and falls – from articles that are left on the ground or on working platforms

- danger from vehicles such as **MEWPs**, dumper trucks, or forklift trucks moving around a site; wearing a high-visibility jacket will make you more visible to the operator.

Remember that cleaning up is part of the job and all waste materials should be removed from the work area and the area kept clean throughout the work process.

A **risk assessment** is a good start to thinking about safety, and is a legal requirement under the Health and Safety at Work Act (HASAWA) 1974. This is a way of identifying the risks of carrying out a piece of work and minimising the chances of an accident happening. An example of this could be removing a brick from a wall. In carrying out this task a variety of risks are present. For example, in cutting a brick out of a wall with a hammer and chisel, particles could become airborne and hit you in the eyes. There is also a chance that a piece of masonry could fall on your foot. The process

Debris

Rubble or waste, eg which could be the product of cutting out a wall with a hammer and chisel

INDUSTRY TIP

Petrol needs to be kept in a purpose-made container and safely stored to ensure that there is no risk of fire.

MEWPs

An abbreviation for mobile elevated working platforms

Risk assessment

A document that lists all of the risks involved in carrying out a piece of work and identifies ways of reducing the risks to the lowest possible level. Chapter 1, page 5 shows a typical example of a risk assessment document

Access equipment	Description
Stepladders 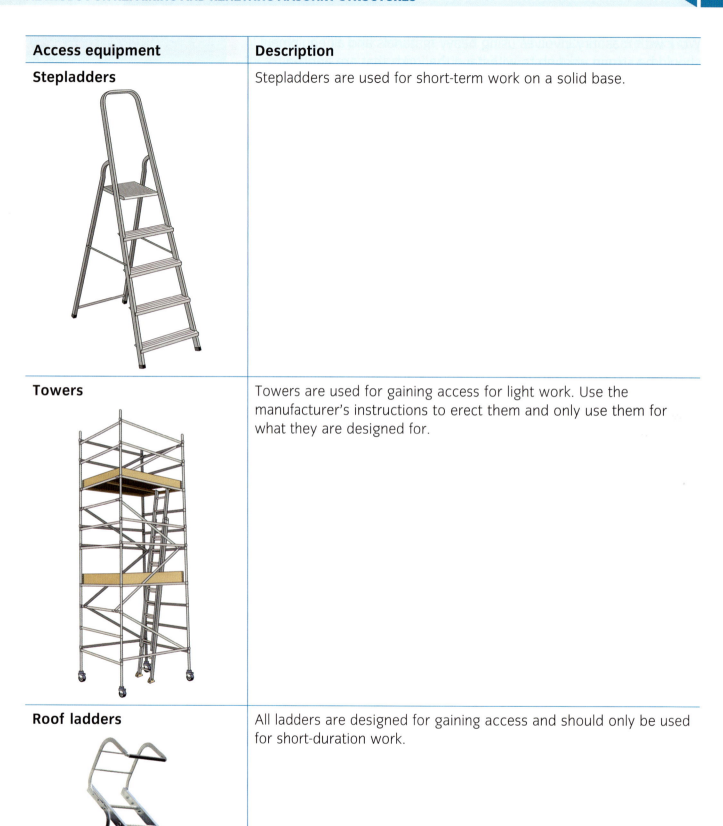	Stepladders are used for short-term work on a solid base.
Towers	Towers are used for gaining access for light work. Use the manufacturer's instructions to erect them and only use them for what they are designed for.
Roof ladders	All ladders are designed for gaining access and should only be used for short-duration work.

Access equipment	Description
MEWPs 	Mobile elevated working platforms are sometimes used for gaining access for repairs and maintenance. Remember you must be properly trained to use this equipment.
Independent scaffold 	This is purpose-built scaffolding which is erected by trained personnel to provide working platforms for operatives to work from.
Stack scaffold 	This is a purpose-built scaffold for gaining access to a chimney.
Cradles 	Access cradles can be used for gaining access to the face of buildings. They are specialist pieces of equipment and should be erected by trained and qualified personnel.

Refer back to Chapter 1 to read up on the Work at Height Regulations 2005 (as amended) on page 24.

Remember that you cannot work safely from a ladder and you should ensure that ladders are used only for gaining access to platforms or scaffolding and not used to carry out work.

If you are not sure about the safety of any access equipment, you should always consult your supervisor before you begin working on it, or refer to the method statement for the work.

Keeping the work area separate by the use of temporary barriers will provide protection, as will signage, by raising awareness of the fact that work is in progress.

FUNCTIONAL SKILLS

Produce a risk assessment to carry out a repair on a garden wall where bricks are to be replaced on the front boundary wall of a property adjacent to the pavement. Discuss the considerations that should be made prior to starting the job.

Work on this activity can support FE2 (2.3.2 and 2.3.3b/2.3.4b).

REMOVE AND RENEW MASONRY MATERIALS

Some repairs will involve removal of existing materials in the structure. These may be bricks, blocks, stones, cills, lintels, windows and door frames.

Some small-scale repairs, such as the removal of a single brick, block or stone, can often be carried out without providing temporary support for the structure above. However, when removing larger areas of masonry or changing components such as lintels, temporary supports may be needed to provide extra support for the structure. The type of supports required will vary according to the job but some examples of temporary supports are shown later in this chapter. These have been divided according to the kinds of jobs that are regularly carried out to maintain buildings.

CRACKING IN WALLS

Walls may crack for a variety of reasons, such as settlement in the foundation, movement due to thermal gain, **lateral pressure** or impact.

Lateral pressure

Pressure that is exerted from a sideways, usually horizontal, direction

Stitching

Careful inspection of the wall can often provide clues to the cause and this can influence the type of repair that is most suitable.

If the crack is following the line of the joints, then the ability of the wall to spread load is not compromised. If, however, the crack has continued vertically through the bricks or blocks, then the damage is more serious and the wall has lost its ability to spread load evenly. This is termed as a failure.

The scale of the repair will be dependent on the type and extent of the movement. Sometimes bricks or blocks can be replaced and joints reinforced by '**stitching**' them with stainless steel rods and cement grout. There are a number of proprietary brands that can be used for this process.

The work is carried out by removing and replacing broken bricks and inserting helical bars in the joints. The joints are then filled with cement mortar or epoxy resin grout. This method provides reinforcement to the wall.

BULGING WALLS

Where walls are bulging, it is possible to reinforce them to avoid the need to take them down and rebuild. This sort of work will normally involve consultation with a structural engineer who will provide calculations and detailed instructions as to how the work should be carried out.

Stitching

A method of inserting reinforcement into the bed joints of a wall to provide added strength

ACTIVITY

The owner of a house has discovered that the area below the suspended ground floor of his house is very large and could be used for storage. A door opening is to be formed in an external wall of the house to provide an access and form an underfloor basement area. In pairs, discuss what will need to be considered before the work begins. Produce a sequence of work to show the order of operations from the start to the finish of the job.

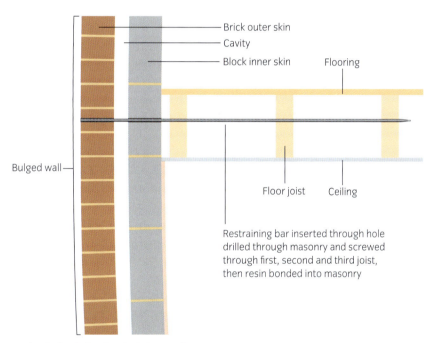

Brick outer skin
Cavity
Block inner skin
Flooring
Bulged wall
Floor joist
Ceiling

Restraining bar inserted through hole drilled through masonry and screwed through first, second and third joist, then resin bonded into masonry

Method of reinforcing bulging walls

REPLACING BRICKS IN A GARDEN WALL THAT HAS SUFFERED FROST DAMAGE OR SPALLING

Often when bricks in a wall are affected by frost damage, the brick faces fall off. As discussed earlier, this is known as spalling. This could be due to the wrong selection of bricks or to the exposed nature of the building. It could also be because of a design fault such as a missing coping or a leaking gutter or downpipe.

The effect of this is unsightly and often the bricks need to be replaced with new ones. Careful preparation for this work is essential if the finished job is to look good. The area of work needs to be prepared and consideration should be given to whom this work may affect. This should be covered in a risk assessment.

Correct selection of materials is also important. Where possible you will want to identify the type, colour and make of bricks that will best match the existing work. This can be done by visiting a builder's merchant and taking a sample of the bricks to be replaced. You can also look at manufacturers' catalogues to find a match. If you have one of the bricks, it may contain a manufacturer's code which will help to identify its origin. You will also need to decide the type of sand that has been used to construct the wall originally to enable you to produce the closest possible match for the replacement mortar.

Removal of the damaged brick should be done with care and you must ensure that you wear the correct PPE. Details of this will be found in the risk assessment. A jointing chisel and lump hammer can be used to remove the joint around the bricks so that the damaged unit can be replaced.

STEP 1 First remove the mortar around the damaged brick using a jointing chisel.

STEP 2 Remove the damaged brick.

STEP 3 Clean out all of the old mortar to ensure that the new brick will fit easily.

STEP 4 Place the bedding in position for the new brick. Wet the area and lay the bed for the new brick.

STEP 5 Place the brick in the gap and fill the mortar **perp joint** and the joint above, making sure the mortar fully fills the joints.

Care should be taken that all of the old mortar is removed so that the new brick can be positioned and aligned to the existing work. The bed of the brick can be laid by using a small trowel and the perp joints can be applied to the brick before placing. The joints should then be carefully filled by pushing the mortar into the joints until compacted.

The joints should be finished to match the existing work.

INDUSTRY TIP

When mixing the mortar, do not add too much water, as wet mortar will stain the face of the wall more.

REPLACING A LINTEL

Sometimes it is necessary to replace a lintel over a door or window because the material it is made from has failed.

Some examples are as follows:

- *Timber lintel:* timber may have rotted over time.

- *Concrete lintel:* steel reinforcing is often affected by water penetration causing oxidisation of the steel; this makes it swell and forces the concrete surface to crack and shell off.

- *Steel lintels:* these are often affected by water causing them to rust and weaken.

Replacing a lintel will mean that the masonry above the lintel will need to be temporarily supported while the replacement is being installed. Each individual job will need to be treated separately to assess the **load** that is to be supported and the building's condition; a decision can then be made as to the best method to adopt to provide the support.

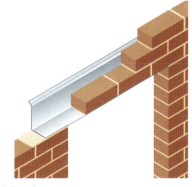

IG lintel

Load

The weight applied to the walls of a building

To assist in understanding how load is transferred in a building, it is worth considering that load is distributed across the length of a wall by the bonding of the units (bricks, blocks, stones). The drawing below indicates how the load of a wall is transferred through the wall through the bonding arrangement of the bricks, blocks or stones.

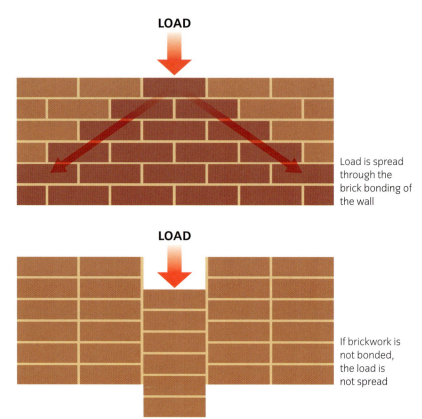

LOAD

Load is spread through the brick bonding of the wall

LOAD

If brickwork is not bonded, the load is not spread

How load is distributed through bonding of brickwork

METHODS OF PROVIDING TEMPORARY SUPPORT

ADJUSTABLE STEEL PROPS AND NEEDLES

Masonry above an opening can be supported temporarily while a lintel is replaced, by inserting a needle through the wall which can be propped with adjustable steel props. To use this method you must have access to both sides of the wall.

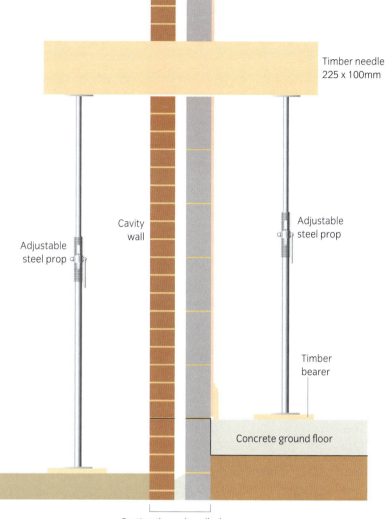

Timber needle
225 x 100mm

Cavity wall

Adjustable steel prop

Adjustable steel prop

Timber bearer

Concrete ground floor

Section through wall where opening is to be cut out

Section through a wall with a needle inserted, supported by steel adjustable props

Dead shore

An upright timber used as a temporary support for the dead load of a building during structural alterations, commonly used to support a needle

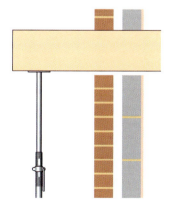

Dead shore

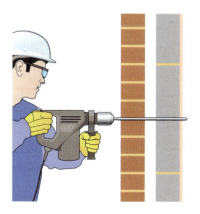

STEP 1 Cut a hole in the wall, above the lintel to be replaced, of sufficient size to thread a needle from one side of the wall to the other.

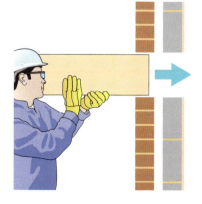

STEP 2 Next, thread the needle through the wall.

STEP 3 Now fit the adjustable props to support the needle on either side. Tighten the props under the needle until they are providing support for the area of masonry above the door or window.

INDUSTRY TIP

When using a concrete lintel, the minimum bearing required by Building Control is 100mm. If the lintel is steel then the minimum bearing is 150mm.

Strongboy®

A proprietary adaptation that is added to an expanding prop to provide support for brick/block structures

Strongboy®

Stitch drilling

A method of drilling a number of holes along a joint to ease its removal

The lintel can now be carefully removed by cutting it out, removing it and replacing it with a new lintel. Remember that the type of lintel used will determine the amount of **bearing** that is needed. Once the new lintel is in place and levelled, the gap between the lintel and the brickwork needs to be filled, ensuring that the gap is well filled with mortar. Slate slips can be used to pack the joint to ensure that it is properly filled.

The adjustable props should remain in place until the mortar has fully set (usually 24 hours); they can then be removed. Once the props have been removed, masonry that has been removed to insert the needle can be reinstated. Make sure that all joints are filled and mortar is well packed into the joints.

OFFSET PROPS (STRONGBOYS®)

An alternative method of providing temporary support for masonry over an opening is to use offset props, the most commonly used being **Strongboys®**. This method is particularly useful when you have access to only one side of the wall, eg when forming an opening in a wall to gain access under a floor.

1 Before you begin using the Strongboy®, remove the bed joint in the brick or block wall in the centre of the wall directly above the lintel to be replaced. This can be done in several ways:

- with a jointing chisel
- with a mechanical disc cutter
- by **stitch drilling** the joint and removing the remaining mortar with a jointing chisel.

Using a jointing chisel

Using a mechanical disc cutter   Stitch drilling the joint

2 Place the Strongboy® on the adjustable prop and insert it into the joint to the full wall thickness. The number of props used will vary according to the opening width; for small openings, under 1.5m, a single prop will suffice but for wider openings more props should

be provided at regular intervals. For wider openings in stable structures, the Strongboys® should be placed at a maximum of 900mm apart. If the mortar in the wall is not considered to be stable, then it may be necessary to place them closer together.

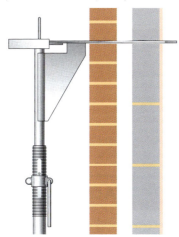

Strongboy® fitted on the adjustable prop and inserted into the joint

3 Carefully tighten the prop to provide support for the masonry above. If there is any doubt, then advice should be sought from a structural engineer. Before using this type of equipment, always ensure that you make reference to the manufacturer's instructions.

4 Once the props and Strongboys® are in position and secured, the lintel can be removed and replaced.

If you are forming a new opening it will be essential to ensure that you close the **reveals** properly; this will include inserting a vertical DPC, making good any insulation to maintain sound and heat insulation, and sealing the cavity to prevent air movement.

Reveal

The position where the inside leaf of a cavity wall returns to meet the outside leaf and seals the cavity

FIXING AND SECURING DOOR AND WINDOW FRAMES

On some occasions the bricklayer will be expected to replace a window or door frame at the same time as the lintel is replaced. It is extremely useful to know the methods that can be used to fix the frames.

In most cases the frame is fixed on the outside leaf of the cavity and plumbed and levelled in position. Care should be taken to ensure that the vertical DPC is in place and not damaged during the fixing of the new frame. The frame can be fixed in place to the side of the frame with brackets or alternatively holes can be drilled through the frame into the brick reveal and the frame secured by using window frame fixings which include an expanding plug (fischer type). The two methods are shown in the illustrations below.

INDUSTRY TIP

Often engineering bricks are used to provide a horizontal DPC, as they are considered the best to use.

Fischer plugs

Brick

Water   25mm

Brick placed in water

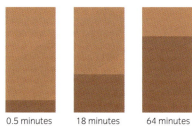
0.5 minutes   18 minutes   64 minutes

Water rising up through bricks

Dense

Closely compacted in substance

If the brick is very **dense**, as is the case with an engineering brick, the water will not find large enough voids to allow it to travel upwards. You can repeat the experiment using an engineering brick and note the result.

When a DPC becomes ineffective it can be replaced in a number of ways. We will look at three.

One method is to remove sections, normally four bricks at a time, insert new DPC, then build brickwork back in place. You must take care to ensure that the mortar is well packed in to the joints of the masonry of the wall.

STEP 1 Remove four bricks at DPC level using a jointing chisel.

STEP 2 After you've removed the bricks, clean the joints away.

STEP 3 Re-bed a new length of DPC.

STEP 4 Replace the bricks on top of the DPC.

A second method is to take out sections of brickwork and replace them with engineering bricks.

STEP 1 Cut out two courses of bricks using a jointing chisel.

STEP 2 Clean out the mortar.

STEP 3 Lay the engineering bricks in the gap and joint the bricks.

A third method is to inject silicone liquid into the body of the wall to fill the bricks.

Silicone injection to provide a DPC

UNDERPINNING A BUILDING

If you need to underpin all, or part, of the foundations of a building then Building Regulations apply. Underpinning is a method of construction that increases the depth of the existing foundations, which may have sunk, settled or failed due to various factors. This could be erosion due to underground springs, shrinkage in the subfoundation caused by prolonged dry weather, or by the water in clay being extracted by nearby tree roots causing the clay beneath the foundation to shrink.

The process of underpinning is very expensive and time consuming but this work is very common and some bricklayers and companies specialise in this work. Remember that before any **excavation** can take place, it is important to locate the positions of **services**. This may involve contacting the electricity company, the gas company, telephone supplier and/or water company, and also locating the depth and position of drainage serving the building as this could be damaged during excavation. Remember that some services may be overhead and these need to be protected from excavator arms and MEWP booms.

The process of underpinning involves excavating trenches around the structure and removing the subfoundation in sections to a lower and more firm foundation base. New foundation is then laid in sections with provision of reinforcing bars to bond the sections of foundation together. New walls are then constructed between the

Excavation

The process of removing subsoil to form a trench

Services

The utilities that serve a building such as water, gas, electricity and telephone

newly formed foundation and the base of the existing foundation. The final joint between the wall and the foundation is packed with mortar to ensure a solid joint is formed.

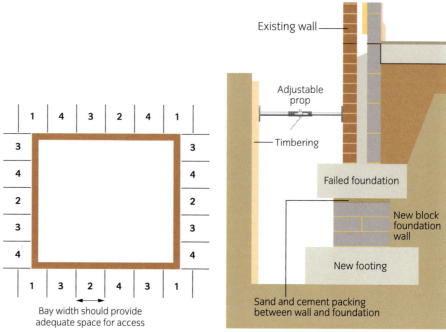

Plan view of a foundation and the order of work numbering the bays to be removed and replaced in specific order

Section view of a foundation being underpinned

REPLACING DEFECTIVE WALL TIES

Wall ties have been built in to cavity walls for almost a hundred years. They form part of the structure of the wall and link the external and the internal leaves of the cavity. Since 1980, wall ties used in cavity walling have been made of stainless steel, which is a very durable material. In early use, ties were galvanised steel. This gave some protection from **corrosion**, but over time, and with constant exposure to moisture in the beds of the external leaf, they would break down and need to be replaced.

If ties corrode in the cavity and break, this could mean that the outer and inner skins are no longer tied together. If this occurs, there is a distinct risk of the outer skin collapsing, especially under high winds which cause suction on the face of the wall.

A more common problem is corrosion of the part of the cavity wall tie embedded in the outer skin. This tends to occur on south- and west-facing elevations which are exposed to driving rain and which are often wet. Rust occupies a greater volume than the original steel and therefore the expansion of the corroding tie in the bed joint forces it to crack. Cracks running along the bed joints, every 450mm up the wall, are a good indication of cavity wall tie corrosion.

There are three distinct processes to be observed, as follows:

Corrosion

The gradual destruction of materials by chemical reaction with its environment

Wall tie tying together the inner and outer walls

1 *investigation* of the type of masonry in each leaf of the cavity and the condition and position of the existing ties

2 *removal* of the existing ties if they are causing movement

3 *installation* of the new ties.

There are a number of ways of replacing defective wall ties, including:

- *Resin grouting:* this system involves drilling through the external leaf of the cavity, inserting specialist ties and resin and grouting them in place.

- *Mechanical ties:* these are fitted by drilling a starter hole into the wall through the external leaf and into the inner leaf. A helical-type tie is then impact drilled into the masonry to the required depth. The hole is then flushed with mortar to match the masonry.

All of this work involves careful planning and needs to be carried out from properly erected access equipment that is erected by competent scaffolders.

INDUSTRY TIP

Resin grouting is a chemical system used to bond fixings and ties to masonry.

A variety of wall ties – helical-types are the 4th and 7th down

STEP 1 Cut out a hole in the cavity wall to establish the condition of the wall ties.

STEP 2 Once the tie positions have been established, remove the ties.

STEP 3 Replace the ties with new drill-in-type ties.

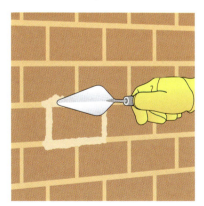

STEP 4 Replace the removed brickwork and make good the joints.

REPAIRING A CHIMNEY STACK WHERE MORTAR HAS FAILED

Chimney stacks tend to be very exposed to the weather and therefore they are prone to erosion over time. Older chimneys were not constructed with liners; instead the inside of the flue was **parged** (see Chapter 6). This method provided protection but constant exposure to carbons and water gradually broke down the strength of the mortar joints in the chimney stack.

This causes instability and movement in some cases, and can lead to chimneys needing repair or replacement.

There are also other areas of the chimney that need to be maintained. The chimney pots are held in place by flaunching. This is a sand-and-cement capping that is laid on the top of the stack and holds the pots in place and also directs rainwater off the top surface of the chimney. This often needs replacement. When chimney pots and flaunching become loose they can be very dangerous and, if they should be blown off in high winds, will cause significant damage to the roof and pose a serious risk to anyone who may be in the area.

Parged

A method of daubing lime mortar on the inside lining of the chimney flue to provide extra protection

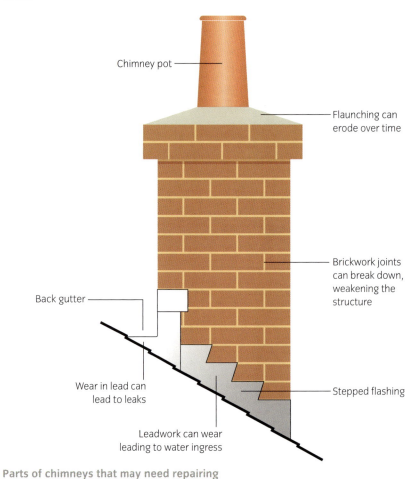

Chimney pot

Flaunching can erode over time

Brickwork joints can break down, weakening the structure

Back gutter

Stepped flashing

Wear in lead can lead to leaks

Leadwork can wear leading to water ingress

Parts of chimneys that may need repairing

Flashings and leadwork around chimneys are fitted to seal the roof around the chimney. Over time the lead can become porous and allow water to pass through into the property. This can cause damage to the timber work and plaster inside the building.

Examples of damaged chimneys

All of the work carried out on chimneys is very difficult due to the problems of access and movement of materials from ground level. Specialist access equipment should be used and this needs to be erected by qualified and competent scaffolders.

Removing faulty materials and providing replacement materials should be carried out by using specialist lifting equipment. Materials that need to be removed should be transported to a skip through a properly erected waste chute to a skip at ground level. New materials can be hoisted by a gin wheel or by a mechanical lift which would normally be installed with the scaffolding. Small amounts of material may be transported to the gin wheel or chute by hand loading into a bucket.

Always ensure that scaffolding has been provided with good ladder access and that no alterations are made to it other than by competent scaffolders.

All of this work needs to be carried out with extreme care and a clear method statement should be produced to outline the methods to be used.

Remember that often a chimney can serve more than one property, so work on a shared chimney can have an impact on neighbouring properties. It is essential to consult with adjoining property owners prior to carrying out any work.

Remember that when working on a chimney, small pieces of old mortar and debris are likely to fall down the flue. Protection should be provided inside the property to prevent damage to furniture and carpets.

ACTIVITY

Discuss in groups of two or three how you would go about identifying how many properties a chimney serves.

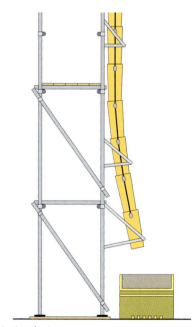

Waste chute

FUNCTIONAL SKILLS

Draft a letter to an adjoining neighbour explaining that you need to carry out remedial work on the chimney and that you would like to discuss how the work will be carried out.

Work on this activity can support FE2 (2.3.1 and 2.3.3a/2.3.4a).

Case Study: Aadil

Aadil is asked for advice about replacing a boundary wall that has suffered damage and needs to be rebuilt. Most of the bricks in the wall can be reused but about 10% of them are damaged and some will break during the cleaning process. Aadil does some research in trade magazines and with local builder's merchants and discovers that the bricks are no longer available in the same colour.

Aadil decides to suggest that the wall is rebuilt with four courses of engineering bricks at the bottom, which will reduce the passage of moisture through the wall, and finish it off with an engineering brick soldier course on the top to create a decorative feature, and waterproof capping. The new bricks will form a contrast with the existing ones.

The customer is delighted with the idea and Aadil gets the contract to replace the wall.

Can you think of any other alternative options to suggest in this case?

Work through the following questions to check your learning.

1   In construction the word 'settlement' means
   a   payment for the work completed
   b   payment at the end of the month
   c   the natural process of the building moving
   d   the expansion of the walls of the building.

2   Efflorescence on the face of walls is caused by
   a   dirty cement
   b   natural salts
   c   dirty water
   d   ground water.

3   Capillary attraction is caused by
   a   surface tension in water
   b   insufficient water
   c   too much water
   d   downward pressure.

4   Spalling in brickwork is caused by
   a   laying the bricks the wrong way up
   b   laying the bricks with large bed joints
   c   water freezing in the body of the brick
   d   rainwater soaking through the brick.

5   A wall has a vertical crack through the bricks and joints; this is classed as
   a   a settlement crack
   b   an expansion crack
   c   a structural crack
   d   a non-structural crack.

6   Sulphate attack is caused by a
   a   chemical reaction with the cement in the mortar
   b   chemical reaction caused by dirty water
   c   reaction between the bricks and mortar
   d   reaction between the sand and the bricks.

7   When replacing a defective lintel over a door opening, the load should be supported by
   a   raking shores
   b   wedges
   c   props and needles
   d   needles and braces.

8   When removing a brick from a wall to replace it, the joint should be removed by using a
   a   lump hammer and bolster
   b   lump hammer and jointing chisel
   c   kango hammer
   d   brick hammer.

9   What is the **minimum** height that horizontal DPC should be placed above ground level?
   a   100mm.
   b   150mm.
   c   175mm.
   d   200mm.

10 A subfoundation is the ground
   a   supporting the foundation
   b   above the foundation
   c   under the water
   d   above the water table.

11 How many bricks are there in 1m^2 of half-brick walling?
   a   60.
   b   105.
   c   1050.
   d   1500.

12 If wall ties are corroded, it can cause the wall to
   a   allow water to enter the building
   b   lose its strength
   c   look unsightly
   d   crack vertically.

13 The **minimum** bearing for a steel lintel is

a   100mm

b   150mm

c   200mm

d   250mm.

14 Before work commences on a job you **must**

a   refer to the risk assessment

b   wash your hands

c   put on your overalls

d   look at the drawings.

15 When selecting materials to repair a garden wall, where would be the **best** place to look to find matching bricks?

a   Trade catalogues.

b   eBay.

c   Local papers.

d   The tip.

16 What is a 'tell-tale' used for?

a   To measure movement in a wall.

b   To find the height of a wall.

c   To determine the depth of a wall.

d   To measure the strength of a wall.

17 The practice of providing support below an existing foundation is called

a   bumping up

b   laying overhand

c   underpinning

d   shoring.

18 The person who checks that building work is carried out to the Building Regulations is the

a   customer

b   building control officer

c   safety officer

d   employer.

19 Which one of the following bricks are the **best** to use for a DPC?

a   Red.

b   Specials.

c   Engineering.

d   Perforated.

20 The regular repairing of buildings to protect the structure is known as

a   maintenance

b   prevention

c   decorating

d   rendering.

Chapter 4
Unit 303: Constructing radial and battered brickwork

This chapter discusses the skills and knowledge you will require to set out and build radial and battered brickwork. Radial brickwork refers to brick walling that has rounded features and can be found for example in arches above windows or curved garden walls. Battered brickwork refers to brick walling that leans inwards from its base and is sometimes used as a pier in supporting solid walling. Radial brick features are becoming more common in new house building as architects are looking to the past for inspiration and more period brick designs are being incorporated into modern homes. A basic knowledge of geometry, attention to detail and the importance of correct setting-out details are covered in this section.

By reading this chapter you will know how to:

1 Set out and build arches including surrounding brickwork.

2 Set out and build concave and convex brickwork.

3 Set out and build brickwork curved on plan.

4 Set out and build battered brickwork.

SETTING OUT AND BUILDING ARCHES

Arches have been in existence for thousands of years in many cultures, but it was the Romans that developed and used arches extensively in their building design to make bridges, sewers, aqueducts and many other structural elements. The main arch used by the Romans was the semi-circular arch. Since then, every period of architecture down the ages has developed more elaborate forms of arches, from the pointed arches associated with Gothic architecture to segmental and flat arches that were used extensively in the seventeenth and eighteenth centuries.

Arches are generally classified by their shape or architectural style. On the next few pages are some examples of arches, but first we need to cover the terminology.

ARCH TERMINOLOGY

In order to set out and build arches it is important that you fully understand the terminology involved. Study the illustration and table below to familiarise yourself with the terms in readiness to set out an arch.

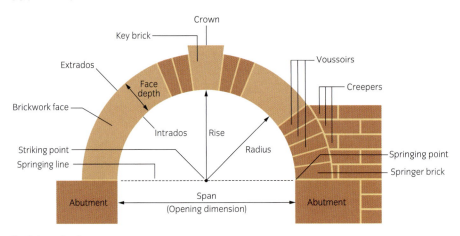

Arch terminology

Axed

A wedge-shaped or tapered brick

Term	Definition
Voussoirs	The wedge-shaped bricks used to form an **axed** arch.
Springer brick	The lowermost voussoir, located at the springing point of the arch.
Striking point	The centre point of the arch from which the voussoirs are set out.
Abutments	The walls beneath an arch that support the load above.
Span	The distance between the abutments.
Springing point	The lowest part of the arch from where it sets out.
Springing line	The horizontal line between the two abutments from where the arc of the arch springs. The rise is set out from the springing line.

Term	Definition
Keystone/key brick	The central brick placed at the crown of an arch and the last brick to be placed in.
Rise	The vertical distance between the springing line and the intrados.
Face depth	The distance between the extrados and the intrados.
Intrados	The underside edge of an arch.
Extrados	The line forming the upper edge of an arch.
Crown	The highest point of the extrados.
Skewback	On a segmental arch, the sloping surface at the springing point on which the springer bricks rest.
Radius	A straight line from the centre to the circumference of a circle.
Collar joint	The joint that runs between the voussoirs and the surrounding brickwork or between two header courses in a double-ringed arch.

TYPES OF ARCHES

SEMI-CIRCULAR ARCH

A semi-circular arch forms half of a circle. It is also known as a Roman arch and this type of arch ensures a very strong structure is maintained over an opening. Forming a semi-circular arch is fairly simple as the striking point is to be found at the centre of the arch.

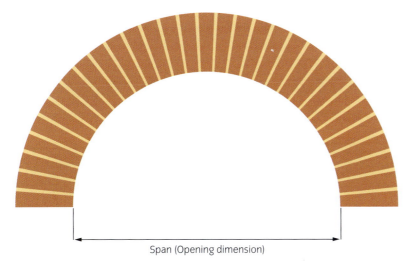

Span (Opening dimension)

Axed semi-circular arch using tapered bricks

The following method can be followed to set out a semi-circular arch.

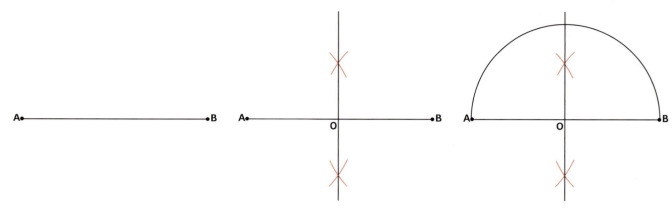

STEP 1 Draw span A–B.

STEP 2 Bisect A–B to produce the radius centre O.

STEP 3 Draw radius O–A to produce the semi-circlular shape.

SEGMENTAL ARCH

A segmental arch is formed from a segment of a circle and has a lower rise than a semi-circular arch. The rise is usually set at 75mm or 150mm depending on the span; this is so that any walling built above the arch works brick courses. Axed segmental, semi-circular and bulls-eye arches always use equal-sized voussoirs. Other arches such as Tudor (four-centered) and three-centered (psuedo-elliptical) arches incorporate different-sized voussoirs within the same arch.

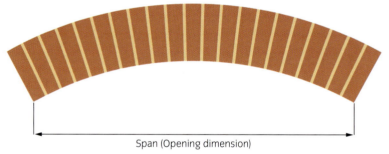

Span (Opening dimension)

Segmental arch

The following method can be followed to set out a segmental arch.

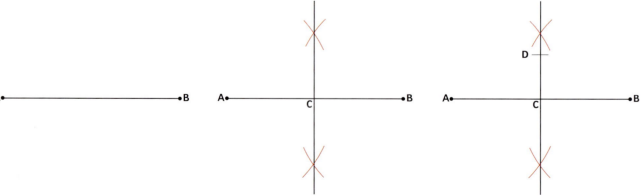

STEP 1 Draw required span A–B.

STEP 2 Bisect line A–B to find the centre point C (extend this line above and below the centre point).

STEP 3 Measure the rise D above the centre point on the bisection line.

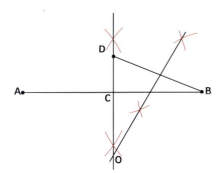

STEP 4 Draw chord B–D and then bisect it. Extend the bisection line to cross the extended line D–C at O.

STEP 5 With O as centre and O–D as radius, strike the arc A–D–B for the arch.

THREE-CENTRED ARCH

Forming half of an oval shape, these arches are less common and are generally seen on period houses and are used to span larger openings. Also known as a pseudo-elliptical arch, the three-centred arch has three separate striking points and is made from a small semi-circular segment on each side and a segmental shape joining them together in the centre. This is a more complicated arch to set out and has two different-sized voussoirs making up the arch.

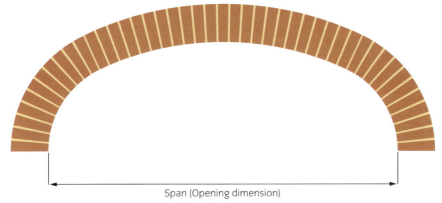

Three-centred arch

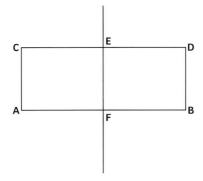

STEP 1 Draw a rectangle A–B–C–D, where A–B is the span and A–C is the rise of the arch. Next bisect A–B to produce points E and F.

STEP 2 Draw a line between points A–E. Using point C as centre and C–A as radius draw an arc to cut C–D at G. Using point E as centre and E–G as radius draw an arc to cut A–E at H.

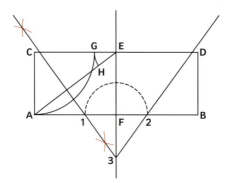

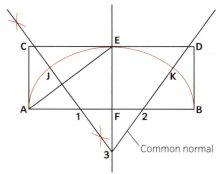

Common normal

INDUSTRY TIP

In Step 4, lines 3–J and 3–K are called 'common normal' and provide the ideal jointing place when producing the curved component.

STEP 3 Bisect A–H to produce point 1 cutting A–B and point 3 crossing extended line E–F. Using F as centre draw radius F–1 to produce point 2 on line A–B.

STEP 4 Using point 1 as centre draw radius 1–A to cut the bisector at J. Using point 2 as centre draw radius 2–B to cut the bisector at K. Using point 3 as centre draw radius 3–J through E to point K.

BULLS-EYE ARCH

This is also known as a wheel arch. This full circular arch is generally used on windows to let more light into a room. There are four key bricks in this arch with the striking point located in the centre of the circle. As all bricks radiate from the same striking point, the voussoirs are the same size throughout. Some arches may not have window openings below them but may be completely filled in with brickwork. These are known as **blind arches**.

Blind arch

An arch whose centre has been filled in with brickwork

Blind arch

Bulls-eye arch formed using tapered bricks (voussoirs)

The following method can be used to set out a bulls-eye arch.

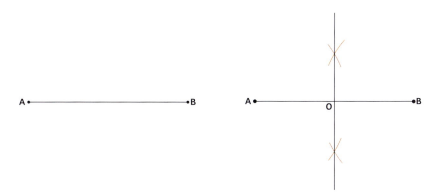

STEP 1 Draw span A–B.

STEP 2 Bisect A–B to produce the radius centre O.

STEP 3 Draw radius O–A to produce the circular shape.

GOTHIC ARCH

Gothic arches are formed from two segmental arches leaning together to form a point. There are three main types of Gothic arch and they are named by the way they are set out. They are called dropped, lancet and equilateral and are different in their spans and heights. Gothic arches are characterised by the position of their striking points. Drop arches have striking points on the inside of the span. Lancet arches have striking points on the outside of the span. Equilateral Gothic arches always have striking points on the springing points located on their span. Gothic arches are always pointed at the crown of the arch. Arches may have a course of projecting bricks or maybe even a tile creasing around the outer side of the arch ring. This is known as a **label course**.

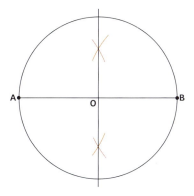

Label course

Label course

This is either a stone or brick feature which sits on the extrados and forms a weathered feature over an arch

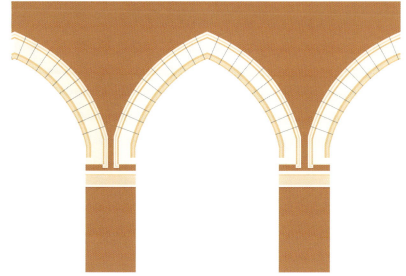

Gothic arch

The following methods can be used to set out the different types of Gothic arch.

Equilateral Gothic arch

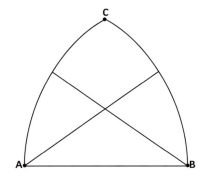

STEP 1 Draw span A–B.

STEP 2 Using the span as the radius draw arcs A–B and B–A to intersect at C.

Drop Gothic arch

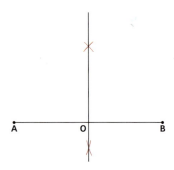

STEP 1 Draw span A–B. Bisect A–B to produce point O. Measure rise C above point O.

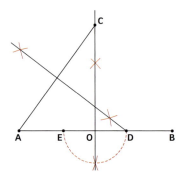

STEP 2 Draw chord A–C then bisect it. Where the bisecting line meets O–B, this marks the first radius point D. From point O use radius O–D to produce the second radius at point E.

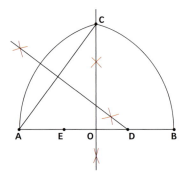

STEP 3 Using a radius D–A and E–B, draw arcs to point C.

Lancet Gothic arch

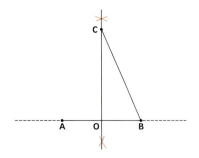

STEP 1 Draw span A–B and extend along springing line beyond the span. Bisect line A–B. To produce point O, measure rise C above point O. Draw chord B–C.

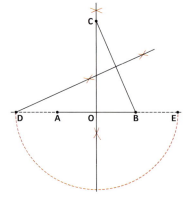

STEP 2 Bisect chord B–C. The bisecting line falls on the springing line past point A. To obtain the first radius point D, from point O draw radius O-D to find the second radius point E.

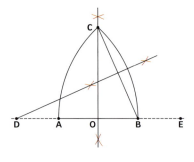

STEP 3 Using a radius E–A and D–B, draw arcs to point C.

TUDOR ARCH

Tudor arches, also known as four-centred arches, were first introduced into England during the fifteenth century. A Tudor arch is a low, wide type of arch with a pointed **apex**. As the span is much wider than its rise this gives the effect of the arch being flattened. Tudor arches can generally be found over wide window and door openings. The structure is achieved by drawing two arcs from a small radius from the springing point and then turning the arcs into a larger radius joining together at the apex.

Apex

The top or highest point of something

Tudor arch

ACTIVITY

Search the internet and list and sketch other designs of arch you can find. Compare your findings with those of your tutor and peers.

The following method can be used to set out a Tudor arch.

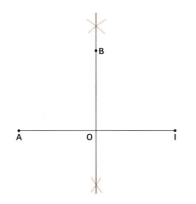

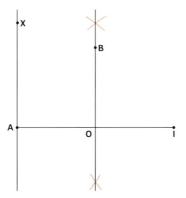

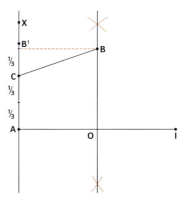

STEP 1 The span and rise are to be taken from the drawing. In this instance, assume that the rise is half of the span. Draw span A–I and bisect to form a perpendicular line. Measure rise above O at B.

STEP 2 Erect a perpendicular line at point A, and extend it to X, parallel to O–B.

STEP 3 From B extend the rise parallel to A-I to cut A-X at B¹. Divide A–B¹ into three and find two-thirds at C.

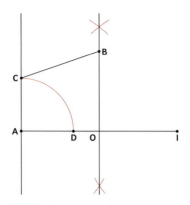

STEP 4 Set up radius A–C and mark point D (first radius point).

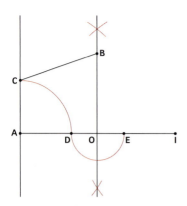

STEP 5 Mark point E as radius O–D to form a second radius point. Radius points D and E are used to mark voissiors.

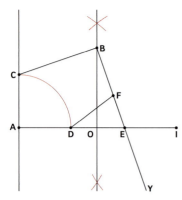

STEP 6 Draw a line at 90° to line C–B at point B and extend beyond line A–I to point Y. Measure distance A–C along line B–Y to produce point F. Draw line D–F.

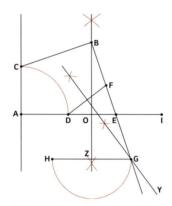

STEP 7 Bisect line D–F. Where this line meets B-Y, mark point G. Draw a line from G, parallel to A–I through bisector B–O. Draw radius Z–G to produce point H. Centres G and H are the third and fourth radius points.

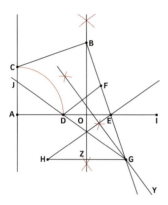

STEP 8 Draw a line through G–D to extend to line A–C at point J. Draw a line through H–E.

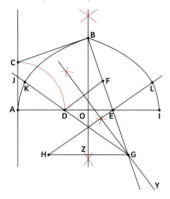

STEP 9 Draw radius D–A to meet G–J at K. Draw radius E–I to meet extended line H–E at L. Draw radius G–K to B. Draw radius H–L to B.

STRUCTURAL FUNCTIONS OF ARCHES

Although the appeal of arches lies mainly in the appearance, arches were primarily designed to span openings and to carry the weight of the load above. Because brickwork is weak in **tension** but strong in **compression**, an arch forms the ideal structural element to span an opening. The curved shape of an arch evenly distributes the compressive forces from above through to the foundations via abutments.

Tension

A force stretching or pulling apart a material

Compression

A force squeezing a material

ACTIVITY

Research what a relieving arch is and its purpose. Report back to a partner or your tutor verbally or in writing.

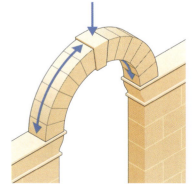

Axial compression of an arch

ARCH CONSTRUCTION TYPES

The two most common forms of arch construction are rough-ringed and axed arches.

Rough arch

Rough-ringed arches are created by using tapered or wedge-shaped joints which are thinner at the intrados and get thicker towards the extrados. This type of arch is generally considered to be less **aesthetically** pleasing. It is difficult to lay soldier courses using this method due to the expanding size of the tapered joint at the extrados. Many rough-ringed arches are constructed by laying bricks as headers across the opening.

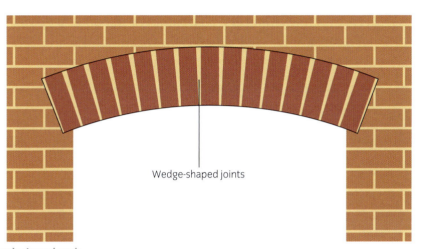

Wedge-shaped joints

Rough-ringed arch

Axed arch

The best looking arches are generally constructed using the tapered brick called a voussoir. All bricks are carefully measured and cut to the same size. The joints are the same thickness throughout from the intrados to the extrados and all joints lead to one central point called the striking point.

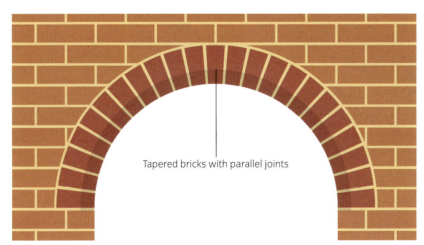

Tapered bricks with parallel joints

Axed semi-circular arch

IDENTIFY COMPONENTS REQUIRED TO SET OUT ARCH CONSTRUCTION

CENTRING

Arches need to be supported properly while being constructed. This can be carried out by the use of temporary timber supports known as **turning pieces**, which are used when constructing a segmental arch, or an **arch centre**, which is used when constructing arches with a greater rise such as a semi-circular arch. These are used to carry the weight of the arch and the **imposed load** above while the arch is being constructed and has time to set. The template needs to be robust when constructed as there will be a considerable weight to be placed upon it during the construction of the arch. A poorly constructed arch centre could lead to a distortion of the arch while the arch is being constructed or even to a total collapse.

It is important to set out the centre correctly as this will lead to the arch having a more pleasing finish, and ensure any doors or windows that will be required to fit into the newly formed opening can be accommodated. **Folding wedges** can be used to adjust the height of the arch centre to the exact requirements.

Timber props can be fastened to the underside of the arch inside the abutment and held together with timber braces (see below).

Turning pieces

Supports that are generally used to construct segmental arches

Arch centre

Supports that are generally used to construct a semi-circular arch

Imposed load

The load that a structure (here, an arch) must sustain

Folding wedges

A pair of wedges used back to back to create a pair of parallel faces; by sliding one wedge against the other the total parallel thickness of the folding wedges can be adjusted to pack out the required gap

A solid turning piece made from solid timber with plywood sheet attached to the upper surface. This makes it easier to mark out the voussoirs

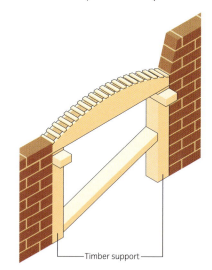

Timber support

Temporary timber used to support the arch during construction. A nail can be fixed to this timber to form the striking point for a segmental arch

Open lagged

Describing the spaced timber laggings (laths) placed onto the upper surface of an arch centre or turning piece

Closed lagged

Describing the unspaced timber laggings (laths) placed onto the upper surface of an arch centre or turning piece

Turning pieces

Turning pieces are generally cut from solid timber and are used in the construction of segmental arches or arches with smaller spans. Arches with greater rises such as semi-circular arches are generally framed up with ribs for segments and are called centres. The top section of the centre can either be **open lagged** or **closed lagged**.

Closed-lagged centres are generally used in the construction of axed arches as the lags are placed close together which helps in setting out and marking the voussoirs on an even surface. Alternatively a sheet of timber ply or hardboard can be used on the outer surface.

Open-lagged turning piece for a segmental arch

Closed-lagged arch centre for a semi-circular arch, framed with ribs

Folding wedges

Folding wedges allow you to adjust the timber centre to the required height prior to the bricks being laid. When positioning folding wedges, ensure that they are placed on top of one another and that the shallow ends taper in opposite directions. Folding wedges also allow the arch centre to be eased once the arch has fully set. This is done by carefully sliding the wedges apart from each other in opposite directions. This allows the centre to gradually fall away from the underside of the arch.

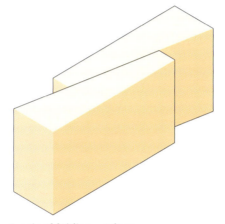

A pair of folding wedges

Templates

When setting out and building axed arches, voussoirs will be required. In order to ensure that all of the cuts are the same size, a template will need to be made.

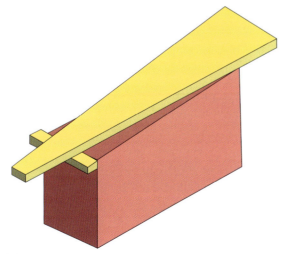

A voussoir template

PROPRIETARY ARCH LINTELS

Many modern properties have arches that are built into cavity walls. As with most lintels, this can bring its own problems, as **bridging** can occur. The bridge can be made up from mortar droppings or a badly fitted DPC tray. This can cause moisture to travel across the cavity into the internal skin. Steel lintels can be made to measure for most openings and are **hot dip galvanised**, ensuring that they will not corrode. Proprietary arch lintels are quick and easy to install, providing strength and stability to the opening. Proprietary arch lintels are now produced to virtually any shape of arch and come with purpose-made cavity trays and stop ends to prevent water penetration.

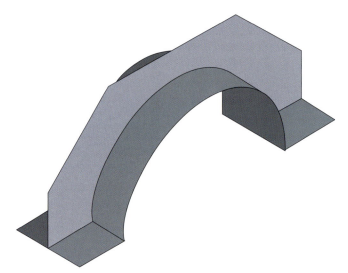

Semi-circular proprietary arch lintel

PROPRIETARY ARCH FORMERS

Arch formers are made from plastic or steel and are used in place of an arch centre. They are used to form the shape of the arch during construction and are made to suit most standard-sized openings. They sit on the centre of the lintel and are usually left in place after the arch brickwork has been built.

ACTIVITY

Look up proprietary arch lintels on www.catnic.com and list the different types available.

FUNCTIONAL SKILLS

Enter 'proprietary arch formers' into an online search engine. Browse the search results and prepare a short presentation about the different types and designs of arch formers that are available.

Work on this activity can support FICT L2 (4).

Rough segmental arch laid onto a uPVC proprietary arch former

OUR HOUSE

Looking at 'Our House', can you suggest a decorative arch that would be suitable for one of the ground floor windows? Give a reason for your choice.

PROVIDING TEMPORARY SUPPORT FOR ARCHES

Before an arch can be constructed, you will need to ensure that you have sufficient temporary supports in place to bear the weight of the arch while it sets. It is important to ensure that the material used to construct the arch centre is robust and will support the weight of the brickwork above. Any braces and props that you use need to be secured tightly to prevent the arch from twisting and buckling under pressure once the work is being carried out.

It is important to ensure that any arch centres are accurately constructed as the finished arch shape of your support will be reflected in the curve of the brickwork. Remember that your arch is to be one of the main decorative features of your wall and needs to be constructed with skill and accuracy. Having a carefully constructed arch centre that is correctly positioned in the opening will help you to achieve this.

SETTING OUT AND BUILDING ARCHES AND SURROUNDING BRICKWORK

INTERPRETING DRAWINGS TO ESTABLISH THE LOCATION, SHAPE AND SIZE OF THE ARCHES TO BE ERECTED

Scale rule

Now that you have a good grasp of the terminology associated with arches and have knowledge of some of the arch templates that can be used, you can get to work on constructing your arch template. First you will need to take a look at the site drawings to determine the shape and size of arch to be constructed. Drawings will generally give you the measurements of the openings but there may be times when you will need to use a scale rule.

Drawings are usually set out in a format where the information is easy to understand. Look at the following types of drawings to ascertain the different types of information that are available to help you set out and build your arch templates.

INDUSTRY TIP

Keep your drawing in a safe place to ensure it does not get damaged. Drawings that do not show dimensions are difficult to get an accurate scale from if they have been folded up and used many times over.

Drawing	Description
Floor plans 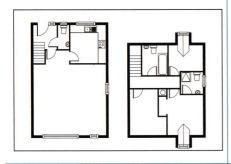	These drawings identify the size and locations of door and window openings in the building. Measurements will be either included on the drawings or they will be drawn to a scale. The scale will be provided on the drawing and measurements will need to be worked out in order to get the correct size of each opening. The opening size will give you the length of the span for your arch template. Written dimensions should always be followed if they are available as these will be more accurate. Floor plans are generally drawn at a scale of 1:50.
Elevations 	These show how the building looks from all sides. The shapes and types of arches can be found from these drawings.
Detailed drawings 	These drawings show the various components that go together to form an opening. This type of drawing nowadays can be drawn in 3D and is supplied by arch lintel manufacturers. Some detailed drawings may show you how various parts of the building are to be constructed. For instance, a window section may show a lintel with a cavity tray and weep holes, with inner and outer skins of brick and blockwork, to give you an idea of what you are to build and where.

GETTING READY TO SET OUT AND BUILD ARCHES

PRODUCING RISK ASSESSMENTS

As with all construction activities it is important that you put health and safety first. The Health and Safety at Work Act 1974 requires all employers to carry out risk assessments to ensure accidents are minimised on construction sites. Your employer can ask you to carry out a risk assessment if they think that you are competent to do this. Risk assessments are important documents that help us to recognise hazards and give guidance on how to make the workplace safer.

INDUSTRY TIP

To prepare a thorough risk assessment of an activity, speak to workers who have experience of carrying out the tasks previously, as they will be able to inform you of anything that could go wrong.

In order to carry out a thorough risk assessment you will need to be familiar with regulations relating to the work being carried out. For instance, arches may have to be constructed to the upper floors of a building so you will need to be familiar with the Work at Height Regulations 2005 (as amended) (see Chapter 1, page 24, for further information). One of the best ways to carry out a thorough risk assessment is to visit the site where you will be working and to go through the steps of the operations to identify any potential hazards that may occur.

It is important in your training that you learn to identify potential hazards associated with your tasks and work in a safe and effective manner. Remember, construction sites can be dangerous places; it is vital that any potential hazards are considered before a project starts so that the necessary precautions can be taken.

The main steps in writing a risk assessment are as follows:

1 Identify actual or potential hazards.

2 Identify who might be at risk.

3 Assess how likely it is that the risk will cause an accident.

4 Design measures that will reduce the risk.

5 Monitor the risk to identify changes.

METHOD STATEMENTS

Let's recap on method statements. Sometimes referred to as a construction phase plan, a method statement will often be linked to the risk assessment and will outline the steps involved in carrying out a task. Depending on the size of the site and the amount of work to be carried out, it can be quite detailed. Health and safety for arch construction may be specified in relation to other activities that take place on site and could involve:

- PPE to be worn during specific tasks
- types of access equipment to be used
- the safe use of power tools and machinery
- security measures to be taken on site
- delivery times and nominated persons for accepting deliveries
- access and egress for the site
- storage requirements for the task
- manual handling requirements
- roles and responsibilities on site
- control of dust and debris
- control of waste materials.

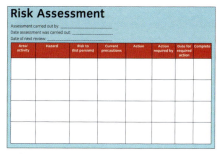

Risk assessment form

FUNCTIONAL SKILLS

Write a risk assessment for your workplace or training area for building an arch above a first-floor window. Produce a table to include the five risk assessment steps. In a separate box below, list which areas are covered by the various pieces of legislation affecting the construction industry.

Work on this activity can support FE2 (2.3.2 and 2.3.3b/2.3.4b).

PRODUCING TEMPLATES TO BUILD AXED ARCHES

Once the span of the opening has been determined along with the type of arch to be built, the arch centre can now be made. It is a good idea to gather all of your tools together ready to set out the arch before you begin. The table below shows the tools you will need.

Tool	Description and use
Trammel heads 	Trammel heads are used to set out circular shapes. A pencil is placed into one end and the other end acts as a pivot point. The heads can be spaced along the timber rod to make a circle larger or smaller depending on the radius.
Sliding bevel 	A sliding bevel is a square that can be set to different angles to aid marking out. It is constructed of a hardwood stock, a sliding blade and a locking screw. It is used to set out and mark the angle of the skewback on the brick.
Dividers 	Once the arch has been drawn, dividers are used to space out evenly the bricks on the extrados of the arch.
Set square 	A set square (or builder's square) is used to set out 90° angles on your template. Folding set squares are ideal as they are easy to store.

Tool	Description and use
Tape measure	Keep your tape measure clean and in good condition. In order to set out the arch accurately you will need to see the lines very clearly on your tape. Using a rusty tape will lead to mistakes.
Straight edge	Use a metal straight edge as it will not twist and warp. Alternatively, a clean spirit level can be used for drawing straight lines onto your plywood sheet.

THE PARTS OF A CIRCLE

In order to set out arches and curved brickwork, you will need to know the main parts of a circle.

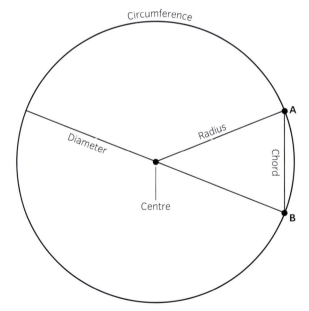

Main parts of a circle

CONSTRUCTING A SEMI-CIRCULAR AXED ARCH CENTRE

The span will be taken from the drawing and the rise will be worked out from the size of the span. In a semi-circular arch, the rise will be half of the span. Ensure that you reduce the size of your template by 5mm so that it does not sit too tight in the opening and is easy to remove. To draw a semi-circular arch, the two curves known as the intrados and extrados are drawn from a centre point on a springing line.

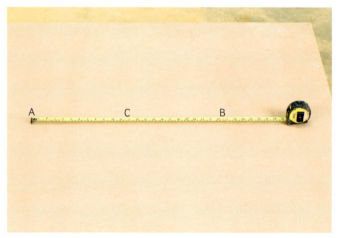

STEP 1 Using your straight edge, draw a horizontal line across the board, then mark the span centrally on this line. Mark the two ends A and B. This is known as the springing line. Next, find the centre point between A and B and mark this as point C.

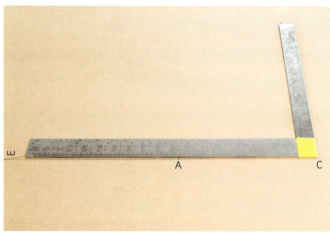

STEP 2 Place a builder's square at point C and draw a perpendicular line at right angles to the springing line. Continue the lines with your straight edge downwards.

STEP 3 Set up the trammel heads and place the compass point at point C and the pencilled end on point A. Scribe an arc from point A round to point B. This is known as the intrados.

STEP 4 Now find the outer curved line: the extrados. To do this you will need to increase the radius by increasing the distance between the trammel points. For example, if the ring is to be one brick thick, then place a brick on the sheet and mark it at the end or alternatively open up the trammel points by 215mm.

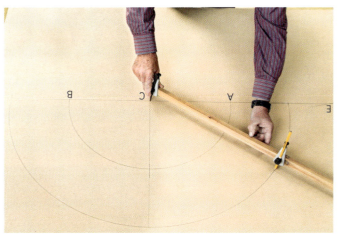

STEP 5 Place the compass point on centre point C and then extend the pencil past point A on the springing line and draw the second curved line around the arch, forming the extrados. The arch is now drawn.

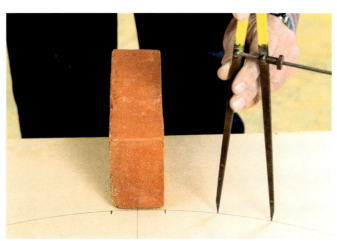

STEP 6 Set the dividers to the size of a brick and mark out the key brick centrally on the extrados on the centre line. Alternatively you can use a brick to get the correct size.

STEP 7 For axed arches, the brick spacing should always be marked around the extrados. This is to ensure that the brick joint can remain the same thickness from the extrados to the intrados and that it is the brick that will get thinner at the intrados to accommodate this. The maximum spacing should always be 65 mm if using standard-sized bricks. Mark along one side of the extrados the other bricks to be laid in the arch. Open or close the dividers to ensure an even spacing of bricks and joints around the extrados.

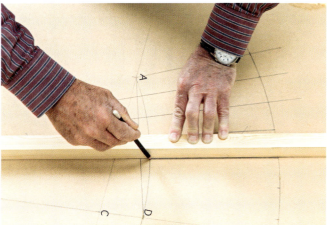

STEP 8 From point C (the striking point) draw lines that intersect through the extrados (approximately 200mm) to form the voussoir template. Mark out the shape of the template.

STEP 9 Once the voussoir has been drawn out, a template can be made. This ensures that all voussoirs will be cut to the same shape, thereby maintaining a consistent appearance.

STEP 10 To make the arch centre, carefully cut out the ply section around the line of the intrados. Sand it down and, using this as a template, draw another semi-circular template the same size to be cut out.

STEP 11 Join the timber sections together with wooden spacers and place the ply around the top of the arch centre (use a 1m × 1m piece of ply and 1m length of rough-sawn timber 40mm × 40mm). Alternatively, cut 19mm × 19mm section timber laggings and fix them around the outside of the centre, remembering to deduct the thickness of the laggings from the intrados radius.

CONSTRUCTING A SEGMENTAL AXED ARCH TURNING PIECE

The dimensions for this arch can also be taken from the plans. When forming a segmental arch it is important to note that the rise is usually one-sixth of the span. For example, if the span of the opening is 900mm wide then the rise will be 150mm. This is to ensure that the compressive load is adequately dispersed through the correct angle of the arch into the abutments. If the rise is too low, the point load above the arch will cause it to collapse.

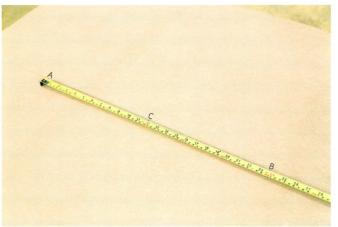

STEP 1 Repeat the same process as for the previous semi-circular arch. Using your straight edge, draw a horizontal line (a third of the way up the board) across the board, then mark the span centrally on this line (remember to reduce this dimension by twice the thickness of the ply covering the top of the centre to compensate for the ply when it is placed around the centre). Mark the two ends A and B, creating the springing line. Next, find the centre point between A and B and mark this as point C.

STEP 2 Draw a perpendicular line at right angles to the springing line using your builder's square.

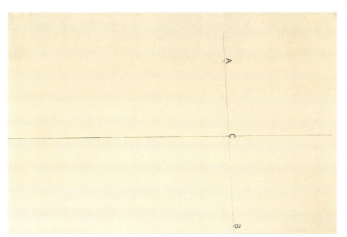

STEP 3 Continue the lines with your straight edge downwards as shown.

STEP 4 Next, you will need to mark the height of the rise. This information may be shown on the working drawing. If it is not available, then, as a general rule, using the measurement of the span and finding one-sixth of this, measure upwards on the perpendicular from point C and mark point D.

STEP 5 Draw lines from D to A and D to B forming the chords.

STEP 6 Using the trammel, place the compass point on point A and the pencilled end on point D. Scribe an arc at the two points shown in the photo. Turn the compass point to point D with the pencilled end on point A and scribe two arcs intersecting with the previous markings. Repeat this process on the opposite side of the arch.

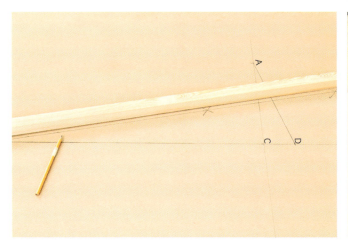

STEP 7 Then scribe lines through the arcs continuing down through the lower perpendicular. Both lines should join at the same point. This is the striking point (mark as point E). This process is known as bisecting an angle.

STEP 8 Set up trammel heads and place the compass point on point E with the pencil end on point A.

STEP 9 Scribe an arc from A to B. This line is the intrados.

STEP 10 Draw lines from point E through point A and from point E through point B to form the skewbacks.

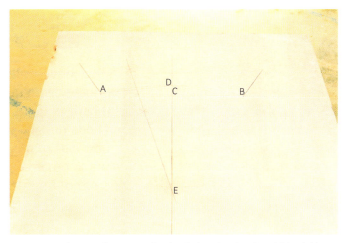

STEP 11 This is what your finished skewbacks should look like.

STEP 12 Extend the trammel points to the required length (ie 102mm if using headers or 215mm if using stretchers on the face) or alternatively place a brick at the springing point on the skewback line and mark this point F.

STEP 13 Again, place the compass point on the striking point E and the pencil end on the line of the skewback at point F. Scribe the extrados through to the opposite skewback. You now have the shape of the segmental arch.

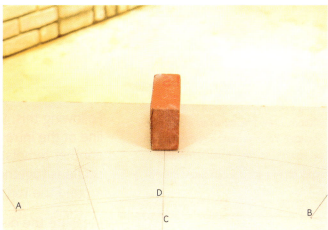

STEP 14 Now repeat the process that was described for the axed semi-circular arch by marking the key brick centrally at the crown of the arch. Then mark along one side of the extrados the other bricks to be laid in the arch.

STEP 15 Open or close the dividers to ensure an even spacing of bricks and joints around the extrados. Alternatively a tape measure can be used.

STEP 16 From point E draw lines that intersect through the extrados to form the shape of the voussoir template. Mark out the shape of the template.

skewback. From this the correct angle of the skewback bricks can be marked out. This line can also be used when laying voussoirs to ensure that the bricks and joints are at the correct angle.

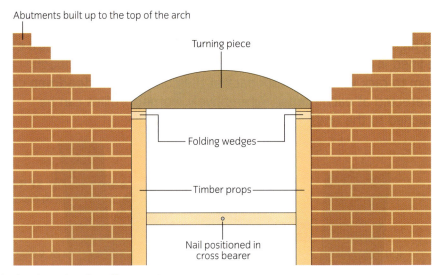

Abutments built up to the top of the arch

Turning piece

Folding wedges

Timber props

Nail positioned in cross bearer

Arch set up showing all supports

To find the striking point, plumb down from the centre of the key brick located on the arch at the distance previously worked out on your template. This point can be worked out from the springing line to the striking point from your template. (See Step 14, 'Constructing a segmental axed arch turning piece', page 179.)

WORKING TO STANDARDS

When constructing arches, you should ensure that you have checked the accuracy of your setting out before laying any bricks. You also need to ensure that you have all of the correct tools, materials and equipment to hand before starting the job. This will save you time. You need to ensure that your cuts are accurate and that you have a specified 10mm joint showing throughout, especially at the skewback angle and when laying the **creepers** at the extrados to form the **collar joint**. If not, it is best to remeasure and cut the bricks again. Do not use any bricks that have chips as this will show up in the finished product. Remember that your work will be on show and your reputation and that of your company will be affected if the standard of work is poor.

If any problems occur during the construction you should always notify your supervisor or line manager. It is their responsibility to offer assistance and they will consider that you have taken the right steps in asking for help.

Creepers

The cut bricks around the extrados of an arch

Collar joint

The joint that runs between the voussoirs and the surrounding brickwork or between two header courses in a double-ringed arch

INDUSTRY TIP

Before placing your arch centre into the opening, set out and mark the position of the bricks onto the centre where they are to be laid. This will help you to lay the bricks evenly as the work progresses.

CONSTRUCTING AXED ARCHES

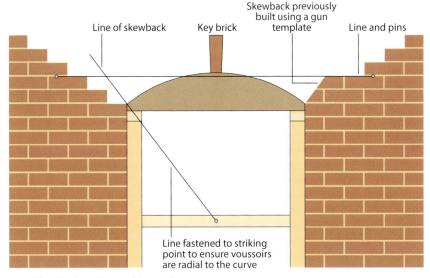

Set up of arch showing striking point

Labels: Line of skewback · Key brick · Skewback previously built using a gun template · Line and pins · Line fastened to striking point to ensure voussoirs are radial to the curve

Once the turning piece has been securely positioned and corners built ready to line in the arch, the arch can be constructed.

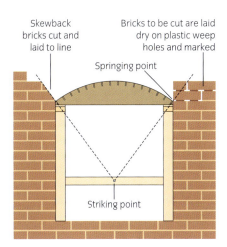

Labels: Skewback bricks cut and laid to line · Bricks to be cut are laid dry on plastic weep holes and marked · Springing point · Striking point

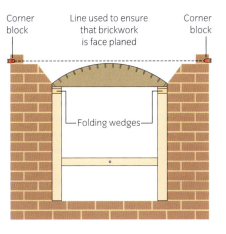

Labels: Corner block · Line used to ensure that brickwork is face planed · Corner block · Folding wedges

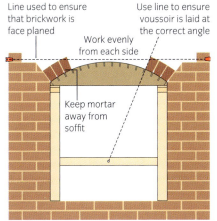

Labels: Line used to ensure that brickwork is face planed · Use line to ensure voussoir is laid at the correct angle · Work evenly from each side · Keep mortar away from soffit

STEP 1 Start by marking out the skewback bricks, which form the angle from which the arch will spring. To do this, attach a line from the striking point and hold it just past the springing point, making sure it connects with this point. Lay bricks out dry onto the wall at the springing point, making sure the bricks to be cut are raised by the thickness of a bed joint and are a cross joint thickness from the previous brick. Mark and cut the skewbacks. Lay the skewback bricks in either side using the string line from the striking point to ensure they are laid in accurately.

STEP 2 Place the line onto the wall ensuring that it spans across the centre line of the arch to be constructed. This will ensure that the face of the arch is in line with the wall.

STEP 3 The first brick to be laid on the skewback is called the springer brick. Next, lay in the voussoirs three at a time, working alternately from each side. This is done to prevent the arch overloading on either side and prevents any lateral movement of the template in the opening. Use the string line set up on the striking point to ensure the voussoirs are laid at the correct angle. Ensure that the underside of the brick sits evenly on the arch so that when the template is removed the arch soffit has a rounded underside. If the underside of the arch is to be seen, the facing side of the brick must sit on the arch centre.

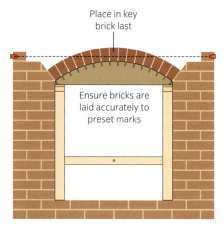

Place in key brick last

Ensure bricks are laid accurately to preset marks

Carefully ease wedges to cause arch to settle slightly

STEP 4 Continue to lay the voussoirs, working from side to side, ensuring the correct spacing and face plane are maintained. Be careful that you lay the bricks to your marks on the centre, otherwise the key brick may not fit. The key brick is the last brick to be placed in.

STEP 5 As soon as the arch is built, ease the centre slightly to allow the arch to settle. Once the key brick has been laid, the centre can be lowered slightly by loosening the wedges, causing a slight displacement of the centre. This will help to compress the mortar joints, pressing the voussoirs more tightly together, and will help to ensure that there are no further settlement cracks in the arch once it sets.

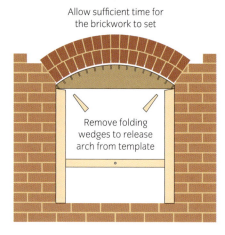

Allow sufficient time for the brickwork to set

Remove folding wedges to release arch from template

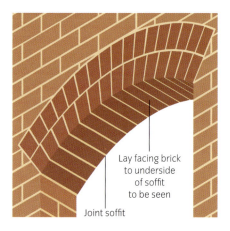

Lay facing brick to underside of soffit to be seen

Joint soffit

STEP 6 Ensure that the folding wedges are secure, then continue to build the arch completing the brick courses above the arch. Allow sufficient time for the brickwork to set before removing the arch centre. In order to allow the arch centre or turning piece to be removed, folding wedges are used. This is known as 'striking the centre'.

STEP 7 Lastly, joint the soffit of the arch. Ensure that you always read the specification for the job carefully to see what joint finish has been specified.

When striking the centre, under no circumstances should the centres be removed from the openings until the arch and brickwork above have had time to set. On site you should follow guidance given, but as a general rule this should be at least seven days, as premature removal can lead to the collapse of the arch. Longer curing periods may be necessary in cold weather.

MEASURING AND MARKING THE CREEPERS

Creepers is the name given to the cuts that are placed over the arch. In order to mark these correctly, a line must be placed from corner to corner across the top arris of the brick to be laid.

A measurement is taken from the previous brick to the bottom of the brick at the lower edge of the arch. The same action is carried out at the top of the brick.

The distance is reduced by 20mm on each point to compensate for cross joints either side of the brick and new measurements are transferred onto a brick which is then marked and cut.

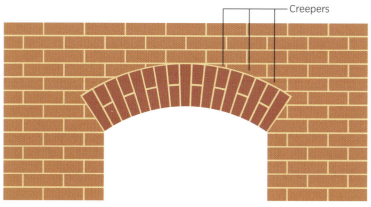

Arch creepers

Make sure that the brick is placed in dry to see if further cutting is necessary before laying. It is important to get the joint correct around the extrados of the arch as this will be seen clearly and will make a difference to the finished appearance of the arch.

CUTTING THE VOUSSOIRS

Consideration should always be given to the type of bricks to be used to build an axed arch. If the bricks are hard, for instance engineering bricks, the most appropriate way to cut these is with a table masonry saw; even then it will be difficult to get the cut completely accurate. If it is absolutely necessary to use engineering bricks, these can be produced by the brick manufacturer and are known as 'specials'. Ideally, you should select bricks that can be cut with hand tools. Below is the step-by-step process for cutting voussoirs.

ACTIVITY

Go to the Brick Development Association (BDA) website and find its image gallery at www.brick.org.uk/resources/image-gallery. Look at examples of arches and see how well they are constructed. Discuss with other students the standard of work, especially in relation to the cuts around the various arches and bulls-eyes.

ACTIVITY

Have a look around your local area at public buildings and see how well arches have been constructed; pay particular attention to the creepers and the quality of the collar joint set at the extrados. Capture images on your smartphone and discuss these with your class.

STEP 1 Using the voussoir template, scribe the outline to be cut onto the face of the brick.

STEP 2 Using a lump hammer and a sharp bolster, cut downwards onto the face of the brick on the marked line.

STEP 3 Cut away any excess from the sides of the brick with a scutch.

To end, rub down the edges with a piece of carborundum stone to leave a neat sharp arris that will be seen on the face of the arch.

FOLLOWING ENVIRONMENTAL AND CURRENT HEALTH AND SAFETY LEGISLATION

It is the responsibility of everyone on site to ensure that safe working practices are adhered to at all times.

Awareness of health and safety on construction sites has been greatly increased in recent years. Many construction sites carry out site inductions and regular **toolbox talks** (refer back to Chapter 1, page 6, and Chapter 2, page 87). Risk assessments and method statements ensure that safe control measures are in place and are monitored. On many sites nowadays, employers will give warnings and will eventually dismiss employees for failing to adhere to safe site procedures (see Chapter 1 for further information).

Toolbox talk

A health and safety talk carried out on site to highlight any potential hazards and precautions to be taken. This will usually be carried out by the site foreman and recorded in writing

Construction of brick arches is sometimes carried out when working at height. It is important that as much of this work is carried out on the ground as possible, such as the setting out and cutting of bricks.

ENVIRONMENTAL PROCEDURES

The construction industry in the UK last year generated and used over 400 million tonnes of construction materials. A hundred million tonnes of that went to waste. Although there is a good awareness of recycling and reusing materials on construction sites, 30 million tonnes were still sent to landfill sites. The costs of construction materials are rising rapidly and recycling and reusing materials is a good way to keep costs down.

INDUSTRY TIP

The most important pieces of PPE when using a disc cutter are dust masks, safety glasses and ear protection.

There are many types of legislation governing the disposal of waste on sites and these are updated regularly. The main ones include:

- *Hazardous Waste Regulations (England and Wales) 2005:* these define what hazardous waste is and how it should be correctly disposed of or collected from sites.

- *Environmental Protection Act 1990:* this defines a legal framework for the duty of care for waste materials and contaminated land.

- *Controlled Waste Regulations (England and Wales) 2012:* these classify waste as household, commercial or industrial and list the types of waste for which Local Authorities may make a charge for collection and disposal.

- *Site Waste Management Plans Regulations 2008:* these require a waste management plan for construction sites with an estimated cost of over £300,000.

Many waste disposal companies provide skips to enable construction workers to segregate waste.

Segregating waste

Your Local Authority will give you guidance on the best ways to dispose of hazardous waste or chemicals. Materials such as asbestos should be moved only by specialist contractors. Many companies will use toolbox talks and display posters in the workplace to ensure that correct disposal of waste is carried out. To cut down on waste on your construction site, consider the following options:

- Segregate waste on site and reuse offcuts for things like props, wedges and trammels. Have a dedicated storage area for offcuts.

- Minimise material movement on site to avoid damage to materials.

- Be accurate with your calculations to ensure that you do not order more materials than you need for a job.

- Store and reuse things like timber arch templates for other work.

Waste has been poorly discarded in this skip

SETTING OUT AND BUILDING BRICKWORK CURVED ON PLAN

Curved walled in a garden

Many new buildings nowadays incorporate curved features as architects and designers look to enhance the appearance of their projects. Curved features provide an attractive look and give added interest to a building. Curved walling is also used extensively in garden projects for ponds, flower beds and low-edged walling. Boundary walling, bow windows and even extensions to buildings can also incorporate a curved design.

When constructing curved walling the space available will dictate the methods to be used for setting out. Accurate and skilful construction techniques are essential to ensure the wall is pleasing to the eye.

Header bond boundary wall curved feature

As no lines can be used to lay the bricks it is also important to establish plumbing points and level the walling as accurately as possible. Also, great care needs to be taken to ensure that the brick cross joints are 10mm wide as extra wide joints look unsightly and will be difficult to joint up.

Standard bricks are straight with flat surfaces (facets), so in order to create curved walling, the cross joints will need to be tapered. **Faceting** becomes more of a problem as the radius is reduced. Depending on the tightness of the curve, this could lead to a certain amount of overhang at the cross joints. This can be removed by introducing headers into the wall by using a variety of bonding arrangements. Another way to overcome this is to use special radial bricks.

Faceting

Maintaining an even surface with no protruding edges

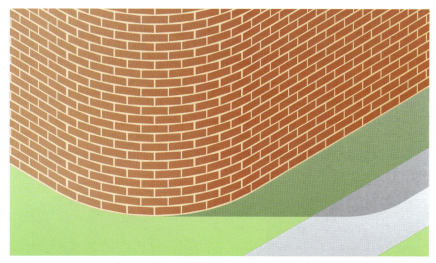

Brick faceting and overhang effects accentuated in strong oblique light

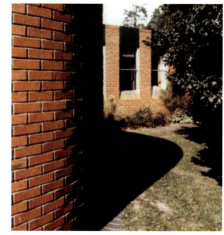

Overhang effects are showing due to the wrong selection of bonding on thin tight radius

DETERMINING THE BOND IN THE WALL

The bonding of the brick walling will alter depending on the tightness of the curve. Headers can be introduced into the wall to prevent the edges of bricks 'overhanging' on tight curves. One way to reduce this on curved walls is to introduce Flemish bond (see picture below). As the wall will have a tighter curve on the inside, you will need to make sure that the stretcher bricks are cut down to size to fit between the headers.

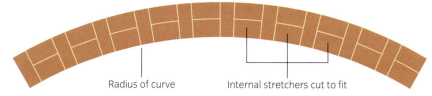

Radius of curve   Internal stretchers cut to fit

Flemish bond curved wall

Where the curve on the wall is very tight, header bond can be used. This bond incorporates only header bricks across the wall.

Header bond curved wall

In some cases, if a solid wall has both faces showing then **snap headers** can be introduced. This will enable the wall to have even-sized joints on both faces. Remember though, when using this method, to place wall ties across the wall to hold both skins together.

FUNCTIONAL SKILLS

In your workshop, try dry bonding out bricks to form curved walls using small and larger **radii** and see how you can overcome any bonding and joint problems using different brick bonds. Record your findings on a table or chart that lists different-sized radii with suitable bonds. Display the findings in your work area.

Work on this activity can support FICT L2 (7B).

Radii

Plural of *radius*

Snap headers

Bricks cut in half and placed in one single skin of a wall. Mainly used in half-brick walling

SPECIAL BRICKS

For work that is to be of a first-class standard and may be on show, eg in a public building, then **radial bricks** can be used instead of standard bricks. Although considerably more expensive, these bricks are made in a curved shape and allow the wall to be constructed in a more accurate manner. Radial bricks can be designed to any radius of curvature and can be manufactured using the same bricks as those used to build the main body of walling. These can be obtained from the brick manufacturer.

Radial stretcher   Radial header

CALCULATING QUANTITIES OF CURVED BRICKWORK

Using the formulae shown below you can work out the circumference and area of a circle or part of a circle. This will enable you to work out the required quantity of bricks to build curved walls.

The formula for calculating the circumference of a circle is:

$$C = \pi d$$

circumference of a circle = π × diameter

π (pronounced 'pi') is the number of times that the diameter of a circle will divide into its circumference. Remember that π = 3.142. This is equal to the number of diameters in one revolution of a circle. It is the same for any sized circle.

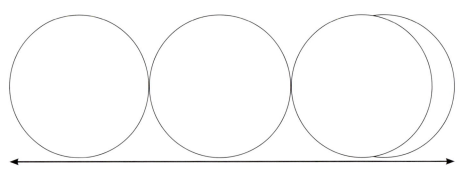

There are 3.142 diameters in one complete revolution

If the wall is to be constructed using tapered joints, then the dimensions can be taken from the internal radius or the diameter for the wall.

If the brickwork to be constructed is to have parallel joints and tapered bricks then the measurements will have to be taken from the extrados. This can be done by adding the depth of the brickwork; for instance, if the wall is to be one brick thick then add 215mm to the radius.

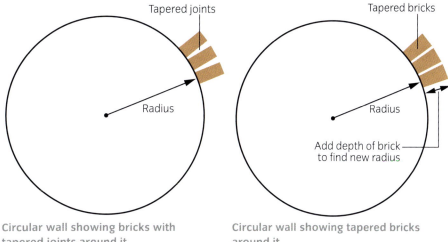

Circular wall showing bricks with tapered joints around it

Circular wall showing tapered bricks around it

Example 1

A bricklayer is building a circular one-brick-thick wall using tapered joints. The wall is 900mm high and the diameter is 2.5m.

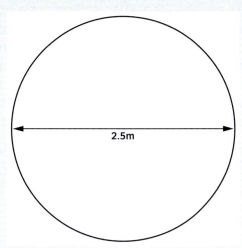

C (circumference, here the perimeter of the wall) = π (3.14) × D (diameter) 2.5m

$$3.14 \times 2.5 = 7.85m$$

Now we will work out the area of brickwork multiplying the perimeter by the height, then calculating this figure by the amount of bricks in a square metre of one-brick-thick walling.

perimeter 7.85m × height 0.9m = 7.065m

There are 120 bricks per m² of one-brick-thick walling.

7.065 × 120 = **848 bricks**

Cutting bricks by hand

When cutting bricks by hand we need to take care that we wear the correct PPE and use all tools correctly. It is advisable that you cut all of your bricks in one operation. First, this will cut down the time it takes, as you will not be stopping and starting your work and secondly, if you clean up the area immediately after cutting the bricks, you will avoid working in an area strewn with tools and broken bricks which could cause a hazard.

STEP 1 Make sure you are using the right PPE (safety glasses or goggles and safety gloves) and that workers nearby are aware that you are cutting masonry materials.

STEP 2 Mark the position of the cut on the face, the opposite side and the bed of the brick with a pencil. For blocks, it is usually sufficient to mark the position of the cut on the face only, unless you prefer to mark it all around.

STEP 3 Placing the blade of the bolster slightly on the *waste* side of the pencil mark, strike the brick lightly but firmly with the club hammer. For blocks you will need to use several more powerful and decisive strikes across the full face of the block.

STEP 4 Now do the same on the opposite side of the brick or block. For blocks, if you've used sufficient strength in your blows, the block should break as desired.

STEP 5 For bricks, turn the brick so that the face is uppermost again and strike the last blow. If the strength of the blow is adjusted correctly, this should complete the operation.

STEP 6 If the brick or block doesn't break as desired, repeat from step 3 until a clean break is achieved.

SETTING OUT AND BUILDING BATTERED BRICKWORK

Battered brickwork refers to any brickwork that angles inwards from its base. Battered brickwork is generally used as a supporting pier on a retaining wall. It can also be used to form chimney breasts, pillar supports and in some cases even to finish off gables. Battered walling can also be built as a retaining wall. This is because the wall is wider at its base, where more support is required. The wall reduces in thickness as it gets higher.

CONSTRUCTION METHODS USED TO DESIGN BATTERED WALLING

BUTTRESSES

Buttresses are built to provide lateral support to walls. They are mainly seen on long boundary walls to provide extra stability and support. It is important that the buttress is fully bonded into the main wall. Many brick buttresses are finished with a brick on edge to prevent rainwater penetration.

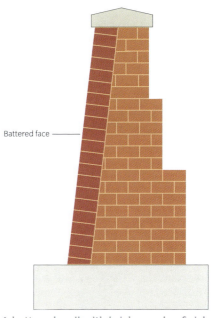

Battered face —

A battered wall with brick on edge finish to prevent weather penetration

Buttresses have been attached to the wall to provide lateral support

TUMBLING IN

Tumbling in is a useful method for finishing off a ramped wall. It can be used as a brick on edge to reduce the wall and form a decorative, weatherproof finish. The dimensions and angle of the walling can be taken from the drawings.

> **INDUSTRY TIP**
>
> As the brick on edge is used to provide a durable weatherproof finish on a buttress it is best to use a hard, frost-resistant brick such as an engineering brick to finish the wall.

INDUSTRY TIP

When setting out different-sized cuts, number the back of the brick with chalk and the corresponding point on the template. It can be easy to forget which brick goes where when they are moved.

FUNCTIONAL SKILLS

Draw a section of tumbling in on a piece of paper to a scale of 1:10. Use a protractor to mark the angle at 45°.

Work on this activity can support FM2 (C2.3).

ACTIVITY

Produce a drawing on a piece of flipchart paper of a section of tumbling in at 45° to the main wall. Draw in the main wall and a projecting feature for a rainwater drip.

INDUSTRY TIP

Mark out the gauge of the brick on edge to be laid on the angled part of the gun template. This will ensure you have evenly spaced bed joints throughout.

ACTIVITY

Construct a gun template for a wall to be constructed at 45°.

Templates used for tumbling in

If you are only constructing a small area of tumbling in, the cuts can be set out on a piece of ply board. Draw out the angle of the wall onto the template to the actual size to be built. The bricks can be laid onto the board at the angle they are to be laid. Then they are marked and cut. Lay them back onto the board to check that the cut is accurate.

Constructing tumbling in

When laying the bricks to angled brickwork a special wooden template can be made called a gun template. This is made by screwing two pieces of timber together at the desired angle to form a gun shape.

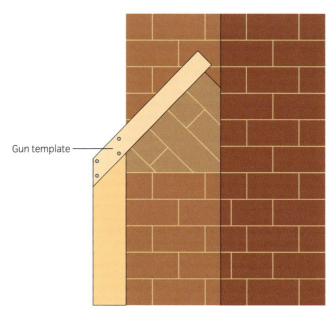

Gun template

Small section of walling with gun template attatched

Tumbling in usually has an overhang; this is to allow for rain to run off the wall without it running down the face.

CONSTRUCTING BATTERED BRICKWORK USING A LINE

A timber batten can be attached to the wall and the line stretched out to the desired angle and fixed to a point at the top of the wall, enabling the brickwork to be built to a line. Once the angle for the cut brickwork has been marked out, the line can be extended outwards from the edge of the wall to form the angle for the brick on edge.

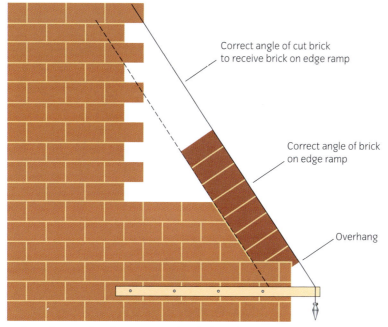

Correct angle of cut brick to receive brick on edge ramp

Correct angle of brick on edge ramp

Overhang

Constructing a battered wall using a timber lath with a line attatched

CONSTRUCTION USING A BATTER BOARD AND SPIRIT LEVEL

Once the angle of the wall has been determined from the drawing, a batter board can be constructed. This is made from a thick piece of plywood to the desired angle of the wall. You will need to ensure that the angle to be set onto the wall is a correct 90° to ensure that the batter board fits squarely onto the wall. The spirit level is then placed onto the angled section of the board to ensure that the wall is straight and plumb.

PREVENTING THE BUILD-UP OF HYDROSTATIC PRESSURE IN BATTERED WALLING

Battered walling can be used to prevent lateral forces being imposed onto the side of a wall. These types of walls are called retaining walls. Every retaining wall holds back a wedge of soil. When it rains, the ground behind the wall swells, which could cause the retaining wall to bulge. This is known as hydrostatic pressure. It becomes significantly worse in freezing temperatures. In order to prevent this, hardcore can be placed at the bottom of the wall to act as a soakaway and a drainage pipe inserted through the face of the wall to help drain away any water.

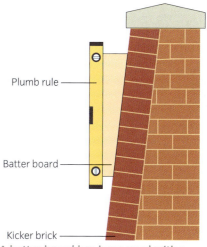

Plumb rule

Batter board

Kicker brick

A batter board has been used with a spirit level to maintain accuracy

Kicker brick

A term sometimes used to describe the first brick placed in a battered wall, cut and laid to form the angle for the rest of the wall to follow

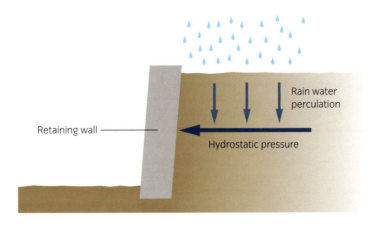

Rain water perculation

Retaining wall

Hydrostatic pressure

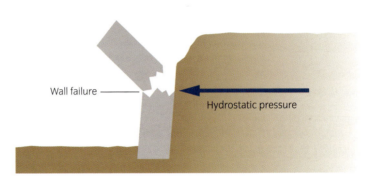

Wall failure

Hydrostatic pressure

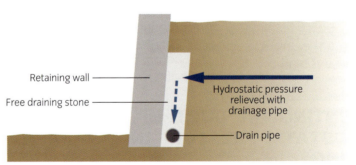

Retaining wall

Free draining stone

Hydrostatic pressure relieved with drainage pipe

Drain pipe

How build up of water behind a wall can lead to damage. This can be relieved by inserting drainage stones and drainage pipes at the bottom of the wall

Case Study: James and Alec

James and Alec work as apprentice bricklayers for a small construction company. Their boss, Alan, has bought a small plot and they are helping him to build a four-bedroom detached house on the site. James and Alec have been shown the plans which include many decorative brick features such as axed segmental arches over the doors and windows, a bulls-eye, and decorative oversailing courses to the house and adjoining garage. Alan has stressed to them that they need to take their time, not only to get the decorative features right but all of the face brickwork needs to be to a high standard. They are told to develop their speed on the boundary walls to be built around the plot.

Meanwhile, on the plot next door, another house is being built by a building contractor. The work on this plot has been subcontracted to a brickwork team on a price work contract. James watches them at work and is impressed with their speed.

Later that morning Alan goes around to the rear of the house to see how James is getting on. He is not happy with James's brickwork and notices that he is rushing. Alan tells James to stop work and tells him to take down the work and to rebuild it the next day, taking his time. Alan tells James not to try to keep up with the speed of the contractors and to concentrate instead on accuracy.

A couple of months later James and Alec stand back and look at both buildings. Their build has taken longer. The differences are obvious. They notice that the building on the other plot has large, uneven joints around the arches. James then looks at his own brick arch and feels proud of his work. James has learned that it is important to take your time when building decorative brick features.

Work through the following questions to check your learning.

1   A correctly constructed arch is an ideal element to span an opening because

   a   arches are strong under tension

   b   the arch shape spreads compressive forces through to the abutments

   c   arches have high lateral strength

   d   bricks are weak under compression.

2   An axed arch can be identified as having

   a   joints that are thinner at the intrados and get thicker towards the extrados

   b   a collar joint that is even throughout

   c   joints that are the same thickness throughout from the intrados to the extrados

   d   two rings of bricks to prevent joints tapering too much at the extrados.

3   Tapered bricks used to construct axed arches are known as

   a   radial bricks

   b   segments

   c   angled bricks

   d   voussoirs.

4   What is the name given for a permanent support used when forming a brick arch?

   a   Turning piece.

   b   Arch centre.

   c   Proprietary arch former.

   d   Timber props.

5   When setting out axed arches, the voussoirs should be marked on the

   a   extrados

   b   springing line

   c   intrados

   d   skewback.

6   Which one of the following items of equipment is needed to set out an arch centre?

   a   Optical level.

   b   Trammel.

   c   Gauge rod.

   d   Pinch rod.

7   What is the **best** way to keep the face of an arch in line during its construction?

   a   Straight edge.

   b   A spirit level held level against the arch centre.

   c   Raised corners or deadmen with a line attached.

   d   By using your builder's eye.

8   Loosening folding wedges once the arch has set is known as

   a   tightening the centre

   b   striking the centre

   c   lowering the centre

   d   easing the centre.

9   The special shaped bricks used in curved walling are known as

   a   skewback bricks

   b   cant bricks

   c   radial bricks

   d   header bricks.

10 If the radius of a circular wall is 1.5m, what is its circumference?

a   4.71m.

b   5.75m.

c   8.75m.

d   9.42m.

11 When building a curved on plan wall with a tight radius, what is the **most** appropriate way to prevent bricks from overhanging the courses below?

a   Introduce header bricks and alter the bond of the wall.

b   Introduce wider cross joints and open out the brick spacing.

c   Cut the back edges of the brick to make the cross joint tighter at the back of the brick.

d   Joint the wall flush to overcome any edges that are sticking out.

12 What is the name given to the sloping surface on a segmental arch where the springer brick sits?

a   Face depth.

b   Rise.

c   Skewback.

d   Soffit.

13 What items of equipment can be used to set out and build a wall that leans in from its base?

a   A spirit level and builder's lines.

b   A plumb bob and gun template.

c   A batter board and spirit level.

d   A protractor and sliding bevel.

14 What is the name given to the special wooden template that can be made to aid the building of a small-angled wall?

a   A trammel.

b   A batter template.

c   A gun template.

d   A turning piece.

15 Battered walls are built to resist

a   tensile forces

b   lateral forces

c   compressive forces

d   axial compressive forces.

16 A build-up of hydrostatic pressure on a retaining wall can be caused by

a   a lack of reinforcement being introduced into the wall

b   the wall not being wide enough at its base

c   lateral pressure exerted from the force of soil behind the wall

d   a lack of drainage provision at the base of the wall.

17 Which piece of legislation is concerned with the protection of the environment when working on construction sites?

a   Construction (Design and Management) Regulations 2007.

b   Work at Height Regulations 2005 (as amended).

c   Hazardous Waste Regulations (England and Wales) 2005.

d   The Confined Spaces Regulations 1997.

18 A wall that curves inward and outwards along its length is known as a

a serpentine wall

b tumbling in wall

c battered wall

d semi-circular wall.

19 A pivot point is a fixed point on

a an arch where a line is attached to set out the angle of the voussoirs

b a wall or floor onto which a trammel is placed to set out curved walling

c the bottom of a battered wall where the kicker brick is placed

d an angled wall to show a change in direction.

20 Which one of the following **must** be carried out before starting any work activities on site?

a A quote for the work.

b A programme of work.

c A materials list.

d A risk assessment.

Chapter 5
Unit 304: Carrying out decorative and reinforced brickwork

In this chapter we will look at how we set out and build decorative brick features and reinforced brickwork. Many new buildings now incorporate decorative features into their designs such as decorative brick panels, oversailing courses, the use of specials and even different coloured bricks. Also, in recent years there has been a growing interest in conservation work with many houses requiring original brick features to be either repaired or restored to their original specifications. Expanding your knowledge and skills in these areas will enable you to be more effective on site as a bricklayer. Knowledge of setting-out procedures, accuracy and attention to detail are key features of your work.

By reading this chapter you will know how to:

1 Set out and build decorative brickwork features.

2 Set out and build obtuse- and acute-angle quoins.

3 Set out and build reinforced brickwork.

SETTING OUT AND BUILDING DECORATIVE FEATURES

Brick terrace facade showing decorative red dentil and combination stonework

Brick is one of the oldest building materials. It was around 3500BC when people first began to fire bricks; bricks made of clay-containing earth or mud and dried in the sun had been used for several thousands of years before that. Firing made them strong like stone as well as allowing them to be made into regular-sized shapes. This then meant that bricks could be formed into decorative patterns and bonds. Brick is still one of the most versatile and resilient construction materials available even today. The different colours, shapes and textures allow brick to be used in an endless number of imaginative and innovative ways. The decorative bonds and patterns that you are about to discover in this chapter have been around for centuries and are still very much in use today.

When you stand back and take a look at brickwork, what draws your eye? Colour, lines, contrast? Yes, all of these things appeal to the eye and make brickwork look more interesting. That is why it is important when setting out and building decorative brick features that the work is of a high standard to ensure that the correct visual effects are created.

PLANNING AND PREPARATION

INTERPRETING DRAWINGS

Before any physical work is carried out on site, correct planning and preparation are essential to ensure a successful outcome of the job. In order to ensure the work is carried out in the correct manner, you need to follow the drawing to establish the correct location and type of work required. See Chapter 4, page 169 for further guidance on types of construction drawings.

Construction drawings are the best means of passing on detailed and complex information to the bricklayers on site. As a tradesperson you need to be able to read drawings correctly. As drawings form a part of the legal contract between a client and a contractor, any mistakes in the interpretation of the drawing could prove costly. On smaller work, where no formal contracts have been made, mistakes in interpretation could lead to a loss of goodwill between the client and the contractor. When reading drawings, study the whole drawing first to establish an overall picture of the work that needs to be carried out. Then look at the details. Do you need to order any special bricks or components in advance? Is there any part of the drawing that needs further clarification before work starts?

INDUSTRY TIP

If you are in any doubt about the types of decorative features to be used or where they are to be located once you have read the drawing, you must get further clarification from either your supervisor or the architect. Don't wait until after you have started the work.

Any changes to the drawings should made in writing and it is important to keep drawings for a period of time after work is complete in case any queries arise at a later date.

SAFETY

Producing risk assessments

In the workshop and on construction sites it is everyone's responsibility to maintain a safe, accident-free workplace. Before any type of construction work is carried out, a thorough risk assessment needs to be prepared (see Chapter 4, page 170 for further information). Ensure that you read and follow any risk assessments before you start any work on site.

Method statements

The method statement for the work will be provided by the contractor carrying out the work. This will give you all of the details of how the work should be constructed in a safe manner. It is important that all staff are made aware of any potential dangers and that all safe working methods are clearly explained (see Chapter 4, page 171 for examples of the types of information to be found on a method statement).

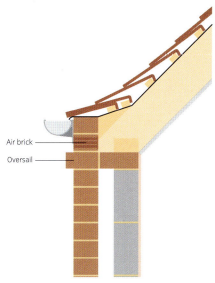

Section drawing showing oversailing detail

Cutting bricks to form decorative features

Carrying out work to build brick decorative features can often require the use of cut bricks which are normally required at the top of buildings. To reduce the risk of accidents, any cutting of bricks should be carried out at ground level. It is also important to ensure that the appropriate safety checks are carried out by a **competent** person when using any mechanical cutting.

Competent

Having the necessary training, skills and experience to carry out a job safely and effectively

Health and safety considerations

Many bricks required to carry out decorative brickwork will require cuts formed to an angle. Engineering bricks or perforated wire-cut bricks are best cut by mechanical means. Any mechanical means of cutting bricks should also be carried out by a competent person.

- You must be fully trained and competent to be able to use disc cutters and table-top cutting equipment. Under no circumstances are you allowed to change a blade on a cutter without full training.

- When using any mechanical cutting equipment it is important that you follow the manufacturer's guidance on the safe use of the equipment. This includes wearing the correct PPE.

- Safety boots are mandatory on all construction sites and should have steel toe caps and non-slip soles.

- Clothing should be sturdy and snug fitting: any loose clothing could get caught up in the machinery. For the same reason long hair should be tied up and scarves and jewellery should not be worn.

Steel toe cap boot

Dust mask   **Respirator**

- Hard hats are to be worn where there is a risk of falling objects.

- Safety glasses must be worn to prevent any loose chips or debris entering the eyes.

- Wear a suitable dust mask if any dust is to be generated. If fumes and smoke are generated, then ensure that suitable respiratory protection equipment (RPE) is worn.

- Hearing protection will prevent you from damaging your ears. Remember that hearing loss is permanent!

It is the responsibility of the employer to ensure that employees are correctly trained in the use of power tools used to cut masonry and that supervision is given, especially to new trainees. All items of equipment must be properly maintained and safe to use. It is the responsibility of the employee to ensure that all instructions are followed and that any situation presenting a risk to themselves or others should be reported immediately to the employer.

Even once you have been trained, you must take your responsibilities seriously, as mistakes could prove fatal.

Environmental and safety considerations

Brick cutting can be a noisy and dusty business. Cutting bricks with a disc cutter often gives off an enormous amount of dust. Materials like bricks, concrete and stone can contain large amounts of crystalline silica. Cutting these materials produces airborne dust particles that can penetrate deep into the lungs causing serious health effects such as lung cancer or silicosis.

Water suppression systems

With these systems, water is sprayed onto the disc cutter to keep dust to a minimum when cutting bricks, blocks and stone

Local exhaust ventilation (LEV)

An engineering control system that reduces exposure to airborne contaminants by sucking the dust and fumes away from the workplace

Under COSHH (2002) employers not only have a duty of care to protect workers but also the general public. **Water suppression systems** and **local exhaust ventilation (LEV)** systems along with the appropriate respiratory protection equipment should be considered to control dust.

Another important safety factor that you will need to consider in the workplace is the control of noise. Brick cutting can be noisy, especially if disc cutters are being used. Adequate hearing protection should be worn at all times.

INDUSTRY TIP

Try rotating who is responsible for cutting bricks on site to minimise the hazards caused by dust and noise.

Try to eliminate waste from brick cutting on site by reusing offcuts or saving them to be crushed and used as hardcore. Disposing of waste is costly. However, if you have large amounts of leftover brick waste many waste disposal companies will now let you dispose of this at their facilities without charge.

CUTTING ANGLED BRICKS BY HAND

When cutting bricks by hand ensure that you are wearing the appropriate PPE. Try to have a separate cutting area away from where you are working so as to keep your working areas clear from debris and to keep any brick splinters away from other workers.

STEP 1 Place the brick in position on the wall 20mm (two cross joint thicknesses) from the brick, next to where it is to be laid.

STEP 2 Mark with a pencil on the brick at either end of the string line.

STEP 3 Draw a straight line between the two pencil marks to identify the cut.

STEP 4 Transfer the marking onto the rear of the brick also to ensure that the brick is cut accurately across its width.

STEP 5 Mark the part of the brick that is wastage with an 'x' or a 'w', then place it onto a cutting mat.

STEP 6 Put on your safety glasses and cut the brick with a hammer and bolster, placing the bolster edge slightly onto the waste side of the brick.

STEP 7 Now do the same on the opposite side of the brick.

STEP 8 Turn the brick back onto its face side and give one final sharp blow. Cut off the angled waste with a hammer and bolster.

STEP 9 Then trim down any excess using a scutch. If the brick doesn't break as required then the whole process will have to be repeated again.

STEP 10 Put the final brick in position on the wall.

DECORATIVE BRICK PANELS

Decorative panels are frequently built to enhance the overall appearance of large plainly bonded walls. They are usually formed in the half-brick outer skin of a cavity wall or on the face of a solid wall. They can also be incorporated into timber-framed houses as infill panels. The most common types of decorative panels are herringbone and basket-weave patterns.

SETTING OUT HERRINGBONE PANELS

The herringbone pattern resembles the shape of fish bones; the zigzag pattern is created by setting the bricks at 90° to each other. This can be carried out either vertically, horizontally or diagonally. It can be achieved using single or double stretcher bricks laid at angles to each other.

Diagonal herringbone panel   Horizontal herringbone panel   Double diagonal herringbone panel

In order to build an effective herringbone panel it must first be set out on a plywood panel on the floor or other flat surface. First you need to mark the size of your panel opening. Deduct 20mm from the width to allow for a 10mm cross joint at either side of the panel and 10mm from the height of the panel to allow for the bottom bed joint. You do not need to take 10mm from the top of the panel as the brickwork at the top of the panel should finish flush with the top of the wall.

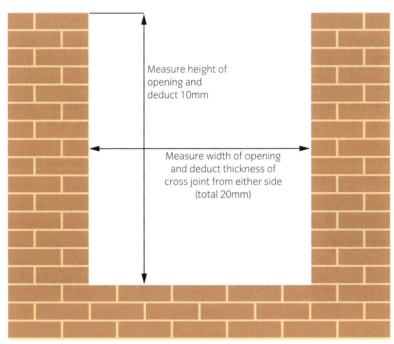

Measure height of opening and deduct 10mm

Measure width of opening and deduct thickness of cross joint from either side (total 20mm)

Wall with opening in ready to receive panel

SETTING OUT BASKET-WEAVE PANELS

Horizontal basket weave

Horizontal basket weave is created by laying three bricks vertically and horizontally in alternate groups throughout the panel. This type of panel is quite straightforward to set out and build. It is important when setting out this panel to ensure that the bricks are carefully selected to be exactly the same size as one another; otherwise this will affect the appearance of the panel and the joints will end up out of alignment. Also, if contrasting bricks are to be used, then colours in each section stand out from the colours on the adjoining section. Any variations in the colours can lead to the contrast being lost. Bricks have a tendency to have multiple colours within them and one colour can merge into another.

A variation of a horizontal basket-weave panel inserted into a wall

Horizontal basket-weave panel

To set out this panel, mark out the size of your opening as described in the previous section, remembering to take away 20mm for the sides and 10mm for the bottom bed joint. Lay the bricks onto the flat surface starting from the bottom-left corner of the opening, working your way to the top right and making any necessary adjustments to the bricks as you place them down to ensure that all joints are the same thickness throughout. Take a look to see how this contrast looks from a distance and whether all joints are in line. At this point, change any bricks that do not line up or give you the required colour contrast.

Diagonal basket weave

A variation of basket-weave bond is diagonal basket-weave bond. Bricks can be laid at 45° to the main wall to form the diagonal basket weave. Like horizontal herringbone panels, diagonal basket weave requires a great deal of cutting.

Diagonal basket-weave panels are set out in the same way as horizontal herringbone panels. The bricks are just laid in a different arrangement within the opening before being cut. How you want your panel to look and the types of cuts that it leaves at the edges of the panel will determine whether the first brick sits centrally in the opening or not.

ACTIVITY

Try to find as many different varieties of panel as possible, keep a record of them and attempt to set them out. Try out variations of herringbone and basket-weave panels in your work.

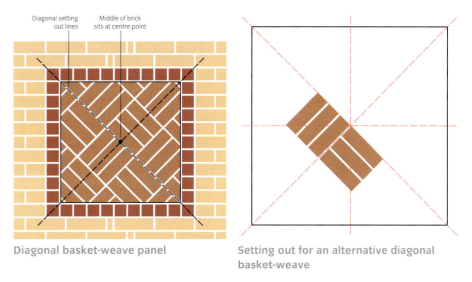

Diagonal basket-weave panel

Setting out for an alternative diagonal basket-weave

SETTING OUT AND BUILDING PANEL SURROUNDS

A panel surround can be added as a decorative border that can allow the panel to be built inside it. Panel surrounds are generally built from bricks laid as headers and can project from the face of the wall to further enhance the decorative effect. If the panel is to be projected it is important to plumb the outer edges of the brick panel and also the front face to the border.

Attach lines to the top and bottom arrises of the border to ensure that the projecting arris of the brick is straight with the eye line (see below).

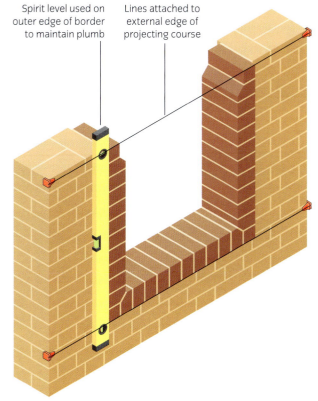

Panel with inset border

It is essential when building the surround to ensure that the sides are plumb and the correct width of the opening remains the same throughout. This can be achieved by using either a tape measure or a **pinch rod**. The panel also needs to be checked for square using a builder's square. Once the panel surround has been built the size of the opening can be marked and set out on a plywood sheet or concrete floor.

Pinch rod

A piece of timber cut to the width of an opening and used to check that the opening size stays the same width throughout the construction of the panel

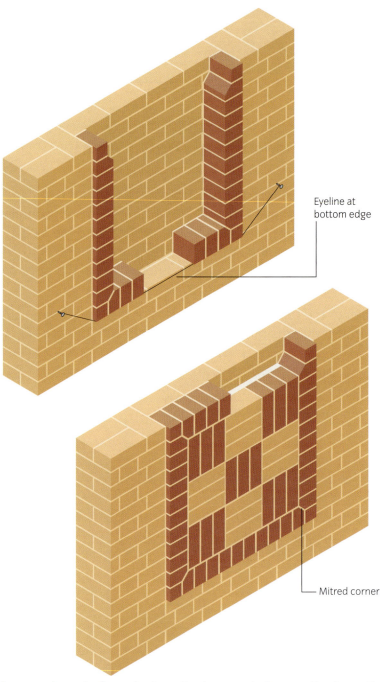

Eyeline at bottom edge

Mitred corner

Panel surrounds can be formed using mitred corners to improve the decorative appearance

THE CITY & GUILDS TEXTBOOK

CONSTRUCTING BRICK PANEL SURROUNDS

Before laying any bricks into the panel it is good practice to cut small lengths of timber lath that fit the length and width of the opening. These can be used as gauge rods for laying the bricks into the panels. Mark on the timber lath the joint markings for each brick. This will ensure the bricks are laid into the panel exactly as they are positioned on the floor.

Constructing horizontal basket-weave panels

As most brick panels are usually formed as the outer leaf of a half-brick cavity or an unattached single skin of a thicker wall, it is important that stainless steel wall ties are placed into the joints to tie the panel to the backing masonry.

It is important when constructing basket-weave panels to ensure that the bricks run in a straight line throughout the panel. Equally important is that the cross joint forms a straight and consistent line vertically throughout each section of the panel. When constructing panels it is best to have the panel laid out next to where you are working so you can easily transfer the bricks from the floor into the panel. As mentioned earlier, a timber gauge rod can be made with the markings on showing where each brick is to be laid on the first course of the panel.

STEP 1 Set up the lines and pins horizontally at either side of the wall at the height of the top of the first soldier bricks to be laid in the panel in order to keep a consistent bed joint line throughout the width of the panel and to maintain face-plane (generally every third course of bricks).

STEP 2 Place a timber batten on top of the panel held down by placing blocks at either end.

STEP 3 A line can be placed vertically from the batten at the top of the wall and fixed beneath the panel at the bottom of the wall. Make sure that your line sits at the end of the first full brick and is made plumb using a spirit level (also shown in Step 4). This will help you to lay your bricks plumb and ensure that any bricks and brick joints line up vertically throughout the panel.

STEP 4 Starting at the bottom corner, lay the first three bricks ensuring each brick is plumb level and that the three bricks laid are to gauge.

STEP 5 Continue to lay the first course ensuring all bricks are plumb with even joint spacings. If the joint spacings are uneven throughout the wall, then take the bricks out and start again.

STEP 6 Move the line up to the top of the next set of bricks and lay in the next course ensuring that bricks line up vertically as well as horizontally throughout the panel.

STEP 7 Continue until you reach the top, working from left to right. Check that your panel is flat. Joint up the brickwork.

As with any panel, during construction take a look to see that it is true to your eye and make any amendments before continuing.

INDUSTRY TIP

Have a boat level handy when building panels. Single bricks can be plumbed using this. Refer back to Chapter 3, page 127, for an image of a boat level.

INDUSTRY TIP

Develop your 'builder's eye' by regularly checking your work to make sure that the work looks 'in line', as this is how others will see your work.

Constructing vertical herringbone panels

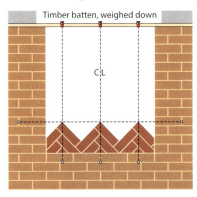

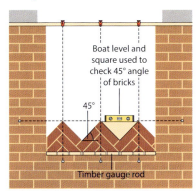

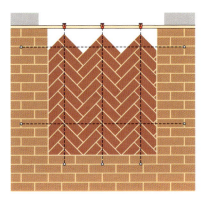

STEP 1 Set out the lines for the panel (see page 223), this time making sure that the lines intersect at the corner point of each brick. The measurement for the height for each line can be taken from the bricks laid dry on the floor. Vertical lines can also be placed in to ensure that the bricks line up accurately. Use a spirit level to check.

STEP 2 Mark a gauge rod with the position of the bricks to be laid into the first course. Use the rod as a template to lay in the first course ensuring the top corner of each brick finishes on the line. Lay the bricks starting from the bottom corner working along the wall from corner to corner.

STEP 3 Continue with each course until the panel has been built up to the point where the last course needs to be placed in. Remember to tie in your panel to the masonry behind to ensure a secure fixing. Visually check your work to ensure that the joints line up with one another.

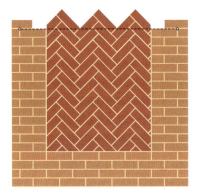

STEP 4 Place the line at the top of the panel in line with the surrounding brickwork. To ensure complete accuracy on the top course you may find that you have to remark and cut these bricks to ensure an even bed joint across the top.

STEP 5 Joint up the work neatly taking care to ensure that you form a continuous line around the border line of the panel.

Constructing diagonal basket-weave panels

Bricks are positioned accurately by using a boat level resting on a small timber square. This will ensure that a true 90° angle has been maintained between the bricks. A level can be used to ensure that the brick joints line up diagonally. If the joint line is located centrally within the panel, a line can be attached diagonally from corner to corner to ensure correct alignment of the brick joints. It is important also to check the face-plane of your work with a straight edge as the work proceeds or alternatively place a line horizontally running through the brick face as the work proceeds.

If the panel is to be recessed then a timber template can be made to fit into the opening which will then work as a straight edge for the panel.

Once plinth bricks have been laid it is important to cover them up with a polythene sheet as the work proceeds as any mortar droppings from the work carried out above will stain the bricks. This can be achieved by inserting a polythene sheet into the brick course above the plinths by 10mm. This will secure the sheet as the work proceeds. Once the work is complete the sheet can be cut out with a knife and the joint filled in.

Plinth bricks are also manufactured with plinth internal or external returns, as shown below.

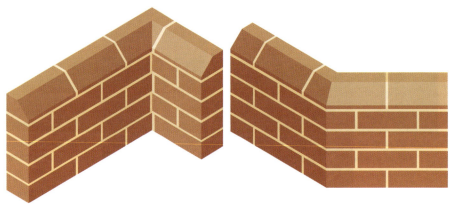

An internal plinth return   An external plinth return

USE OF CANT BRICKS

Cant bricks have 45° angled faces on both the header and stretcher faces. They are made with either one angled face known as a single cant or with both faces angled known as a double cant. They are used to form a cill for a window or a brick-on-edge coping for a boundary wall. When laid flat, cant bricks can also be used to form chamfered corners at right-angled piers.

Single cant bricks

Double cant bricks

      THE CITY & GUILDS TEXTBOOK

Cant bricks on cill

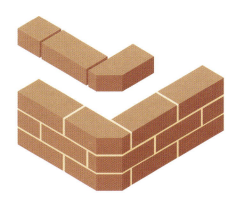

A chamfered corner using single cants laid flat

RAMPED WORK (CIRCULAR AND STRAIGHT)

Ramped work is constructed from brickwork that has a sloping face. This can either be carried out in a straight line as in a gable end or used to change the height of a boundary wall. It can also be carried out in a curved shape and is normally seen as an inverted feature on a garden wall.

Setting out for sloping straight ramps is carried out in the same way that battered brickwork is set out (see Chapter 4 for further information). The main walling will have to be constructed first with the sloping angle racked back from the line. Bricks are then cut to form the angle. The top of the wall can be then finished off in a variety of ways.

A gable end with decorative oversailing courses

CONCAVE RAMPS

Concave walls are generally used as a decorative feature in garden walls. Concave walls need first building up to the height of the striking point. A timber beam is then supported onto the wall which will be held down with bricks or blocks (see next page). Next you will need to find the striking point and set up a trammel at this point. The dimensions for the striking point should be found on the working drawing. The trammel will have a small nail projecting from it in order to mark the bricks. The cut bricks that form the curve can be laid in using the trammel as a guide. As with arches, the size and shape of the curved brickwork will have a bearing on whether a V-shaped joint or a tapered brick is used.

Concave

Curving or hollowed inwards

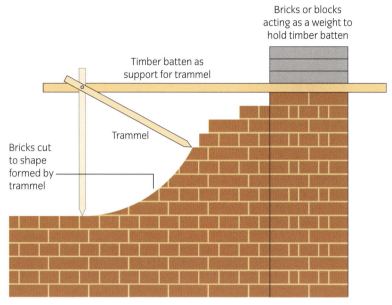

A timber batten sat on top of the wall with a trammel attached at the striking point, forming the concaved curve to the wall

CONVEX RAMPS

Convex ramps have a similar use to straight ramped brickwork in that they are used to reduce the height of a wall and again are generally found on garden or boundary walls.

The striking point for a convex wall will be located on the main section of brickwork below the curve. A timber wedge can be driven into the bed joint at the location of the striking point and the trammel fixed to this. The trammel must be allowed to swing freely and has a nail fixed at one end with which to scribe the shape of the curve.

Convex

Curving or bulging outwards

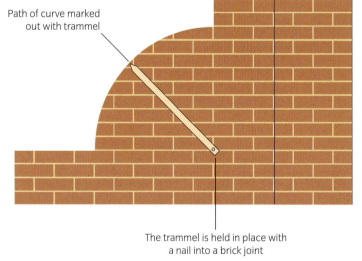

Trammel set up at the striking point, marking the curve for the brickwork

GOOD PRACTICE FOR BUILDING DECORATIVE FEATURES

- Ensure that any projecting bricks are lined in along the 'eye line'. Most times the line will need to be attached to the underside of the bricks, especially on upper floors.

- Dentils and dog-toothed bricks need to be cut accurately so as not to protrude into the cavity.

- Ensure all decorative work is plumb and level. Remember this is the type of work that catches your eye so it needs to look 'in line'.

- Ensure that you make full use of any templates to maintain accuracy in the work.

- Ensure that you use bricks with close dimensional tolerances and have neat square arrises with no chips.

- Any work that has cuts involved should be laid out dry to check the accuracy before being laid.

- Projecting bricks are prone to weather damage so ensure that they are hard-wearing.

- Make sure that joints are fully filled especially where there are recessed bricks.

- Ensure correct bonding arrangements are maintained.

- **Frog bricks** should not be used for string courses.

Frog brick
Bricks with an indentation (frog)

SETTING OUT AND BUILDING ACUTE- AND OBTUSE-ANGLED QUOINS

Not all walls and buildings are built square at 90°. There are many times on site where a wall needs to be built at an irregular angle such as one under a bay window or a boundary wall that follows various directions on a site. These irregular-shaped angles are known as **obtuse** and **acute** corners.

In many cases the angle of brickwork to be built will have been predetermined by the architect and this information can be found on the site drawings. However, there will be times when you will be required to set out and build walls with angles greater or less than 90° where you will be required to find the angle yourself.

Obtuse
An angle between 90° and 180°

Acute
An angle less than 90°

INDUSTRY TIP
Walling featuring obtuse and acute angles is also known as 'splayed walling'.

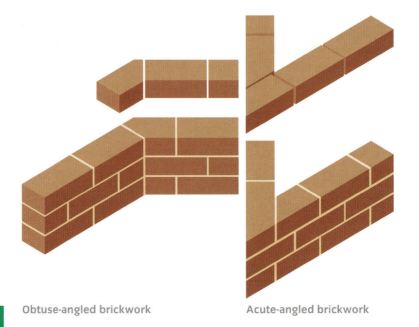

Obtuse-angled brickwork   Acute-angled brickwork

GEOMETRY

Having a basic knowlege of geometry will help you to work out acute and obtuse angles.

Angles can also be worked out by **bisection**. Many obtuse and acute angles can be worked out by bisecting other angles. Let's take a look at some examples.

Most angles on site are set out using a builder's square and tape measure and a set of trammel rods. When setting out obtuse or acute angles it is best to start with a 90° angle.

1. Acute angle: less than 90°
2. Right angle: exactly 90°
3. Obtuse angle: between 90° and 180°
4. Straight angle: exactly 180°
5. Reflex angle: greater than 180° but less than 360°
6. Full angle: exactly 360°

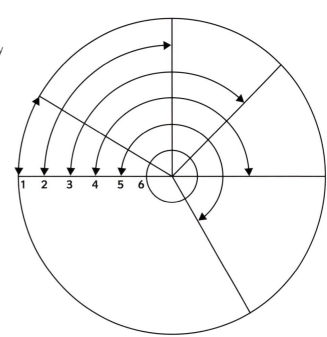

Circle with angles by bisection

BISECTING A 90° ANGLE

A 45° angle can be found by bisecting a 90° angle.

STEP 1 Establish a base line (frontage line of the wall) using a straight edge.

STEP 2 Mark point A on the far left.

STEP 3 Use your square to draw a perpendicular line; this will give you a 90° angle.

STEP 4 Using the compass or trammel rods, mark a point from the corner (point A) at equal lengths along the vertical and horizontal lines points B and C.

STEP 5 Keep the compass at the same width opening and place the compass point on point B. Scribe a small arc. Repeat the process placing the compass point on point C joining the two arcs together to form point D.

STEP 6 Draw a line joining point A to point D forming a 45° angle.

You have now bisected a 90° angle. Setting out in this way also gives 135° obtuse angles.

45° and 135° angles

FUNCTIONAL SKILLS

Using a pencil, rule and a compass, bisect a 90° angle.

Work on this activity can support FM2 (L2.2.2).

CONSTRUCTING A 30° ANGLE

There may be times when the angle is even more acute than 45° or even more obtuse than 135°, depending on the nature of the site and the type of wall to be built. Acute-angled brickwork can also be formed using 30° and 60° angles.

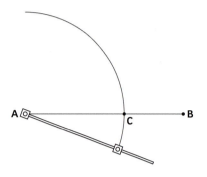

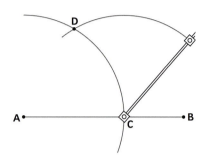

STEP 1 Draw a line that will be the frontage line of the wall and mark the two ends A and B.

STEP 2 Set up the trammel at point A and place the pencil end just past the midway point and scribe an arc; where the arc springs from is point C.

STEP 3 Keep the trammel points at the same distance and move the trammel point to sit at point C and scribe an arc to form point D.

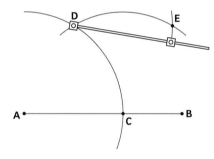

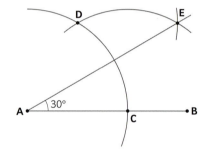

STEP 4 Keep the trammel points the same spacing apart again and move the trammel point to point D. Scribe an arc along line D forming point E.

STEP 5 Join point A with point E to give you a 30° angle.

BONDING OBTUSE-ANGLED QUOINS USING SPECIAL BRICKS

When setting out obtuse corners it is important to set out the brickwork so that the bonding arrangement is correct at the corner. Special bricks can be used to form obtuse angles. These can be formed by using either special shaped bricks called **squint bricks** or by using another type of special brick known as a **dogleg**. These special bricks are generally used for walls that are set at an angle of 135°. Many manufacturers now produce specially made angled bricks to match the facing bricks specified for the work. This information will be found in the work specification.

Squint brick

A special brick placed into the corner of a half-brick wall. Just like a normal **quoin**, the bonding arrangement is then worked out from there

Quoin

Masonry block at the corner of a wall

Dogleg

A special brick used on 135° obtuse corners, also known as an external angled brick

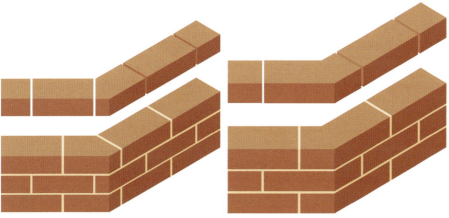

A squint brick placed into the corner of a half-brick wall. Just like a normal quoin, the bonding arrangement is then worked out from there

An external angle brick placed into a wall

ACTIVITY

Go to www.stihl.co.uk/brickjig and watch the video of bricks being cut. Look out this time for how to make a dogleg brick using standard bricks and starter cuts for herringbone panels.

BONDING ARRANGEMENTS USING SPECIALS

On half-brick walls squints and external angles will require a three-quarter brick placing next to them to maintain half-bond. However, if the wall is to be built in one-brick thickness in English bond then a queen closer will need to be placed next to the squint brick to maintain bond.

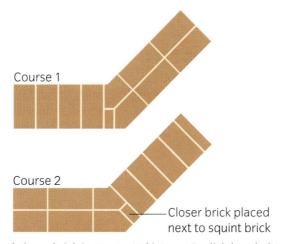

Course 1

Course 2

Closer brick placed next to squint brick

A squint brick and closer brick incorporated into an English bond obtuse wall

The illustration above shows a one-brick solid English bond wall with a queen closer placed next to a squint brick to maintain the bonding arrangement. When building obtuse solid walling it is preferable to use dogleg bricks in the internal angles as the solid brick will provide a strong internal bond at the corner.

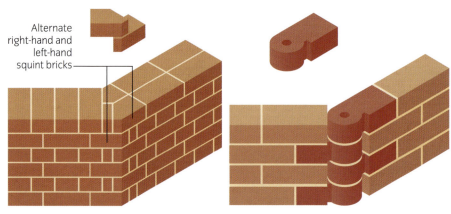

Alternate right-hand and left-hand squint bricks

One-brick-thick wall showing bond changes when wall changes direction

Easy angle special brick and wall showing where brick positioned

The illustration above right shows an easy angle (or universal brick) which can be used to form any angle of wall.

BONDING USING STANDARD BRICKS

FORMING OBTUSE QUOINS USING STANDARD BRICKS

There are a variety of methods that can be used to form obtuse quoins without the use of special bricks. There are a number of advantages and disadvantages associated with these methods. Special bricks can be very costly; however, their addition can improve the appearance of the project. The illustration on the next page (left) shows the bonding arrangement for an obtuse quoin using standard bricks. The bricks have projected from the corners leaving them prone to damage and weathering; however, with this method the angle of the wall can be altered in any way to suit the building lines required for the job.

Here is another method of forming an obtuse angle using standard bricks. The illustration on the next page (right) shows an obtuse quoin with bricks butted together to form the angle and gaps left at the corners. Again, cost savings can be made using this method; however, the disadvantages are that there is insufficient strength at the corner of the wall due to a lack of lapping between the bricks and again the spacing left at the corner is prone to weathering.

Solid wall showing bricks projecting from corner

Obtuse corner built using standard bricks, formed with indents

FORMING ACUTE QUOINS USING STANDARD BRICKS

An alternative to forming acute quoins with standard bricks can be achieved by forming what is known as a 'birdsmouth' feature. Some acute quoins are prone to damage as they have pointed corners, but by forming a birdsmouth, damage can be eliminated. By incorporating mitred bats into the wall (see below), relatively few cuts will be required. This method can be introduced into one-brick-thick walls or thicker. Walls built at one-and-a-half bricks or thicker are generally constructed as retaining walls.

Acute quoin formed with a birdsmouth

TEMPLATES USED TO FORM OBTUSE QUOINS

Templates can be made by the carpenter that fit the exact shape of the wall to be built. In the case of bay windows a profile can be laid into the opening and marked around. During the construction of the bay the profile can be laid on top of the brickwork to check that the angles are still correct. It is important to work in this way as the windows will be specified to a certain size and angle and will be manufactured with measurements taken from a drawing. It is important that the angle of your wall matches exactly with the angle of the window.

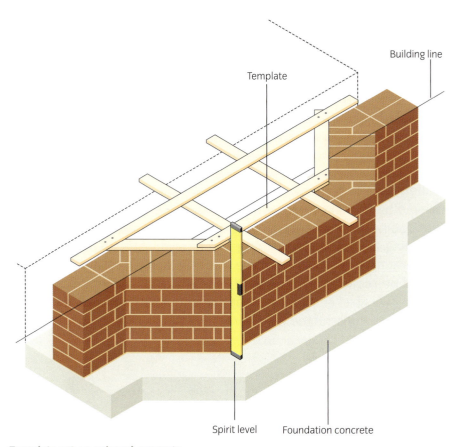

Template sat on splayed concrete

The illustration above shows a timber template sat on the brickwork ensuring the correct angle of brickwork while the work proceeds.

FORMING ACUTE-ANGLED QUOINS

CUTTING BRICKS

Acute angles are formed by bringing the corner to a sharp point. There are no special bricks available for this so the standard bricks have to be cut using a mechanical saw. Cutting a standard brick with a hammer and bolster will leave a jagged face. A table saw will give you the most accurate cut and will be the safest option.

The illustration below (left) shows a one-brick-thick acute-angled quoin built in English bond. Notice that the bond changes when the wall changes direction and the queen closer is always placed next to the quoin header to maintain a quarter bond arrangement. The illustration below (right) shows the bonding arrangement for a one-and-a-half brick thick wall which has a birdsmouth incorporated into the corner.

INDUSTRY TIP

You must have received training before being allowed to operate a table saw or mechanical cutting saw.

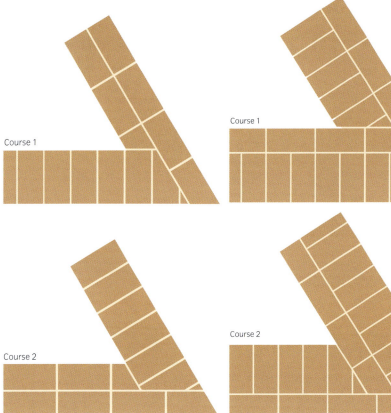

Course 1

Course 1

Course 2

Course 2

Acute quoin formed using standard bricks in English bond

One-and-a-half-brick English bond corner

A digital angle finder can be used to form the exact angle required

SETTING OUT AND BUILDING OBTUSE- AND ACUTE-ANGLE QUOINS

If a template has been made for the work then this must be used to set out the shape of the wall. If there is no template available this will have to be carried out prior to the work starting.

1 Dry bond the brickwork on the first course. Remember to create even-sized joints throughout the work.

2 Lay the first course of bricks, then recheck the angle using a protractor or angle finder.

3 Continue to build the wall. You must take great care to ensure the corner is plumb. Obtuse quoins will usually need special bricks to form the corners. Care must be taken when plumbing these bricks as when you tap one face to adjust the plumb, it can move the opposite face of the brick out of plumb.

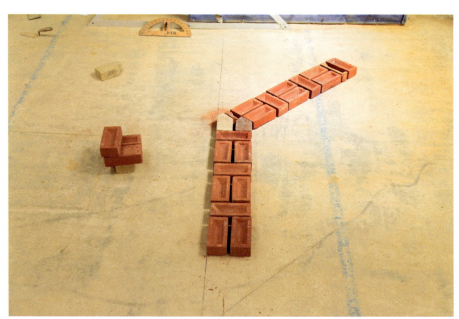

Dry bonded brickwork on the first course

Bay windows can be built using either squints or dogleg bricks. Dogleg bricks are made in both internal and external shapes allowing the work to be faced at all angles.

When constructing acute and obtuse quoins, again care must be taken when plumbing the corner brick as when one face of the bricks is tapped the other side will move also.

Plumbing an acute quoin

SETTING OUT AND BUILDING REINFORCED BRICKWORK

If constructed correctly, under normal circumstances, brickwork is designed to withstand the forces placed upon it. However, there are many situations where loads are placed on a wall that will require added strength and support.

If there is a force pushing downwards on a wall, such as a heavy concrete floor or several courses of bricks over a large span opening, then the wall is known to be in a state of compression.

Brickwork is relatively weak when it comes to being pulled apart. This occurs when forces are placed on a wall from the sides which creates a pulling effect. When this happens the wall is said to be in a state of tension. Under normal circumstances brickwork is strong under compression but weaker under tension.

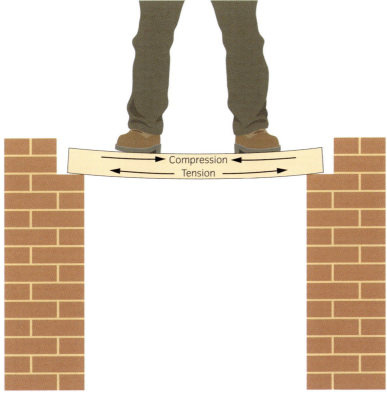

Brickwork under compression

ACTIVITY

Search the internet to find out if there are any other types of forces that can be placed on a building.

Boundary walls with soil piled up behind them, high walls that are exposed to wind, sea defence walls and free-standing pillars that support heavy gates are some examples of where a wall can be said to be in a state of tension.

The illustration on the next page shows these gate piers are under tension from the heavy gates pulling on them sideways.

Gate piers are under tension from the heavy gates pulling on them sideways

INDUSTRY TIP

Reinforcement on site is sometimes referred to as Rebar.

Lateral

To or from the side

Where brickwork is exposed to compressive or tensile forces it can suffer from cracking, bulging, leaning and in severe circumstances may even lead to a total collapse of the structure. In order to prevent this from occurring reinforcement needs to be placed into the brickwork. Reinforcement is placed into the brickwork to increase the **lateral** and compressive strength of the wall, thus helping to prevent any failures at a later date. The type and quantity of reinforcement will depend on the amount of pressure that is on the wall and where the pressure is coming from.

INTERPRETING INFORMATION

Structural engineer

The structural engineer is involved in the design of a building. They are responsible for calculating loads on a structure and will decide on the most appropriate structural systems to use

The most appropriate methods to use for the construction of reinforced brickwork will be recommended by the **structural engineer**. Details of construction methods will be found on the working drawings. This may include accurate and detailed descriptions of spacing and positioning of reinforcement. It is important to follow these instructions as incorrectly positioned reinforcement could lead to wall failure.

INDUSTRY TIP

Drawings can be very technical and at times difficult to interpret. If you have any problems understanding the instructions, ask a more experienced worker or a supervisor for help.

PRODUCING RISK ASSESSMENTS

General site safety should be adhered to when constructing reinforced brickwork. Specific hazards need to be carefully considered before starting any work as no two jobs are the same. Unguarded steel reinforcement on site is dangerous. If you stumble onto unprotected reinforcement you could impale yourself. In general, when working with reinforcement you must ensure that any vertical rods that stick out from the ground have safety mushroom caps covering their ends. You may also want to cover the tops of the caps with a timber sheet for added protection; alternatively vertical rods can also be bent over for safety reasons.

Operative placing mushroom caps onto steel reinforcing rods

Fall protection should also be the first line of defence when work at height is being carried out around reinforcement. Also, general safety precautions need to be taken when working with concrete. Ensure that waterproof gloves are worn and that cement is washed away from the skin as exposure to it can cause burns. Repeated exposure can lead to dermatitis (for further information on risk assessments see Chapter 4, page 170).

CUTTING COMPONENTS FOR REINFORCED BRICKWORK

In general, there are not any angled bricks used for reinforced brickwork so most bricks can be cut using a hammer and bolster (see Chapter 4). Remember though when constructing Flemish and English bonds that the queen closers need to all be cut to the same width to maintain the correct bond in the wall. Bolt cutters are the safest method for cutting reinforcement rods on site. For more information see *The City & Guilds Textbook: Level 2 Diploma in Bricklaying*.

Bolt cutter

TYPES OF REINFORCEMENT

HORIZONTAL REINFORCEMENT

Where walls are prone to compressive loads horizontal reinforcement can be placed onto the bed joints to prevent any movement. This can be found particularly over openings with wide spans where large amounts of brickwork are carried over window and door openings. Expanded metal lath (EML) is an excellent type of bed joint reinforcement for this as it forms a solid bond between the bricks and joints. It counteracts cracking of the brick joints as a result of any movement. The expanded metal lath is stretched out before laying onto the brick bed joint; this is to take out any bends in the mesh that will protrude from the bed joint. This type of mesh has excellent bonding qualities as the holes in the mesh provide a good key with the mortar. When positioning horizontal reinforcement it is important to keep the reinforcement a minimum of 15mm from the edge of the face of the brickwork. This is to prevent any rain from penetrating the bed joint and causing the mesh to corrode. Expanded metal lath can be obtained for both single-skin and one-brick-thick walling.

A roll of expanded metal lath

Another commonly used type of bed joint reinforcement is known as welded fabric. This type of reinforcement consists of two 3mm-diameter stainless steel rods joined together with connecting rods spaced at intervals. This type of reinforcement is similar to expanded metal lath performing a good key between the mortar bed and the brick. The added advantage is that it lies flatter on the bed of the brick than the expanded metal lath.

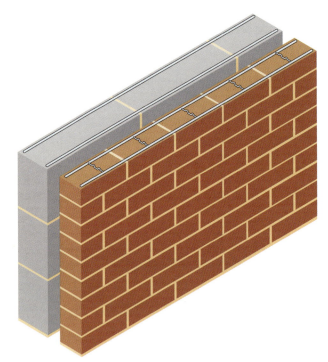

A bed joint reinforcement being used

Hoop iron bond and 4ft thick walls were used in the construction of the hydraulic tower built in 1852. A water tank holding 30,000 gallons of waste exerting a pressue of 100lb per square inch required strong reinforcement to prevent the walls from bulging

An older version of bed joint reinforcement that you may come across is known as hoop iron bond (see below). It is rarely seen nowadays. One band of the hoop iron generally covers one skin of brickwork.

The purpose of the reinforcement was to strengthen the bond especially in areas prone to settlement. The iron reinforcement banding was covered in tar to prevent corrosion and then coated in sand to act as a key for the mortar. However, if the metal strips were insufficiently coated or laid in a damp wall they would become prone to corrosion. The iron strips are joined together at the corners with welt hooks to ensure a continuous band is formed around the wall. English bond or English garden wall bond would generally have been preferred due to the nature and strength of the bond.

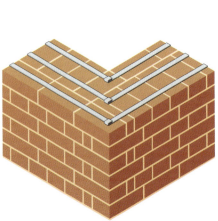

Hoop iron bond used on English bond brickwork

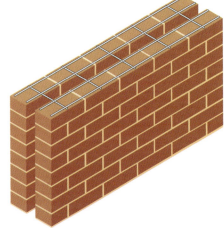

Bed joint reinforcing used to tie both leaves of a cavity together at the same time

The illustration at the bottom of page 246 (right) shows bed joint reinforcement used to tie both leaves of a cavity together at the same time as providing horizontal bed joint reinforcement.

VERTICAL REINFORCEMENT

This type of reinforcement is placed vertically within the brickwork to resist the forces of lateral pressure placed on a wall. Rods are positioned vertically within voids within the bond. The thickness and positioning of the rods generally depend on the type of stresses that are placed on the wall; this again will be determined by the structural engineer. As the work proceeds the pockets are then filled with concrete. Wires are then tied between the vertical rods to further increase the longitudinal stability of the wall.

Quetta bond

Quetta bond is designed to resist the lateral impact of loads placed sideways onto the wall. This bond allows for voids to be formed within the middle of a wall allowing for vertical reinforcement to be placed in as the wall is constructed. The bars are joined together with starter bars that are placed into the concrete foundation. Quetta bond can be formed in either Flemish bond (see below) or Flemish garden wall bond and is generally constructed to one-and-a-half-brick thickness. Quetta bond and other forms of reinforced masonry are commonly used in earthquake-prone countries.

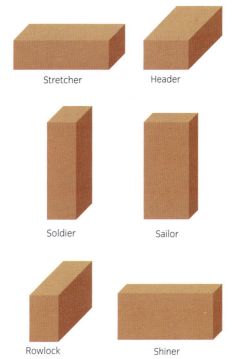

Stretcher   Header

Soldier   Sailor

Rowlock   Shiner

Classifications of how bricks are laid. The pictures show the exposed face of the brick on the finished wall

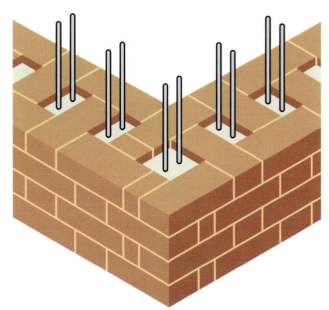

Quetta bond using Flemish bond

The illustration above shows the bonding arrangement for Quetta bond incorporating the use of Flemish bond. This can be seen on both faces of the wall.

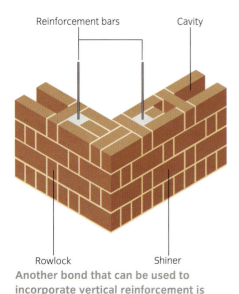

Reinforcement bars Cavity

Rowlock Shiner

Another bond that can be used to incorporate vertical reinforcement is known as rat trap bond

Method statement of work for building walls with Quetta bond

1 Steel starter bars should be placed into the concrete foundation positioned in line with the pockets to be built into the brickwork.

2 Steel reinforcement rods are tied vertically to the starter bars, securing the wall to the foundation.

3 The wall is then constructed.

4 Once the brickwork has fully set the pockets are filled with concrete which should be well compacted around the rods.

The construction of reinforced brickwork requires good quality control due to the amount of hidden work that takes place within the structure. It is important to adhere to all guidelines set by the structural engineer.

English bond in pillars, supporting heavy gates

HOLLOW PIERS

Vertical reinforcement can be used more commonly in supporting piers that have gates swinging from them. Where this is the case piers should be attached wherever possible to the main walling. Where this cannot be achieved then vertical reinforcement will need to be positioned within the pier to prevent it toppling over. As with the method described above for constructing vertical brickwork, steel reinforcement bars should be placed into the concrete to tie the wall to the foundation. A hollow brick pier is then constructed around the bars. Wait for the pier to fully harden before pouring the concrete into the pier. Otherwise, compacting the concrete too early may cause the pier to expand.

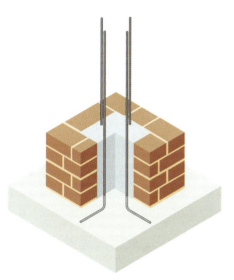

Vertical reinforcement placed into hollow piers

Another method of achieving strength within the pier is to use a solid bond of brickwork. English bond and English garden wall bond can be used to provide lateral support. Brackets can be built into the brickwork as the work proceeds that will support the gate.

ACTIVITY

Take a look around your local area at public buildings and walls. Do you see any piers that are leaning? Take a photo with your smartphone so that you can discuss this with your colleagues and tutor. Can you tell why this has happened?

Case Study: Dayne

Dayne's new brickwork company has really taken off and he is getting a lot of work. He has just started to work on his own after working for a local builder as a trainee for the last few years. His work keeps him busy as when he is not building he is either pricing up work or ordering materials.

Dayne's latest job is to build a one-brick-thick boundary wall with a sloping concaved feature in the centre of the wall. Dayne accepts the work and takes some quick measurements before leaving.

Later in the week Dayne gets started and the main walling is built with the concaved feature being racked back ready for the cut bricks to be placed in. Dayne sets up a timber batten across the wall and holds each end down with blocks. He goes to the van to get some timber for the trammel but it then occurs to him that he has forgotten to order any timber to make the trammel. Dayne quickly comes up with a plan to use a piece of string attached to a nail to form the curve. Dayne draws a mark with a pencil attached to the other end of the string to form the cuts for the curve.

Once the wall is completed Dayne steps back and takes a look at the curve. He isn't quite happy with it and realises that the client is also not going to be happy with the standard of work either. Dayne spends the rest of the day taking down and relaying the curved section of the wall, this time using a wooden trammel for accuracy. Dayne tells himself that in future more time and consideration need to be taken on planning and preparing the work. As Dayne drives away he acknowledges that his mistake has cost him extra time and materials and he puts it down to experience.

Work through the following questions to check your learning.

1 At what angle are herringbone patterned bricks laid to each other?

    a 60°.

    b 45°.

    c 90°.

    d 180°.

2 What decorative pattern are the bricks in the panel shown?

    a Vertical herringbone.

    b Diagonal herringbone.

    c Double diagonal herringbone.

    d Horizontal herringbone.

3 When setting out a panel, what dimensions do you need to account for to ensure the panel fits accurately into the surround?

    a Take off 10mm all around the panel for all joint thicknesses.

    b Take off 10mm at either side and 10mm for the bed joint thickness.

    c Add 10mm at either side and 10mm for the bed joint thickness.

    d Take off 10mm at the top and bottom of the panel.

4 When building a panel surround the correct width of the opening can be maintained by using a

    a gun template

    b gauge rod

    c pinch rod

    d straight edge.

5 A string course, built with alternate projecting headers, is known as a

    a band course

    b oversailing course

    c plinth course

    d dentil course.

6 At what angle is dog-toothing is generally laid?

    a 45 and 60°.

    b 30 and 75°.

    c 90°.

    d 180°.

7 Oversailing courses are generally formed

    a in a zigzag manner

    b in an in-and-out manner

    c in a continuous line

    d flush with the wall.

8 Bricks that can be used to reduce the thickness of a wall are known as

    a engineering bricks

    b squint bricks

    c cant bricks

    d plinth bricks.

9 Where should you start from when setting out brickwork that incorporates plinth courses?

    a Above the plinth course.

    b Below ground level.

    c Below the plinth course.

    d Above DPC level.

10 Which one of the following bricks can be used to form a chamfered corner to a wall?

   a Plinth.

   b Cant.

   c Bullnose.

   d Dogleg.

11 Silicosis can be caused by

   a drinking contaminated water

   b materials coming into contact with the skin

   c breathing in contaminated dust particles

   d working in noisy environments.

12 Walls built with angles set at less than 90° are known as

   a obtuse angles

   b reflex angles

   c acute angles

   d right angles.

13 Which one of the following special bricks can be used to form obtuse angled walling?

   a Plinth.

   b Voussoir.

   c Double cant.

   d Squint.

14 A birdsmouth can be used to form

   a an acute-angled wall using standard bricks

   b an obtuse-angled wall using squint and dogleg bricks

   c a 90°-angled wall

   d an obtuse-angled wall using projecting bricks.

15 Which one of the following is a force pushing downwards when brickwork is placed above a door or window opening?

   a Tension.

   b Torsion.

   c Compression.

   d Shear stress.

16 Which one of the following is reinforcement placed over large spans?

   a Horizontal.

   b Lateral.

   c Compression.

   d Vertical.

17 A one-and-a-half brick thick wall with voids incorporating vertical steel rods can be constructed using

   a English bond

   b Dutch bond

   c English garden wall bond

   d Quetta bond.

18 What materials are used to fill the voids created in reinforced brickwork?

   a Steel rods and mortar.

   b Concrete.

   c Steel rods and concrete.

   d Bricks and mortar.

19 Who has the responsibility of calculating the loads placed on a structure when designing buildings?

   a Structural engineer.

   b Clerk of works.

   c Architect.

   d Quantity surveyor.

20 When should concrete be placed when providing reinforcement to a hollow brick pier?

   a Immediately after being built.

   b As the work proceeds.

   c Once the pier has fully hardened.

   d At the end of the working day.

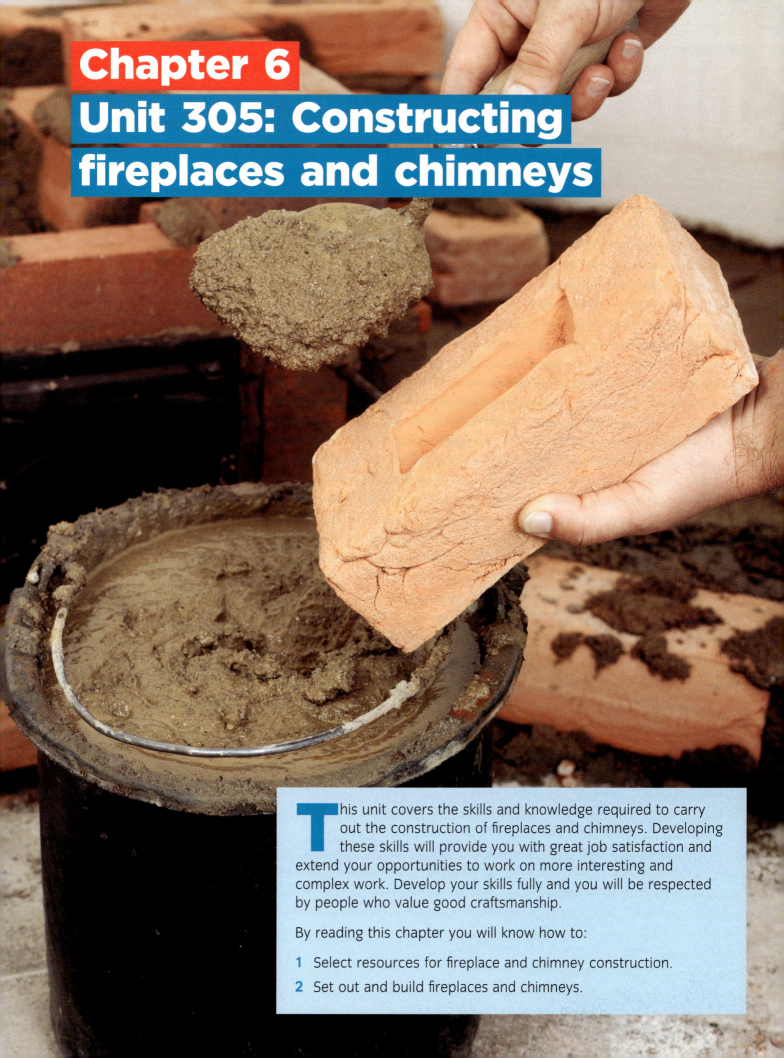

Chapter 6
Unit 305: Constructing fireplaces and chimneys

This unit covers the skills and knowledge required to carry out the construction of fireplaces and chimneys. Developing these skills will provide you with great job satisfaction and extend your opportunities to work on more interesting and complex work. Develop your skills fully and you will be respected by people who value good craftsmanship.

By reading this chapter you will know how to:

1 Select resources for fireplace and chimney construction.
2 Set out and build fireplaces and chimneys.

PREPARING RESOURCES FOR FIREPLACE AND CHIMNEY CONSTRUCTION

As with all construction activities, the preparation required to carry out the work is vital. Understanding the wide range of materials that are used and their properties is also very important; you will also need to become familiar with a wide range of terminology. Remember that becoming a good bricklayer depends on more than just the trade skills. You also need to fully develop your organisational skills and your ability to work well with other trades.

HEALTH AND SAFETY CONSIDERATIONS

As discussed in previous chapters, health and safety is a major factor, especially when working at height. Method statements and risk assessments will provide you with guidance and instructions on how the work should be completed in the safest possible manner. There are a number of specific hazards that you will encounter when constructing fireplaces that will need to be taken into account. Some of the materials are heavy and you will need assistance with them to move them and fix them in place. There are also particular hazards with working at height; ensuring that scaffolding and lifting equipment are fit for purpose and erected by qualified people will be vital.

FUEL AND HEATING

The heating of buildings using solid fuel was very popular during the early part of the last century and many buildings were constructed with fireplaces in every room. This allowed localised heating in individual rooms. With so many people using solid fuel there was an effect on the atmosphere, especially in cities where large numbers of buildings were all heated in this way. This led to high levels of **pollution** which needed to be controlled. In 1956 The Clean Air Act was introduced. This was an Act of Parliament passed in response to the Great **Smog** of London in 1952. It was in effect until 1964 when it was revisited and updated. It was sponsored by the Ministry of Housing and Local Government in England. The Act introduced measures to reduce air pollution, especially by introducing smoke-control areas in some towns and cities in which only smokeless fuels could be burnt. Air pollution and smog were blamed for the premature deaths of hundreds of people in the UK, but at this time there were very few alternative fuels available.

However, as time passed other forms of heating were developed, using alternative fuels such as oil and gas. Over time more complex heating systems were developed that provided controlled heat to

Pollution

The introduction of contaminants into the atmosphere that cause adverse change

Smog

A smoke or fog form of air pollution

every room in a building by heating water from a single heat source and pumping it to radiators. This became known as central heating. Central heating became popular because these systems were more efficient, cleaner, easier to maintain, and also did not have such a high impact on air quality.

There are a variety of fuel types that can be used for heating including the following:

- *Solid fuel:* this is generally wood or coal or a combination of both, normally used in an open fire or a wood-burning appliance.

- *Oil:* this is generally used to fuel a boiler that could serve a central heating system.

- *Gas:* this is generally used to fuel a boiler that could serve a central heating system.

- *Biofuel:* many biofuels are now being produced to fuel central heating systems including wood pellets which are formed from compacted wood fibre with low moisture content and high energy density.

With the introduction of central heating the use of the fireplace as a heating system lost popularity; however, a fireplace is still considered a pleasing addition to the modern home and can form a focal point in a room. With rising fuel costs many people are returning to using open fires and log burners as they can provide an alternative heat source that can be cheaper than other fuels.

Most homes now use central heating instead of fireplaces

Burning logs in an open fire is still a current heat source

SOURCES OF INFORMATION

There are a variety of sources of information that will provide instructions for you when constructing fireplaces, flues and chimneys. The following is a brief overview of what these are and the types of information they can provide.

ARCHITECTS' DRAWINGS

These are drawings produced specifically for the job. They will provide designs, measurements and details of the work to be carried out.

SPECIFICATIONS

These are produced alongside the drawings and specify the types, colours, quality and details of the materials to be used in the construction process; this is also applicable to the materials used to construct fireplaces and flues where the quality of materials or even the particular manufacturer may be specified.

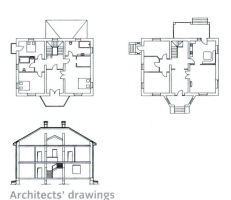
Architects' drawings

BRITISH STANDARD SPECIFICATIONS

These are a set of standards that define good practice. They are agreed ways of doing something, written down as precise criteria so they can be used as rules, guidance or definitions. The original British Standard 6461 provided a wide range of guidance but was superseded in 1984 by the BS EN standards. A BS (British Standard) document is generally confined to the UK and British territories (eg Gibraltar). A BS EN (British Standard Euro Norm) document applies to many European countries and includes the UK.

The following are two examples of British Standards:

- British Standards Institution 1984 – 6461 Part 1, Installation of Chimneys and Flues for Domestic Appliances Burning Solid Fuel.

- British Standards Institution, 1997 Code of Practice for Oil Firing, BSI Herts, England.

INDUSTRY TIP

An example of a British Standard applied to fireplaces is the British Standard for Fireplace Openings, BS 4834.

CODES OF PRACTICE

A code of practice is a set of written guidelines and regulations issued by an official body or professional association to its members. The guidelines are to help members comply with the ethical standards of the official profession, trade, occupation or organisation.

There are many codes of practice that relate directly to fireplaces and chimneys, some of which are listed below.

- British Flue and Chimney Manufacturers Association, *Choosing and Using Flues and Chimneys for Domestic Solid Fuel and Wood*, BFCMA, Bucks, England.

- Hampshire Fire and Rescue Service, 'Thatched Property Safety Guide', 2009.

- Russell Taylor, *The Building Conservation Directory*, 1999, 'Chimneys and Flues'.

MANUFACTURERS' INSTRUCTIONS

Manufacturers' instructions are important as they act as a guide to the correct way to assemble or use an item that you have purchased. Following the manufacturer's instructions will ensure that if the item does not function as it should, you can claim against the warranty and be compensated. It also ensures that the item will wear better, be safe in use and function properly over time. An example of this is a set of instructions providing guidance on how a fireplace should be fixed in position.

ACTIVITY

Look at an example of a set of instructions on fixing a fireplace in position at www.fireplacesareus.co.uk.

HSE GUIDELINES

HSE guidelines are developed for all industries and there are a specific set for the construction industry. These provide information, regulation and guidance on work in construction and help to avoid accidents in the workplace.

These guidelines will provide you with useful information regarding the risks involved with the work you are carrying out, such as moving materials and working at height. All work on chimneys will involve work at height so reference to these guidelines is essential.

BUILDING REGULATIONS

The design and construction of fireplaces and flues is controlled by the Building Regulations Part J. There are many individual components that form fireplaces and chimneys and it is useful to look at the definitions as described in the Building Regulations.

SETTING OUT AND BUILDING FIREPLACES AND CHIMNEYS

GENERAL TERMS FOR CHIMNEYS AND FIREPLACES

Term	Description
Chimney 	A structure (forming any part of a building) enclosing or forming any part of a flue or flues other than a flue pipe, excluding the terminal (chimney pot).
Chimney breast 	A projection beyond the thickness of the wall containing the fireplace and flue(s).

Term	Description
Chimney connector 	An accessory that connects an appliance or flue pipe to a chimney. (This part is shown in context on page 277.)
Chimney jamb 	The pier at the side of the fireplace recess.
Chimney stack 	Part of a chimney enclosing one or more flues that rises above the roof of a building that includes the chimney terminal, but not the flue terminal.

Term	Description
Chimney terminal 	The uppermost part of a chimney stack (pot).
Fireplace lintel 	A load-bearing or throat-forming beam above the fireplace recess.
Fireplace recess 	A space formed in a wall or chimney breast into which an appliance may be placed.
Flaunching 	The weathering formed in mortar on top of a chimney stack or base of a terminal.

Term	Description
Flue 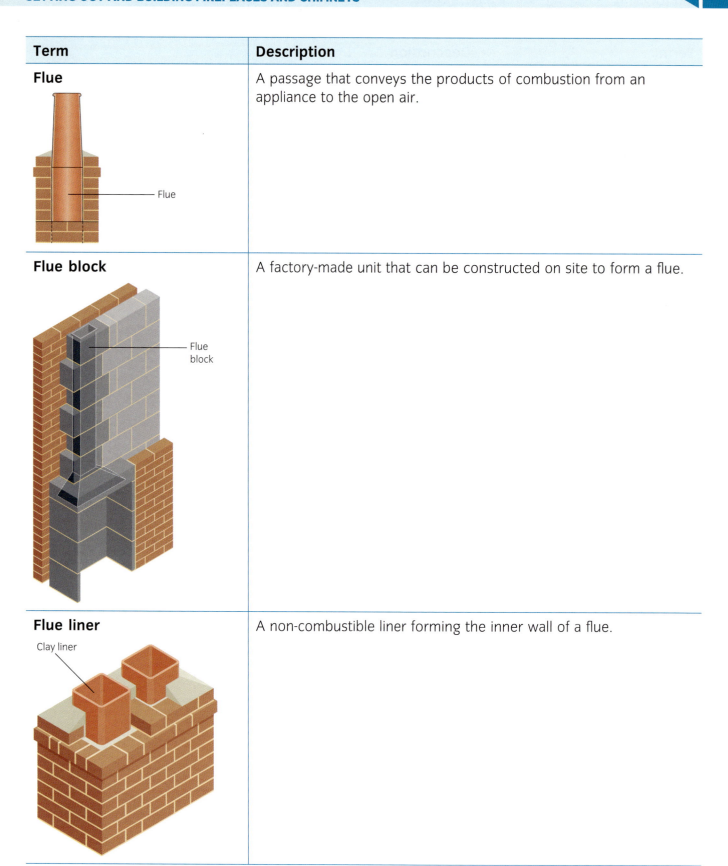	A passage that conveys the products of combustion from an appliance to the open air.
Flue block	A factory-made unit that can be constructed on site to form a flue.
Flue liner	A non-combustible liner forming the inner wall of a flue.

Term	Description
Flue terminal (chimney pot) 	A prefabricated or built-up unit forming the outlet end of a flue.
Gather (oncome) 	A construction over a fireplace to reduce it to the size of the flue.
Throat 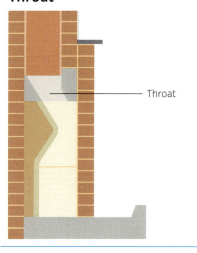	That part of the flue if contracted which is located between the fireplace and the chimney flue.

Term	Description
Throat unit 	A pre-cast concrete product that forms a starter for the flue liners.
Offset 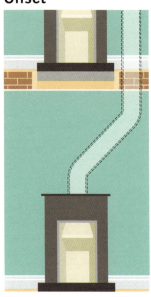	A double bend introduced into a flue so that its direction remains parallel to its original direction (maximum of two in any flue at 30° to the vertical).
Oversailing 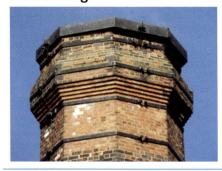	Courses of stone or brickwork (masonry) arranged to project from the face of the wall or chimney stack a minimum of 50mm to protect the face of the masonry or used as a decorative feature.
Parging 	The application of mortar to the inside of a chimney flue to form the inner surface of the flue.

Term	Description
Withe (midfeather, brig or bridge) 	A partition between adjacent flues in a chimney.

MATERIALS USED FOR THE CONSTRUCTION OF FIREPLACES, FLUES AND CHIMNEYS

When constructing fireplaces, flues and chimneys, it is important to understand the types of materials that are used and the reasons for their use. Many developments have been made in the production of materials used in the construction of fireplaces, flues and chimneys and now there are a wide range of specialist materials that make the construction process easier. These also ensure that the components used in the construction are hard wearing and will last over time without the need for expensive maintenance.

The materials used should be selected to ensure that they are of high quality and able to last under the conditions they will be exposed to. This includes exposure to high heat levels, sudden changes in temperature, severe weather conditions, and chemicals and sulphates that are generated in the **combustion** process. Remember that repairs to chimneys are very expensive so choosing the right materials is essential.

Most of the materials used for the construction of fireplaces and flues are purpose made for the job and are manufactured to high standards to ensure that they are fit for purpose.

Remember that some materials that you will be working with will be heavy and you will need to seek help to position them. Items like lintels, throat units, chimney caps and chimney pots are too heavy to lift into position on your own, so team lifting will ensure that you do

Combustion

The sequence of exothermic chemical reactions between a fuel and an oxidant accompanied by the production of heat

Term	Description
Flue liners Clay Concrete Round Square	The component parts of the flue that are joined together to form a flue; these may be made of concrete or clay and could be round or square in section. Sometimes existing flues are lined with metal flue liners to form a new flue within an existing chimney to serve a gas- or oil-fired appliance.
Chimney breast	A projecting wall that surrounds the flue and fireplace opening.
Chimney stack	The masonry above roof level that is surrounding the flue.
Chimney pot	The terminal of the flue.
Flaunching	The sloping mortar finish on top of a chimney stack.
Flashings	The lead material used to waterproof a chimney stack where it leaves the roof structure.

Term	Description
Withes or **midfeathers**	The separation between flues.
Chimney capping	This could be **pre-cast** or **cast in situ** but provides a protective top to a chimney and sheds water from the top of the chimney and away from the stack.
Cowl	A cowl is sometimes fitted to the top of the chimney pot to assist flue gases to escape from the flue in windy conditions. It can also stop rainwater from entering the flue at the chimney.

CHIMNEY BREASTS AND FORMING FIREPLACE OPENINGS

The way that a chimney breast and fireplace are to be set out will be clearly shown on the construction drawings and the materials that are to be used will be detailed in the specification. There are a number of ways that a chimney breast can be constructed according to the design chosen but the following are common methods:

- internal breast with straight outer cavity wall

- external breast with straight inner wall

- as a back-to-back fireplace (usually in semi-detached houses).

Pre-cast

Formed in a mould until hard and then used as a solid item. Such items are often made in a factory, or can be made on site and fitted when **cured**

Cured

A word that describes concrete that has set over time.

Cast in situ

To form a shutter or box and cast in position

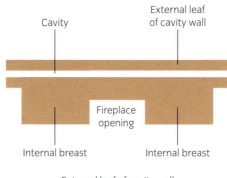

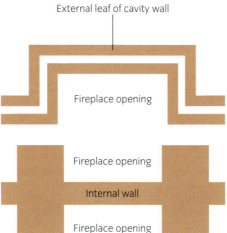

Plans of fireplace layouts

The Building Regulations

Combustion appliances and Fuel storage systems

J

APPROVED DOCUMENT

J1   Air supply
J2   Discharge of products of combustion
J3   Warning of release of carbon monoxide
J4   Protection of building
J5   Provision of information
J6   Protection of liquid fuel storage systems
J7   Protection against pollution

Latest Edition with up-to-date amendments

Building Regulations Part J

Suspended floor

A floor that is constructed of joists and wood covering such as floor boards

Superimposed hearth

A decorative feature, normally part of the fire surround, that is laid to protect the floor from sparks and embers

INDUSTRY TIP

Corrugated cardboard is used in chimney construction because provides a joint between the fireback and the fill to allow for expansion/movement.

LEGAL REQUIREMENTS FOR CONSTRUCTION OF CHIMNEY BREASTS AND FIREPLACE OPENINGS

The construction of fireplaces, flues and chimneys is regulated by Part J of the Building Regulations. This is an Approved Document and is issued by the Secretary of State to ensure that buildings are constructed to a minimum standard. These regulations will be referenced throughout this chapter. Guidance is also available in the British Standards in 6461 and BS EN 15278.

The materials chosen for the construction of various parts of the fireplace flue and chimney are selected because of their individual properties. This ensures that the fireplace when completed will work effectively and be safe to use over the life of the building.

This means that the materials must be of the right quality, strength and fire resistance needed to cope with the demands that will be placed on them.

The fireplace opening will need to have a base that is non-combustible. The way that this is constructed will vary according to the way in which the building is designed. For example, if the floor of the building is solid then the constructional hearth could be formed by the concrete floor; however, if the floor is **suspended** then provision will need to be made to ensure that a constructional hearth is incorporated. The minimum sizes of constructional hearths are determined by the Building Regulations. Usually a **superimposed hearth** is provided on top of the constructional hearth as part of the fire surround.

- *Constructional hearth*: this should have a minimum thickness of 125mm and is normally made of concrete.

- *Projection*: the distance that the constructional hearth must project from the face of the chimney breast is a minimum of 500mm.

- *Opening size*: this will depend upon the type of appliance that is to be used but should be a minimum of 570mm; this opening size may be reduced when the fireback and fireplace are fitted.

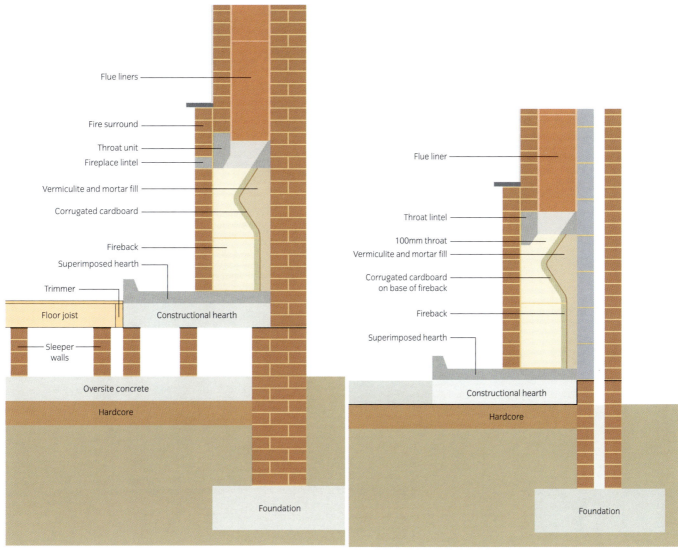

Section through fireplace (suspended floor)

Section through fireplace (solid floor)

CHANGES IN CHIMNEY BREAST CONSTRUCTION OVER TIME

The construction of the chimney breast and the formation of the entry to the flue have changed in recent years. In the early part of the last century the flue was formed with bricks and the fireplace opening was **gathered** across to reduce the opening to the required size of the flue. The inside of the flue was daubed with lime mortar or parged to provide the flue with some protection from the carbons generated from soot. In more recent times liners were introduced. These are made from fired clay or concrete and have socket and spigot ends to form a sealed joint. It is very important that the liners are laid socket uppermost as this ensures that any liquid running down the inside of the flue is not able to carry carbons to the joints of the breast or stack where they could cause erosion to the structure.

Gather

A method of changing the flue direction by using two bends to angle the flue and change the position of the flue in the breast

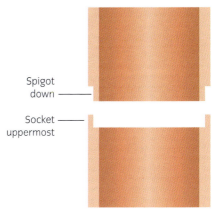

Spigot down

Socket uppermost

Section through flue liner

In most cases chimney breasts in modern houses are constructed with concrete blocks as this is a less time-consuming process. The size requirements of the Building Regulations still apply and the breast needs to be accurately set out at the base to ensure that the sizes will meet the requirements. Some fireplaces will incorporate a **back boiler** within the opening and provision will need to be made within the construction of the chimney breast to allow for pipework to feed this.

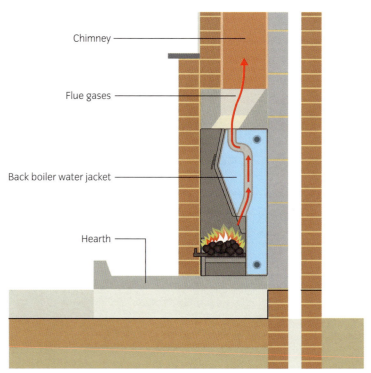

Fireplace with a back boiler

When setting out the base of the chimney breast it is important to ensure that all of the sizes that are used are compliant with the Building Regulations and codes of practice. Sizes for fireplaces and openings will vary according to the type of appliance that is installed. Guidance should always be sought prior to installation to ensure that the requirements for the appliance are met. Some of the sizes that it is important to measure include: the required size of jambs, opening and depth of the breast, as well as the required thickness for walls where the fireplace is constructed back to back with a neighbouring property.

Back boiler

A unit built into the back of a solid fuel fireplace that heats water by heat transfer from the fire

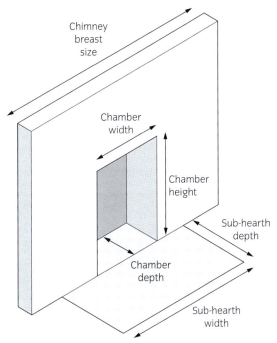

Chimney breast size

Chamber width

Chamber height

Sub-hearth depth

Chamber depth

Sub-hearth width

Fireplace opening

When the chimney breast is constructed to the top of the opening height a lintel is placed over the opening; this lintel is made with an angled rear which helps to form the angle to the flue.

Manufactured throat units are now generally used to reduce the opening size to the size of the flue. These are bedded in place and provide a good joint between the fire opening and the flue. When a single fireplace is being constructed the flue will be constructed vertically with no bends in the flue. This is the best way of construction and allows an easy passage for flue gases to escape to the atmosphere. In more complex situations where more than one fireplace is included within the building it is necessary to angle the flues or gather them across so that they join to form a multi-flue chimney stack.

In a single flue stack, the size of the chimney breast is often reduced at first floor level if there is no fireplace opening above. In this case the breast only needs to be big enough to encase the flue liner by 120mm. This will reduce the amount of materials needed and take up less space in the room if the breast is internal and allow space around the flue for expansion. If the breast is external then the breast will need to be reduced and there are a variety of methods that can be used to do this. Suitable waterproofing will be required to ensure that the lower cavity is sealed and watertight.

Fireplace lintel with an angled back

INDUSTRY TIP

The throat size should be a minimum of 100mm at the fireplace opening.

Chimney breast reduced externally

USING FLUE LINERS

The use of flue liners has made a significant difference to the building of flues to serve solid fuel fireplaces. In 1965 the Building Regulations added a requirement for all flues to be lined. Old fireplaces with parged flues tended to break down due to the presence of carbons in the soot. This had a detrimental effect on the mortar in the structure and often caused the chimney to become unsafe and need rebuilding. The inclusion of flue liners provides protection and ensures that the structures will last for longer without the need for repair. When fitting flue liners care should be taken to ensure that they are bedded in fireproof or sulphate-resistant mortar to ensure a good seal. Cracked or damaged liners should not be used and care must be taken to ensure that the area around the outside of the liner is filled with weak mix mortar or mortar with **vermiculite** added to allow for expansion around the flue when it expands due to the heat generated within the flue.

Care will need to be taken when cutting flue liners as they are made from very dense material that is prone to cracking. Using an **abrasive wheel cutter** or **disc cutter** will be the most effective way of doing this. Remember that these are dangerous tools if not used properly, so ensure that you follow safety instructions when using them and that the blade is fitted by a trained person.

SAFETY CONSIDERATIONS

Other materials will need to be cut using other methods: blocks and bricks should be cut using a lump hammer and bolster, whereas DPC should usually be cut using a sharp knife. Care should be taken when cutting. It's also important to ensure that you are wearing the correct PPE.

Once the breast is built up to roof level, provision for the construction of the chimney stack needs to be made. This is a very difficult job to undertake due to the height above ground level and the added difficulties of transporting heavy materials from ground level to the roof where the stack will be constructed. It is essential that proper access equipment is used to carry out this work and that it is erected by competent scaffold erectors. They should ensure that the scaffolding is constructed safely and that it will be able to withstand the load of the materials that will be placed on it.

They should also ensure that provision for safe access to the platform is provided by means of a ladder or stairway. It is essential that proper lifting methods are used to raise and lower the materials to and from the work area. There are a number of methods that can be used to lift the materials to roof level. Some sites have telescopic forklifts which will lift building materials on to a platform at eaves level. Materials can then be passed up to the roof level by hand. Barrow hoists are also available and can be attached to scaffolding which can be erected to accommodate extra lifts to transport the materials to the required levels.

Vermiculite

A lightweight material that is mixed with mortar to provide insulation and allow expansion in the flue

Abrasive wheel cutter or **disc cutter**

A piece of equipment that is fuelled by electricity, petrol or air power and is used to cut construction materials by the abrasive action of the wheel

ACTIVITY

There are a number of hazards that will need consideration when constructing a chimney breast, flue and chimney. In groups discuss the methods that would be used to carry out this work.

Using the standard method statement template produce three method statements to establish how the work should be completed in the safest possible manner. These should include:

- building the chimney breast and installing flue liners
- constructing the chimney above roof level
- fixing a fireplace.

Now produce risk assessments for each of the activities to show how the hazards will be controlled.

Telescopic forklift lifting blocks

THE CITY & GUILDS TEXTBOOK

Front elevation

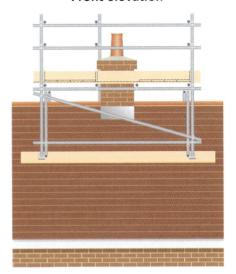

End elevation

Plan

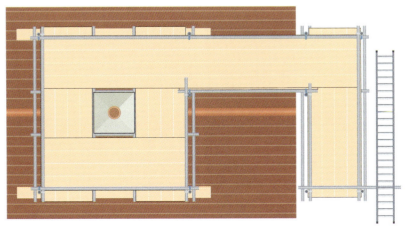

Stack scaffolding

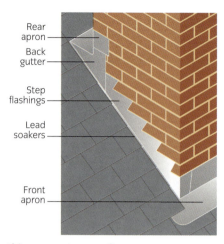

Chimney waterproofing

Labels: Rear apron, Back gutter, Step flashings, Lead soakers, Front apron

Ingress

Entering

Dress up

Verb used for changing the shape of lead, ie when you dress lead around a chimney

Placing soakers

CHIMNEY DESIGN

As well as serving as a means of removing gases from the fire, chimney stacks also form a striking architectural feature to the building and can be constructed in very decorative ways. They are also very exposed to extreme weather conditions so the choice of materials and the quality of workmanship for the construction are very important. A chimney may be built with facing bricks or other masonry materials but whatever the finish it must be durable as it is probably the most exposed point of the building. We must ensure that when the chimney is constructed proper damp proof barriers are provided to stop **ingress** of water into the building.

Careful consideration should be given to the following points when designing a chimney:

- Where the chimney leaves the roof structure a suitable system of waterproofing is needed in the form of damp proof barriers. This normally begins with a lead tray inserted across the bed joints and covering the whole area of the stack and **dressed up** the flue liner to direct the water out of the building.

- The joints around the stack and the roof surface also need to be sealed to prevent ingress of water and this is generally done by placing soakers under the slates or tiles which are dressed to the sides of the stack; the joint between the stack and the soakers is then sealed with a stepped flashing or an apron.

- Soakers are metal or plastic flashings used on pitched roofs. They are used to manage junctions between:
  - □ the slope of the roof and any upright object or structure, for example, a wall or a side abutment roof window
  - □ at a valley or hip between two roof slopes
  - □ at a party wall junction.
  The soakers are installed between each course of plain tiles and double lap slates and the shape of size of the soaker will differ depending on the situation it is used in.

Horizontal lead tray

Leadwork around a chimney

THE CITY & GUILDS TEXTBOOK

■ The height of chimney stacks is determined by the position that it leaves the roof structure. The Building Regulations give clear guidance on the height that chimneys need to be constructed to ensure that gases clear the building and that the chimney is not affected by wind which could cause a **downdraught** in the flue.

The following photos show the recommendations of the Building Regulations with regard to chimney height in relation to the position of the chimney on the roof.

Downdraught

The effect of wind on a flue that causes the flue gases to blow down the flue and into the room

Stack positions on a roof   Necking course

The way in which a chimney stack is constructed will determine how well it will weather over time, as this is a part of a building that is difficult and expensive to repair. Good design and the right materials are essential. Often at the top of the stack oversailing courses are incorporated; this not only provides a pleasing feature but also directs water off the top of the stack and stops it from running down its face. Sometimes a **necking course** is incorporated halfway down the stack to assist the shedding of water off the walls of the stack.

The joint finish to the brickwork will also have an effect on the weathering of the brickwork. Recessed jointing is not recommended as it tends to hold water, so a more flush type of jointing will be more suitable in such exposed positions. A **weatherstruck**, flush, **tooled** or **ironed** joint finish will provide a more weatherproof finish to the stack.

Necking course

A course of bricks around a chimney that are slightly oversailing to provide a decorative feature and also help to shed rainwater

Weatherstruck

A way of forming sloping bed joints to allow water to shed off the wall

Tooled/ironed

A half-round joint that directs the water outwards

Various decorative finishes for chimney stacks

Chimney finishes

CHIMNEY MASONRY (FLAUNCHING)

The top finish to the chimney stack is very important and there are a number of ways in which this can be formed. Often this is formed with a mortar layer that is sloped towards the outside of the stack to assist the shedding of water. The mortar used for this should be mixed from sharp well-graded sand and cement gauged 3 to 1. Plasticiser should not be used as this can affect the strength and durability of the mortar over time. It is important to provide a solid hard-wearing finish that will withstand weather over time.

Concrete cappings can be made or can be cast in situ to provide a top with a weatherproof drip to assist the shedding of the water.

CHIMNEY POTS

Chimney pots are fitted to the top of a chimney; they increase the efficiency of the flue by extending the overall height of the chimney and because of the tapered shape towards the top they increase the updraft through the chimney.

Range of chimney pots

There are many types of chimney pot with a variety of designs. They are manufactured from high-fired ceramic clay, which can withstand the high temperatures that a chimney can generate.

As chimney pots are open at the top they are prone to allow water to enter the flue. To eliminate this problem chimney cowls are often fitted.

CHIMNEY COWLS

Many chimneys are fitted with cowls. A cowl is a fixture that is added to the top of a chimney pot for a variety of purposes. Some chimneys do not always work as efficiently as they should: this may be caused by strong winds which stop the free flow of smoke from the chimney. A suitable cowl fitted to the top of the pot will assist the escape of smoke and stop the smoke from flowing back down the chimney into the building where it could be a hazard.

Chimney cowls

Another use of a cowl is to stop the ingress of water. An open chimney pot can allow rainwater to enter the building and run down the flue into the building causing a mess inside the room. Fitting a cowl will stop this water entering without affecting the free flow of gases from the flue.

Another hazard on chimney tops is bird nesting. Often birds will build a nest in the flue opening and this can cause a blockage in the flue. Fitting a suitable cowl can prevent this from happening.

Specialist types of cowl can be purchased which are specifically made for thatched properties. Due to the combustible nature of thatched roofing some insurance companies used to insist on the fitting of a spark arrester. This is a type of cowl that stops sparks from a fire leaving the flue and landing on the thatch where it could

ACTIVITY

At a scale of 1:20, produce a drawing showing a cross-section through a cavity wall incorporating a gas flue. Show the opening, flue and terminal method for the flue.

cause a fire. However, more recent research has concluded that spark arrestors themselves can be the cause of fires where they become blocked with tar from the fire. Where a spark arrester is fitted it will need regular maintenance to ensure that it does not block. The recommended height of a chimney above the thatch level is 1.8m.

CONSTRUCTION OF A FLUE FOR A GAS FIRE

In some modern properties architects design a system where there is a requirement to build in a flue to serve a gas appliance. In this case it is common to build a gas flue into the block wall as part of the structure.

There are a variety of specialist proprietary flues that can be purchased to use in this situation. The flues are made from refractory concrete and are bonded into the structure of the wall to provide a flue that finishes flush to the structural wall and carries the flue gases to the roof area. Inside the roof a flexible metal flue connects via a special reducer or connector and carries the flue gases to the ridge where they are emitted through a purpose-made ridge vent.

This is a popular system where a gas fire is to be incorporated into a property but it must be remembered that this type of flue is only suitable for specific gas-fired appliances.

It is essential that the building of a flue block system is carried out correctly and according to the manufacturer's instructions. The following information should be considered when constructing the flue:

- The flue should be structurally sound.

- It should ensure the safe operation of the gas appliance installed.

- The maximum overall height of the flue must not exceed 12m.

- Flue blocks can be terminated in the roof space and at this point a reducer is fitted which connects the masonry flue to the metal duct; this then connects to a low-resistance terminal at the ridge, or to a chimney stack.

- Blocks should be laid rebate up with an 8mm fireproof **jointing compound** to be applied into the rebate.

- Joints should be pointed and any surplus adhesive removed from the flue during construction leaving a smooth uniform surface. Ensure joints are completely sealed with jointing compound.

- If the blocks and surrounding courses of masonry fail to meet exactly do not attempt to cut the blocks but adjust the surrounding masonry to suit.

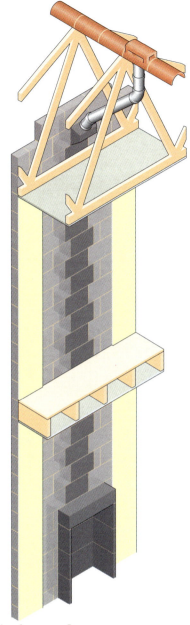

Flue for a gas fire

Jointing compound

Used to join flue liners and provide a sealed flue that will contain the exhaust gases from the fire

Gas flue blocks

Timber-framed

Constructed with a framework of timber that is clad externally with masonry

A fireplace as the focal point of a room

Asbestos

A material that was widely used in construction but is now banned from use due to its very dangerous nature. If you suspect that asbestos is present then you should stop work immediately and inform your employer or supervisor

Example of a fire surround

This system is very adaptable and can also be used to install a flue to serve a gas-fired appliance in a **timber-framed** house.

FITTING A FIREPLACE AND SURROUND

The finishing touch to constructing a flue and chimney is to fit the fire surround in the room.

This provides a focal point in the room and there are many designs manufactured that can be selected. These vary in price but generally they are expensive items and care will be needed when installing them to ensure that they are not damaged during fitting.

When replacing an existing fireplace extreme care should be taken as there may be **asbestos** present in the old fireplace. Asbestos rope used to be used to seal the joint between the fire opening and the fireback. If this is present then it should be disposed of properly by a registered asbestos contractor. If you have any doubts about this then you need to speak with your supervisor or employer before starting work.

Fireplaces can come in a range of shapes, sizes and looks:

This specialist work is often left to the bricklayer and particular skills are needed to ensure that it is carried out correctly. Taking care to store the fire surround and hearth correctly will ensure that it is does not sustain damage and also make it easier to lift into place when fitting it. Some timber bearers placed on the floor will prevent damage and placing packing at the back will prevent damage to walls.

Fitting the fireplace will include fitting the fireback and positioning it correctly, finishing the hearth and sealing the whole unit to ensure it is safe to use.

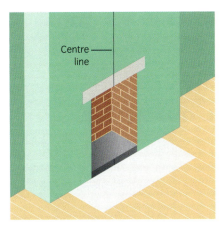

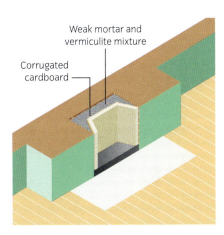

STEP 1 The process begins by preparing the fireplace opening. The base of the constructional hearth will need to be raised to receive the fireback. The superimposed hearth is bedded onto the constructional hearth. Once the superimposed hearth is in place, the position of the fire surround can be established. This is done by determining the centre line of the breast and marking this position on the wall; at this point it is important to check that the opening is central to the breast and this will be seen clearly once the mark is in place.

STEP 2 The fireback can now be positioned to ensure that it is central to the fireplace position and care taken to ensure that the front is upright and far enough forward to meet the fire surround when it is put in place.

STEP 3 The fireback now needs a corrugated cardboard layer applied to its rear and then the area behind the fireback can be filled with weak mix mortar mixed with vermiculite chippings. This will fill the area but will also ensure that any expansion in the fireback is taken up. If the fireplace opening is wider than the fireback then the sides will need to be built up at the same time.

STEP 4 The next stage will depend on the type of fireplace but often the superimposed hearth will need to be laid first. This is achieved by bedding the hearth evenly on a mortar bed centrally to the opening. At this stage you will need to ensure that the hearth is level both ways and is laid centrally to receive the fire surround.

STEP 5 The fire surround can now be placed in position very carefully to avoid causing any damage to the hearth or to the tiles on the fire surround. The joints around the fire opening will need to be sealed between the fireback and the surround; in most cases surrounds are supplied with pieces of fireproof rope fitted around the opening. Once the surround is in place it can be fixed by drilling and screwing the side plates back to the wall. The plasterwork around the fireplace can then be finished.

INDUSTRY TIP

Remember that fire surrounds are very heavy and will probably need two people to lift into place.

OUR HOUSE

Look at 'Our House' and discuss the options for a new fireplace to be fitted in the lounge. Look at manufacturers' catalogues and choose three options that could be offered as suggestions to fit in the property.

CALCULATING MATERIAL QUANTITIES

It is important to be able to calculate quantities of material and components to construct fireplaces and chimneys. Now that you are familiar with the terminology for this topic, we will look at some examples for calculating materials.

USING LINEAR MEASUREMENT

A fireplace is to be constructed in a new property. The flue is to be lined with clay liners 225mm in diameter and 300mm high which cost £7.00 each. The liners are to be installed from the top of the throat unit to the top of the chimney at a total length of 10.5m. Calculate both the number of liners that will be required to construct the flue and the cost for them. Remember to allow 10% for waste and add VAT at 20%.

Example

Divide the total length of liners needed by their height. Make sure you are using the same measurements – in this instance, you need to make sure the height (300mm) is in metres.

Step 1
$$10.5 \div 0.3 = 35$$

Step 2

Add on 10% for wastage. You can either do this using this two-step method, by working out 10% then adding it to the total:

$$35 \times 10 \div 100 = 3.5$$

$$3.5 + 35 = 38.5$$

Or by doing it in one step:

$$35 \times 1.10 = 38.5$$

Step 3

Round this up to the nearest whole number, and multiply it by the cost per liner.

$$39 \times 7 = 273$$

So you need 39 liners, which will cost £273.

Step 4

VAT can be added at 20% using the two-step method.

$$273 \times 20 \div 100 = £54.6$$

$$273 + 54.6 = £327.60$$

Or using the one-step method:

$$273 \times 1.2 = £327.60$$

Both methods give you the result that the total cost for the liners is **£327.60**

CALCULATING MATERIAL QUANTITIES, COSTS AND LABOUR COSTS

A chimney breast is to be constructed in an existing building. You will need to know how many blocks you need to order to carry out the work. The chimney breast is 2.25m wide, 4.5m high and 0.45m deep, and will be constructed in concrete blocks that are 215mm × 430mm × 102mm. The examples below will explain how to calculate the number of blocks needed, the cost for these blocks, and the cost for the labour.

Example 1

Calculate the number of blocks that will be needed to construct the chimney breast and allow 10% for cuts and wastage.

Step 1

Work out the area of blocks needed for the chimney breast, by multiplying the width by the height.

$$2.25m \times 4.5m = 10.125m^2$$

Step 2

The number of blocks required is 10 per square metre on the face × 4 for the depth of the breast, so we need 40 blocks per metre square (ie each 1m² of blockwork 100mm thick contains 10 blocks; therefore a wall four times that thickness contains 40 blocks per m²).

Step 3

Multiply the area of blocks for the chimney breast by the number of blocks that can cover one square metre.

$$10.125m \times 40 = 405$$

Step 4

Add on 10% for wastage.

$$405 \times 1.10 = 445.5$$

Step 5

Round this up to the nearest whole number. The total number of blocks you need is **446**.

Example 2

Calculate the cost of the blocks if they are 56p each. Remember to add VAT at the current rate (20%).

Step 1

Multiply the number of blocks from Example 1 by the cost per block.

$$446 \times 0.56 = £249.76$$

Step 2

Add VAT at 20% using the two-step method:

$$£249.76 \times 20 \div 100 = £49.95$$

$$£249.76 + £49.95 = £299.71$$

Or using the one-step method:

$$£249.76 \times 1.20 = £299.71$$

Both methods give you the result that the total cost for the blocks is **£299.71**.

Example 3

Calculate how much labour would be charged to construct the chimney breast if the price for laying each block is £2.50.

Multiply the number of blocks needed by the price for laying one block.

$$446 \times £2.50 = £1,115.00$$

The total cost for laying the blocks is **£1,115.00**.

INDUSTRY TIP

'Labour charge' is the term used to describe the amount charged for carrying out the physical work.

Case Study: David

David is asked to fit a new fireplace into a customer's house. David collects a range of brochures from the builder's merchants and shows them to the customer. The customer selects a fireplace that they like and asks David to fit it for them.

In order, write a list of the work activities required to carry out the fitting of the fireplace.

TEST YOUR KNOWLEDGE

Work through the following questions to check your learning.

1 The **minimum** thickness of a constructional hearth should be

   a   100mm

   b   125mm

   c   150mm

   d   175mm.

2 Flue liners should be fitted

   a   socket down

   b   socket up

   c   after the socket has been removed

   d   sockets joined.

3 The person that checks buildings to ensure that they comply with Building Regulations is the

   a   building control officer

   b   safety officer

   c   surveyor

   d   health inspector.

4 To what **minimum** height should a chimney be constructed above the ridge of the roof?

   a   300mm.

   b   450mm.

   c   600mm.

   d   900mm.

5 The **minimum** distance a constructional hearth should project from the breast is

   a   150mm

   b   200mm

   c   350mm

   d   500mm.

6 Vermiculite and weak mortar are infilled behind a fireback to

   a   allow for moisture

   b   insulate the fireplace

   c   allow for expansion

   d   save mortar.

7 The weatherproof capping on the top of a chimney is called

   a   flashing

   b   pointing

   c   flaunching

   d   sloping.

8 The division between flues is called a

   a   withe

   b   divider

   c   partition

   d   spacer.

9 The leadwork around a chimney is called

   a   flashing

   b   flaunching

   c   rendering

   d   plumbing.

10 The throat size at the fireplace opening should be a **minimum** of

   a   50mm

   b   100mm

   c   150mm

   d   200mm.

11 To gather in a chimney is a method of

   a   changing the flue direction

   b   widening the opening

   c   finishing the chimney

   d   collecting materials.

12 Before flue liners were used, flues were

  a painted

  b skimmed

  c parged

  d floated.

13 A flue is to be constructed 7.2m high. How many 300mm liners will be needed?

  a 12.

  b 14.

  c 15.

  d 24.

14 The construction of fireplaces and flues is regulated by which part of the Building Regulations?

  a Part A.

  b Part C.

  c Part F.

  d Part J.

15 The **minimum** size of a fireplace opening is

  a 450mm

  b 500mm

  c 570mm

  d 600mm.

16 A concrete unit that reduces the fireplace opening to the size of the flue is called a

  a base unit

  b head unit

  c throat unit

  d flue unit.

17 The wall at the side of a fireplace recess is termed

  a an abutment

  b a surround

  c a jamb

  d a cavity.

18 Guidance on the design and construction of flues can be found in

  a BS 1984

  b BS 6164

  c BS 6461

  d BS 8491.

19 A cowl is fitted to a chimney to

  a make it easier to clean

  b retain the heat

  c help the flue gases escape in windy conditions

  d make the chimney look more attractive.

20 A necking course would be found

  a above the throat unit

  b where the stack leaves the roof

  c at the top of the stack

  d halfway up the stack.

TEST YOUR KNOWLEDGE ANSWERS

Chapter 1: Unit 201/601

1 c Risk assessment.
2 d Blue circle.
3 b Oxygen.
4 a CO_2.
5 b Control of Substances Hazardous to Health (COSHH) Regulations 2002.
6 c 75°.
7 c Glasses, hearing protection and dust mask.
8 d Respirator.
9 a 410V.
10 b 80 dB(A).

Chapter 2: Unit 301/701

1 b Objects can be reproduced quickly.
2 c 1:1250.
3 a A0.
4 b Isometric.
5 b Quotation.
6 b Preliminaries.
7 d Quantity surveyor.
8 a Quote.
9 b Pre-contract.
10 d method statement
11 c lead time
12 b Costs are increased in the long term.
13 c Variation order.
14 c method statement
15 d during a toolbox talk
16 c Sender's address.
17 b heat loss
18 a Timber frame.
19 c A–G.
20 b L.

Chapter 3: Unit 302

1 c the natural process of the building moving
2 b natural salts
3 a surface tension in water
4 c water freezing in the body of the brick
5 c a structural crack
6 a chemical reaction with the cement in the mortar
7 c props and needles
8 b lump hammer and jointing chisel
9 b 150mm.
10 a supporting the foundation
11 a 60.
12 b lose its strength
13 b 150mm
14 a refer to the risk assessment
15 a Trade catalogues.
16 a To measure movement in a wall.
17 c underpinning
18 b building control officer
19 c Engineering.
20 a maintenance

Chapter 4: Unit 303

1 b the arch shape spreads compressive forces through to the abutments
2 c joints that are the same thickness throughout from the intrados to the extrados
3 d voussoirs
4 c Proprietary arch former.
5 a extrados
6 b Trammel.
7 c Raised corners or deadmen with a line attached.
8 d easing the centre
9 c radial bricks
10 d 9.42m.

11 **a** Introduce header bricks and alter the bond of the wall.

12 **c** Skewback.

13 **c** A batter board and spirit level.

14 **c** A gun template.

15 **b** lateral forces

16 **d** a lack of drainage provision at the base of the wall

17 **c** Hazardous Waste Regulations (England and Wales) 2005.

18 **a** serpentine wall

19 **b** a wall or floor onto which a trammel is placed to set out curved walling

20 **d** A risk assessment.

Chapter 5: Unit 304

1 **c** 90°.

2 **d** Horizontal herringbone.

3 **b** Take off 10mm at either side and 10mm for the bed joint thickness.

4 **c** pinch rod

5 **d** dentil course

6 **a** 45 and 60°.

7 **c** in a continuous line

8 **d** plinth bricks

9 **a** Above the plinth course.

10 **b** Cant.

11 **c** breathing in contaminated dust particles

12 **c** acute angles

13 **d** Squint.

14 **a** an acute-angled wall using standard bricks

15 **c** Compression.

16 **a** Horizontal.

17 **d** Quetta bond.

18 **c** Steel rods and concrete.

19 **a** Structural engineer.

20 **c** Once the pier has fully hardened.

Chapter 6: Unit 305

1 **b** 125mm

2 **b** socket up

3 **a** building control officer

4 **c** 600mm.

5 **d** 500mm.

6 **c** allow for expansion

7 **c** flaunching

8 **a** withe

9 **a** flashing

10 **b** 100mm

11 **a** changing the flue direction

12 **c** parged

13 **d** 24.

14 **d** Part J.

15 **c** 570mm

16 **c** throat unit

17 **c** a jamb

18 **c** BS 6461

19 **c** help the flue gases escape in windy conditions

20 **d** halfway up the stack

INDEX

Every effort has been made to acknowledge all copyright holders as below and the publishers will, if notified, correct any errors in future editions.